Under Too Long is a great read. The more people read about people who deal with life and death situations every day and have found ways to deal with it- long after the danger has ceased-gives hope to us that still deal with the injuries we've suffered, both mentally and physically.

—Joe Gleba, Retired Vietnam Vet, and PTSD Sufferer

Billy the Liquor Guy, between thrilling moments and levity, made this book impossible to put down. This was one of those books you down want it to end.

—Frank Canoro. Retired Master Sergeant with the United States Air Force and. Vietnam Vet.

Utilizing Bill's undercover skill against criminals makes crime fighting like fishing in a hatchery.....they always get caught.

—"Experienced Crime Fighter"

Since I have known "Billy the Liquor Guy" for almost 25 years and worked alongside of him for six years, I must give major kudos to him for his exciting undercover real-life stories about his experiences in the undercover world of drugs, untaxed cigarette and alcohol products that finance commingle or lead to other dangerous and nefarious crimes that have jeopardized our society and our country. BUT I particularly applaud the ghost writer, Tennille, for telling Billy's story in a most amazing way that captures the essence of who Billy is-a man of courage possessing great heart for his friends and co-workers and even a little empathy for the criminals he rounds up while depicting his extraordinary sense of humor and his obvious dedication to good versus evil, but all the while keeping him true to himself as an ordinary kind of a guy with amazing " street-smarts." When I worked with Billy, there was no other investigator I knew that I could count on to always have my back. With that being said, I could hardly set this book down. I hope that while you may not know Billy or his story, you will be engaged and walking with him from the first paragraph to the last just as I was.

—Bobbi Paye NYS Investigator

Under Too Long is a "CPD" (Can't Put Down). It contains absolutely invaluable insight into the unique and extremely dangerous role that government undercover agents undertake on a daily basis. It is a must read.

—Peter Karl, Attorney

UNDER
TOO LONG

BILLY THE LIQUOR GUY

Los Angeles, California

Published by:
Genius Book Publishing
31858 Castaic Road, #154
Castaic, CA 91384
GeniusBookPublishing.com

ISBN: 978-1-947521-17-9

200128

DEDICATION

This book is dedicated to my family, friends, doctors and PTSD therapeutic support group that made me smile again. Thanks to them I realized that every day is a gift and that life is worth living.

CONTENTS

INTRODUCTION

"Who's the guy that just intercepted the bar?" the New York State Attorney General inquired.

It was late, 3 a.m. to be exact, and the General was annoyed. Within minutes of exiting a bar his team had spent months trying to intercept, he'd gotten word of my license plate and car make. And, when those numbers came up as an operating vehicle for the Petroleum, Alcohol, and Tobacco Bureau, he went straight to my superior.

"It's Billy," Staton, the Director of my unit, replied. "Best undercover we've got."

"I want to meet him," the General instructed. "Have him to my office by morning. I want to meet the agent that's infringing on my team."

Infringing was an ironic choice of words since I'd been in the bar to complete a liquor buy—and a measly buy at that. The bar had been so run down and lackadaisical with liquor purchases that my partner, Tony, and I had written it off as a waste of time. To say that we thought there was any suspicious activity going on inside was a stretch. But the New York State Attorney General was interested, so whatever he was looking for must be good.

I glanced at the clock, which now read 6 a.m.

"How early you want us there?" I asked, my body exhausted from the late evening my crew and I had pulled.

"I'd like you here before 10," Staton said. "We'll work out the details on the drive over."

"I'll call Tony and arrange it," I said, wiping the sleep from my eyes. I wasn't ready to start my day, but curiosity had me on my feet and ready to go.

"Billy," Staton said before we hung up, "let's keep this under wraps until we know what's going on. Got it?"

"Got it, boss," I said and hung up, dialing Tony seconds later.

Whether we were ready or not, our undercover careers were about to be put into overdrive. Keeping it under wraps was just a momentary diversion. Soon enough, we'd have over 10 agencies, like the FBI, the United States military and ATF, assisting us to take down bombs, drugs, untaxed liquor and a multi-terrorist unit. And it all stemmed from my ability to transform, relate and bullshit with degenerates at any given time.

CHAPTER ONE

ATTORNEY GENERAL

Tony and I reached Staton's office five minutes after his recommended time.

"You two are late," Staton said, looking directly at Tony.

I could see the heat spread across Tony's face. I felt bad for him in a way. He was a timely guy, built on schedules and factoids. I, meanwhile, required an extra stop for coffee and a breakfast bagel from my favorite spot in Troy.

I could feel Staton's eyes on me. I had on my day-to-day wears: wind pants, sneakers and a wrinkly t-shirt.

"You couldn't run an iron over your shirt, at least?" Staton said, shaking his head.

He wasn't one for fashion, either. However, today he sported a crisp white shirt and black dress pants.

"What do you want from me?" I mumbled. "You woke me up at 6 a.m. I didn't have time to go shopping. And no one told me they were dressing up!"

Staton shook his head and let out an aggravated sigh.

"Tony, thank you for dressing respectable," he stated.

"See, there you go. You've got one well-dressed guy on the team." I smiled.

Staton mumbled something and pulled a file from his briefcase.

"Okay, boys. Here's what I've got," Staton said, leaning forward. "The governor created a task force designed to shut down a drug distribution ring throughout New York State. His task force is huge, but from what I can tell they haven't been able to find the link in the Southern Tier area. Somehow, you two have stepped into something they've been trying to uncover. This can be a win-win, for you, the state, and the Attorney General—if you get this one right."

Staton prepped us with facts, names, and requirements as we headed to the state office building in Albany, or the Ivory Tower as I liked to call it.

As we walked through the sterile hallways, glares from suits passed my way.

"They probably think you're our criminal." Tony laughed.

"Maybe I should have tied my sneakers before I got out of the car."

Tony looked down at my laces, which were flopping with each step I took, and sighed. Before Staton could scold me, two gentlemen, both sporting black business suits and sharp ties, stepped in front of us.

"Mr. Staton," they said, their hands extended.

Staton, who knew both individuals by name, shook their hands and introduced us.

"It's a pleasure," the gentleman introduced as San said, shaking my hand. "We heard about you breaking into Soft Tail like it was your home base. Kudos on a job well done. That's one bar we've yet to get into."

Soft Tail was a low-grade bar that seemed easy to infiltrate, so the acknowledgement took me off guard. Yet, by the time I was introduced to Bloom, San's back-up, who excitedly praised my work as well, my ego was swimming. It was a great decoy, since once we made our way into the Attorney General's office my body seemed to trip over itself.

"So, this is what my team was up against?" the Attorney General smirked, gesturing to my outfit. "I must have really picked from the bottom of the barrel, huh."

His jab put me at ease. He was a ball buster, just like any other guy.

Along with Staton, Tony, San, Bloom and the General were the heads of the Narcotics Task Force.

"Some of the bars we've found you in have been heavily involved with the Narcotics Task Force for some time," the General said as we all took a seat around the oval table in his office. "They've had everyone from the State Police to local law enforcement trying to get in. All unsuccessfully. As I am sure your director has informed you, the Governor has been adamant about uncovering and stopping drug traffic across the state. What you may not be aware of is the high volume of drugs that run through the Southern Tier of New York. Drugs are coming into NYC through various points, which we're working on, and then following a line straight into Elmira—a major distribution point for the rest of New York State and Pennsylvania. We believe one of the bars you landed yourself into is part of the wheelhouse in this operation."

San went on to discuss the dispatches they'd set across points in Binghamton, Syracuse, Rochester, and various towns that border Pennsylvania. It was clear the Attorney General was desperate to break down the distributions, and San and Bloom were responsible for making sure that happened.

The head of Narcotics broke down the patrons they'd been pursuing, particularly those who frequented Soft Tail. As he flashed pictures across his PowerPoint screen, he stopped to display a shot of me, dressed in sweatpants and a dirty t-shirt, talking with the Jamaicans we'd encountered the evening prior. These guys were said to be relevant drug dealers and extremely dangerous. The smiling one I'd warmed up to was the leader.

Tony's mouth was hanging open and he was whiter than I'd ever seen.

"We want to assign you on the case with us," the head of Narcotics said, displaying more pictures of Tony and me outside Soft Tail and The Thirsty Bear. I'll admit we did appear to look buddy-buddy with Nash and the Jamaicans. There was even a shot of Tony cleaning broken liquor bottles out of the van. Staton eyed us about that picture. I guess we'd forgotten to tell him about that one.

"Billy, we have to ask," San said, leaning forward, "how the hell did you get to be so friendly with these guys so quick? You're in there laughing like you're long lost friends."

"Gentlemen, I don't know," I said, putting my hands up in defense. "I think so many people have referred to me as a low-life degenerate all my life that I'm actually not pretending to be one anymore."

"I don't buy it for one minute," San said. "You seem to be in the right place at the right time, and we don't think that's by chance. You're a lot smarter than you're playing it."

"Look guys, I can't say that I'm not impressed by all of this," I said, looking around. "But we've just been selling untaxed liquor and cigarettes. From what you're telling me, there's a major drug operation going on that we weren't even aware of. That's not our area of expertise, so anything we've stumbled upon happened on dumb luck."

"Again, we have to respectfully disagree," Bloom replied. "You're forging relationships with owners who trust you, and that's what we need to get inside. We need someone they feel comfortable with and trust enough to bring us in."

"And you think that's something Tony and I can do?" I questioned, even though deep down I knew damn well we could.

"That's why we've asked you here," the General replied. "We need your help."

"That's something you're going to have to speak with my director about," I said, looking at Staton. "My loyalty is with my unit and with the operation we've been successfully building."

The General highlighted the respect our agency would hold with the Governor, the Narcotics Unit and his own office, should Tony and I assist them. He spoke about advanced video and sound equipment that they'd yet to grant any other agency, additional manpower, vehicles and a handsome raise. It was hard not to be impressed.

"Before we proceed, I have to be clear that his first alliance would remain with his agency," Staton said. "As hard as you guys have worked to crack this case, we've worked just as hard to crack ours, and we're close."

"That sounds reasonable," the General responded.

"I'd also like to be able to keep my original crew," I stated. "You said more manpower, which is great, but the guys I've been working with have busted their ass with me from the start. We have a good rapport with each other. That's how we've gotten as far as we have. I won't come without them."

"Again, that doesn't seem like a problem," the General said, though I watched the head of Narcotics slump back in his chair.

San tossed a key fob across the table.

"The mic is inside. We can track your audio, location, and deliver video surveillance without raising suspicion with this."

I glanced at Staton who smiled in approval. Until now I'd been hiding a wire in a beeper. Imagine having to explain why you wore a beeper in this day and age to a group of bad guys.

"We want to start working with you as soon as possible. We can have cars and equipment to you within a day," Bloom said.

"If my partner and I do agree to sign on, we'll also need agreements to the terms of our schedule. We run a consistent itinerary so people know when to expect us. That makes them feel safe."

"We were hoping to have you back in Soft Tail in a few days. While the fire is still hot, so to speak," San said.

"You can hope for whatever you like, but I won't be going back to Soft Tail or Thirsty Bear until next week. If I begin pushing in or looking eager it can raise questions and we've worked too hard to jeopardize that for our agency."

The General and the rest of his crew weren't happy, but they knew that for the mission to be effective they had no choice other than to adhere to what I wanted. And what I wanted was to wait.

"I respect your discipline, Billy," the General said, rising from his seat and extending his hand. "I have no doubt it will all be worthwhile."

The General excused himself, leaving San and the head of Narcotics to finalize vehicle and equipment arrangements.

"Off the record," the head of Narcotics said as we prepared to depart, "how the hell did you look at the guy from Soft Tail with a straight face? Kid looks like the fucking Elephant Man."

"I chose one eye and focused on that." I smiled. "I didn't dare let my eyes wander anywhere other than that eye for fear it would throw me off."

"Well, the real bad asses in that bar are the Jamaicans, not your Elephant Man. They control that bar. It's a thick crowd, so be careful."

ⅎ

"We're fucking working for the New York Attorney General!" Tony screamed as we pulled out of the garage. "The New York fucking Attorney General!"

The smile plastered across Tony's face acted as a mirror for mine.

"I can't fucking believe we just sat with the fucking head of Narcotics asking us for help!" I laughed.

"Can you imagine the look on their faces when they saw you walking out of the bar with those guys? They must have been shitting their pants!" Tony laughed.

"I guess looking like a slob is a good look for me after all, Staton!" I joked.

"And I knew those Jamaicans were up to no good!" Tony continued. "I almost shit myself when he pulled their faces up on the screen."

"I guess no good depends on which side of the fence you're standing on, because their no good just got us into the Attorney Fucking General's office!"

Tony and I laughed and rehashed the whole meeting while Staton quietly sat back, taking in our excitement. Though he didn't join in on our stories, his smile was just as large.

"This can be huge for you guys," he said after we'd toned down. "The equipment they have and the unlimited vehicles are crazy, but it's something you need to talk to your family about. Take a night and make sure you're comfortable with this. You're talking drugs and gangs here, so it can become very dangerous and extensive."

I could taste the opportunity on my tongue. Regardless of what my family had to say, I was in.

I spent the rest of the drive home going over the past 24 hours in my head. Almost overnight, I went from slumming cigarettes in a back parking lot to receiving a job proposal from the General's office. Thoughts and scenarios swirled through my head, and in what seemed like minutes rather than hours, I pulled into the driveway of my home.

I never said a word to my family.

CHAPTER TWO

LINE OF COCAINE

While I'd lied through my teeth to my family about what I was doing for work, Tony had been more candid with his. So candid in fact that his wife was a little apprehensive of Tony signing on.

"It's the chance of a lifetime," I reassured him. "Tell her if shit gets bad you can back out. And you have my blessing on that."

"Billy, we've never dealt in drugs before," Tony said. "We don't know the first thing about what to buy. And now they just expect us to go in and demand it? How is that going to work?"

"I've already got a plan." I smiled.

"The fuck you do," Tony muttered.

"It came to me last night. It's simple and brilliant."

"Brilliant," Tony questioned, raising his eyebrows.

"I'm going to bring it right back to the ladies." I smiled. "I'm going to tell them I have this hot young chick who's only into it for a line."

"A line," Tony reiterated.

"A line, a bump. It means cocaine. I looked it up."

Tony shook his head.

"Anyway, I'm going to tell them my dealer has fallen short and I need a little help or else I ain't getting laid."

"You're going to use getting laid as your forefront to get us in the drug business?"

"Yeah," I smiled, proud of my genius plan.

"You're going to get us fucking killed," Tony said, gripping the steering wheel. "That's the dumbest plan you've had yet!"

"Tony, trust me. We make it complicated or somehow walk in saying we need shit for ourselves and they're not going to believe us. This plan is more believable than anything else we could do."

Coming up with strategies like this was something I'd been producing since my career in undercover began. They were sharp, quick and effective, although if you asked outside of the police realm they'd call them volatile and offbeat. But that's what made me who I was. I didn't think like cops, never did. I thought like a criminal, which brings me back to the line. Did it work, you wonder? I think it's fair to wager over two million dollars in sales and the largest takedown in New York State as collateral.

∾

Tony and I spent the next two days reloading our liquor and playing with all the little accessories that came with our shiny new van. It was fair to say we'd gotten the better end of the stick as our surveillance crew had to spend their days learning how to maneuver all the new materials and camera equipment.

"It's a better deal until we get held up at gunpoint for making a bad deal," Tony stated.

"That'll never happen," I said naively, patting his shoulder. "We won't be in it long enough to get that deep. Remember, we say when. And if it gets too risky, we bounce. It's our unit before theirs, remember. That was the deal."

Tony didn't respond. Deep down, I wondered if I believed my own lies as much as I thought.

The morning of our delivery to Thirsty Bear, Tony was nervous. He questioned what we'd say about the new van, what we'd do if Nash got mad about my drug inquiry, and who would bring the liquor inside if Nash banned us for life.

"Tony, you're living in the future," I said, searching the radio station for FOX News. "We have a new van because the other one broke down. We need drugs because I have women problems…

and unless Nash's short-staffed, he's never allowed us to bring the liquor down to begin with."

Tony remained quiet, chewing on the end of his fingernails. By the time we pulled into the parking lot there was nothing left for him to bite off.

℘

Our time within the bars hadn't always been so smooth. Tony and I had been brought into the operation with Staton under the premise of uncovering untaxed liquor sales through liquor distribution centers. I'd sat idly, waiting for any type of new gig, while mourning the crew and supervisor we'd recently lost in the towers, so I wasn't as quick to jump up and give my unimpressed input at first. Frankly, I was just happy to have been taken from my desk and the watchful eyes of Internal Affairs, and brought back onto the field. Sitting in a quiet office every day, imagining supervisor Mills helping several people down the stairs and out of the crashing towers, haunted me. I'd try and look through old files and drum up a new case, but his wife's eulogy would pop into my head.

"He died remaining true to who he was and doing what was instilled in him. He died a hero."

For months, stories emerged of the man who'd pulled co-workers off an elevator and down the stairs, helped a frantic woman who was being trampled, and yelled for people to keep moving as the roar of the building caved in above them. I kept those stories, and his wife's words, with me as I tried to imagine how to go on. And then, just when I seemed to reach a mental breaking point of day-to-day nothingness, Mill's appointed replacement, Staton, called.

As the previous Assistant Director for our New York City agency, Staton was recognized for the strong moves he'd made in the field. He was bold, daring and known for his high intelligence and successful reverse sting operations. However, his appearance left people thinking otherwise. This guy had long white hair pulled into a low ponytail at the back of his neck and a long beard. He didn't dress like other superiors. Instead of a suit, Staton sported cargo pants and flannel shirts.

Rumors had spread that Staton was pulling files on all employees for a large internal investigation he was conducting. It was a method said to be responsible for the renewed success of two downstate operations he was running. It was also a method that made us wait nine long months after 9/11 before our phone rang. Only the call wasn't for a case, it was for my pulled file.

The battle of emotions on the drive down to Staton's office had left me nauseous. I knew he was going to be onto something big, and I wanted nothing more than to be a part of that. Yet, as the desire for a future filled with possibilities crept into my head, so did the negative connotations. I assumed Staton had asked around about me and my reputation was less than par. I'd taken some inappropriate digs with my superiors, refused direct commands from Deputy Chief Booth, and didn't always play by the books. Agree with those ideals or not, I spent the ride up the marble elevator wondering if my pulled file was about to be my long-awaited dismissal from the agency.

"Welcome, Bill," Staton said as he rose from his brown leather seat to shake my hand. "I was just going over your file with a few of the agents. Pretty interesting stuff you've got here."

As I took a seat across from him, I noticed my file, spread open on his desk, full of highlights and Post-it notes.

"I called you here because your file shows you took a break during your career to operate a bar."

"That's correct," I said, twisting my hands together.

"I'd like to know a little bit more about your role in the bar, if you don't mind."

"Well, I owned it," I stated, shifting in my chair. "My buddy and I thought it would be a good idea at the time. The bar was for sale, in a decent location, and we knew a lot of people so, against better judgment, we bought it."

"Your file says that you stayed there for four years. That doesn't sound like poor judgment to me."

"No, it was a good fit at the time," I said, meeting Staton's stare. "But as the years went on I realized that I wasn't doing what

I truly enjoyed. I'd always wanted to be in the investigative field. I think I just got distracted for a bit."

"Billy," Staton said, leaning forward, "for the record, I'm not here for the history bullshit. I don't care why you left the field or why you came back. What I want to know is how much of a presence you held within the bar?"

"Well, I showed up every afternoon around two or three and stayed until we closed. It was my business, so I was there every day."

"So I'm sure you saw things that weren't always ethical," Staton said, his long ponytail falling over his shoulder.

"I think it would be hard to miss, yes."

"Let me cut right to the chase, Billy," Staton said. "I'm looking to tap into the untaxed liquor distribution that's been hitting New York State, and your past makes me think you might be an interesting fit."

Staton sat back, studying my reaction, which jumped from shock to excitement. I wasn't losing my job!

"I'm interested!" I said, sitting forward a bit too eagerly than I liked.

"I'm glad to hear you say that." Staton smiled. "I've been watching you. I think you've got what it takes to be a good undercover officer. Have you ever thought about dipping into that side of law enforcement before?"

"It's never been presented in a serious manner before, but I think I would be great at it. I've never had your typical cop demeanor."

"I agree," Staton stated. The dress pants and tie I'd worn, thanks to my wife, had been closing in on me since the moment I stepped out of the house.

"I think your upstate office gets the brunt end of the stick. I'll admit, I dismissed your unit as small-town civil workers as much as anyone else. But after evaluating your unit, I realized that philosophy is wrong. You guys are up there working hard, not giving a shit about the other stuff that goes on inside the office. I saw an openness and desire to learn and grow from every one of your guys. And let's not forget to mention how huge everyone is.

There wasn't one person who appeared to be under six foot! You're all big and burly, like you ate trees or some shit. We need a little ass kicking like that down here."

What Staton said was true, we were harsher than your typical downstate cops. None of my guys cared about what shoes matched their uniform or if their hair was fixed. They cared about going to work, busting out their shit and heading back home or down the street to their favorite bar. They were dirty, rough and not always the most articulate, but they meant business and they always got the job done—no matter what the cost.

"I do have one question I need to know before we move any further," Staton asked. "What's the deal with you and Booth?"

There it was, the question I'd worried would spear my file.

"Well, he's my superior, and I respect him in the field, but that's about it," I stated.

"Really? Because he didn't have the nicest things to say about you. In fact, he said you were a bullshit artist with no real skills."

"That's because he's a jealous asshole!" I spat, happy to finally say the words out loud. "I had a chance for Booth's position. I turned it down, and he can't get past that. He's so worried about everyone learning that I scored higher than him on the chief test, a test he didn't even pass, that instead of doing right and making a name for himself, he'd rather go out of his way to bust my balls. He's a prick who opts to sit back and complain, rather than make something for our agency and himself. That I can't respect."

"That's what I was hoping you'd say." Staton smiled. "Now that I can trust you, let's get to work."

The job, Staton informed me, required me to go to undercover school, a school I never knew existed.

"It's a formality," Staton said. "I can't send you on the streets without it. But it's only a few weeks, and it'll teach you things to keep you out of trouble."

I agreed to go before Staton finished his sentence. I'd never been one for classes or tests but, for the first time in my life, I couldn't wait to get started.

CHAPTER THREE

U.C. SCHOOL

Undercover school was held in an old police academy in Rochester, NY. The program was scheduled to last for two weeks and, if all went well, would grant me certification as a New York State registered undercover officer.

There were 40 other individuals in line to take the course, and every one of them dressed the part. They each had their own colored version of creased khaki pants, button down dress shirts, crew cuts and laptops. I'd showed up as myself: wind pants, an old t-shirt, an overdue haircut, and a yellow pad and pen. It's fair to say I stood out like a sore thumb.

I took a seat towards the back of the room as the instructor walked in. Without a word, the 5' 10", 185-pound and approximately 50-year-old—I guessed due to his slight gray coloring—instructor stood in front of his desk and surveyed the room.

For five minutes he held everyone captive with his gaze. When he stepped away from his desk, walking towards the rows of students, a strong anticipation for an introduction or class preparation speech lingered. You could feel the discomfort in the room as he scanned each person. Then he stopped in front of me.

"What's your name?" he said, hovering in front of me, his voice deeper than I'd imagined it to be.

"Bill," I said.

"Bill," he said, stepping back to look me up and down. "Did you think about what you were going to wear this morning or did you just pick any old shit up off the floor?"

The room filled with laughter.

"Actually, sir, I called your mother first to see what she suggested." I smiled.

The instructor's face fell flat, but I held my position. As much as I wanted to be here, I wasn't going to play in the bullshit, and I wanted that to be clear.

"It's a good thing you did," he said after a few minutes of silence. "Because my mama always knows best. Now, I want all of you to turn and look at Bill."

Forty bodies twisted around to get a better visual of the sloppy guy in the room.

"This is what you should all strive to look like," he said. "This is an example of a good undercover."

A smile cracked on the instructor's hard face as he reached out his hand.

"Pleased to meet you, Bill. I'm instructor Sullivan," he said, shaking my hand. "Together we're going to show the rest of these assholes how to enter a room NOT looking like a cop."

All forty faces looked at me in disgust while Sullivan walked the room talking about what we'd learn while we were there.

"The first," he said, "is not to get caught. You know how you do that?"

"By dressing like a slob," a tall asshole with a freshly shaved buzz cut yelled out.

"By not dressing like a cop, dipshit," Sullivan said, walking towards him. "You idiots dress like this asshole here and you're going to get caught, or killed. Bill, can I ask you why you think this schmuck here is not a street person?"

Every eye was on me once again.

"Well, for starters I'd look at his shoes," I said. "He's wearing black tactical boots. All law enforcement individuals have those shoes. They're not exactly what you'd find a street person wearing.

The second thing that strikes me is his hair. It's styled and freshly shaven, which lets me know looks and stature are important to him. That doesn't work in the criminal world."

"How about his outfit?" Sullivan said. "Anything strike you here?"

"Other than the fact that he looks wound up? No." I laughed.

"So you're saying wound up has a look?"

"What I'm saying is that's not what we'd find him wearing on a Sunday. We'd probably find him in a pair of old sweats and his college sweatshirt."

"Well, I didn't realize it was dress down day," Buzz Cut sneered.

"See, and here I thought working undercover was an automatic dress down day," I replied. "But that's because I don't want to be pegged for a cop, like you will be. I walk into a bar like this and they're going to dismiss me as a lowlife. They're not going to give me a second look. You walk in and you'll be lucky if they let you sit at the bar, let alone talk to you."

"Bill has a very good point," Sullivan said, stepping away from Buzz Boy. "Your first impression can be your last. You have to act, think and be the undercover you're portraying way before you walk through the door. Before you even meet the guys you're there to take down you have to be comfortable with yourself and steady in your presence, both mentally and physically."

Sullivan paced the room, spewing shit that seemed like second nature to me. As he talked about knowing your surroundings and playing the element, I kept wondering if I was the only person who found this shit easy. As I looked around the room, watching most of my fellow pupils furiously taking notes on their fruit computers, I realized I might have stumbled onto my career.

The next few days continued as the first, though Buzz Cut and other officers began arriving in casual attire. Sullivan covered the basics. He discussed dress, demeanor and automobiles.

"When you're undercover the state will supply some of you with cars," he said, his hands in his pockets as he paced the room. "The first thing you want to do when you get your vehicle is to study it. Spend an afternoon driving around to test it out. Learn where the windshield wiper button is. Figure out how to play with the radio, how to adjust your seat and your mirrors, and learn which side of the car your gas tank is on. The guy you're trying to get close to will notice if you're driving and you can't figure out how to turn on the wipers or change the radio station. Learning small, simple details such as these can save your life."

He also addressed using our backgrounds in a role.

"Here's where your real life comes into play," he said. "If you were an asshole in high school, be that asshole again. If your mama made you scrub your brother's piss off the toilets every week, use that anger. Pulling part of who you really are into who you are portraying can help form a connection between you and your target."

A small snicker escaped my lips.

"Bill, did you say something?" Sullivan inquired.

"No, sorry. I was just thinking about using my past in my role."

"Well, let's share what you're thinking then. Is there something you think you could use?"

"Well, my agency hired me because of my past. I'm a former bar owner. So working inside the bar seems like an appropriate fit."

"But what about your other background parts? Most of the guys are here because they know about motorcycles or they're an avid smoker or their daddy played with guns in the basement. That's a given. That's what makes them a perfect fit for the job. But what I believe you sneered at, and I'm going to use some of my undercover skills here, was in regard to something else. If you thought I was just addressing your job-related skills, you would have slept through my lecture or thought about what you had to get done this weekend. Instead your body reacted to what I said, which lets me know you've got more to say than you're sharing this minute."

"That's pretty good." I smiled, folding my arms across my chest.

"I want to hear it. And I'm certain everyone in this room wants to hear it now too. What's your story, big guy? You have a happy go-lucky family and decided to become a cop to save the world or did you see and experience some rough shit that made you want to go blue?"

"Well," I said, uncRossong my arms and sitting up, "I didn't come from a happy-go-lucky family, that's for sure. My family is as fucked up as they come. Dad was an alcoholic, Mom was quiet and took out his abuse both on me, and particularly on herself."

"So you became a cop to end domestic abuse," Sullivan interrupted, attempting to move on with his conversation before I cut him off.

"No. I became a cop because I was conflicted. I grew up surrounded by the mafia and the police. My grandfather was the driver for one of the top mafia guys in my neighborhood, as were some of my cousins and uncles. My uncle, my grandfather's son, was the Deputy Chief of Police. You want to talk about having family dinners with police members and mafia collectors every Sunday? I grew up not knowing if I wanted to be the good guy or the bad guy. I watched how they played off each other, saw the perks and angles from both sides, and battled with the constant desire to be both—hence my sneer. Being able to play a bad guy and feed that side of myself while doing good, well, let's just say it seems too good to be true at the moment."

Sullivan stared at me for a minute, taking in what I'd said.

It was true. I'd spent every afternoon until the age of nine going to stores and businesses with my grandfather. When I asked him why I always got a free soda or a piece of candy when we walked in, he would tell me it was out of respect. I was nine years old, what the hell did I know about respect and a free ice cream? But I idolized it. So much so that I awoke to my father and grandfather having a fight one evening about how my father did not want me riding with my grandfather any longer.

"You're not invisible, Dad," my father yelled. "You've got him with you everywhere. It's not safe."

The breakfast table was quiet the next morning. Only my father, who'd been busy reading the paper, spoke.

"You're no longer allowed to go with Pappi," he said, his face buried behind the black and white ink. "I don't want to hear one word about it."

That was the first time I knew what it felt like to hate a parent. As the years went on, my grandparents' passing on and my father's drinking becoming more extensive, I knew what the feeling of hate truly was. It was the loathing of the sound of his car door when he arrived home, his steps up the stairs, and his fists to my body when it wasn't my mother's turn. It didn't matter that there were three children in the house. I, the middle, odd-looking son, was the target of his abuse. My height, broad stature and awkward nature embarrassed him. Today, I would have been a father's proud sports prodigy. But then, in a neighborhood filled with Italians who were shorter and slimmer than I was, my look was awkward and a reminder that my mother had Polish blood in her—a fact my Italian father never liked to admit.

"That right there," the instructor said, bringing me back to the class, "is an agency's dream. He understands the look, understands the nature, and has the right background to pull off a major sting. That right there is an undercover fantasy. If he plays his cards right everyone in this room will be hearing some major shit about operations he'll take down. If we don't, then that's one man who truly fucked up the talent the world laid out for him. Now the rest of you won't be so lucky. But you'll be lucky to study with him now and possibly work with him at some point along your career."

Sullivan raised his eyes over the crowd and looked directly at me.

"I'm going to expect a lot from you, as is everyone in this room," he said. "If your shit is real you won't let us down."

I nodded my head, taken aback by the sudden turn of conversation. It was the first time anyone in my life addressed my skills and my background in a positive light.

The final days of school were spent on field assignments. Outside of the classroom, we took driving classes, learned speed tactics and how to remain discreet during a pursuit, studied with former undercovers, and my favorite—shadowing detectives on a current operation.

By the time I was introduced to my two detectives, Barrett and Romaro, I was practically foaming at the mouth. The excitement to be on the field again, shadowing two prominent detectives on an active case, made me feel alive.

Barrett and Romaro were by the book. They both had firm handshakes, broad smiles and wore the same black leather gloves. Even their statue was about the same, with Barrett holding a slight edge up. After our brief introductions, I swiftly followed them to their patrol car, where Barrett took lead in the driver's seat. Romaro opened the back door, gesturing for me to slide in, before settling into the front.

Sullivan had made it clear that we were there to observe and listen. He discouraged us from attempting to aide in the detectives' work, unless we were invited, and I respected that. After all, while I knew these guys were making a few extra bucks escorting wannabes around, at the end of the day they still had a job to do. And, if I were in their seat, the last thing I would want is some two-bit ride-along offering advice on my case.

Knowing my place, I nestled into the hard backseat and listened as Romaro explained their case in detail. An illegal manufacturing plant, responsible for producing tobacco, had been discovered two miles off the interstate. The plant, which had been home to several canning and bottling operations in the past, had been linked to a few illnesses and one death as a result of mixed material found in the faux cigarettes they were distributing. The detectives had one informant ready to testify, but needed something stronger to insure they went down for the crime. They'd received word that the next shipment of cigarettes would be coming from the warehouse within two days. They had around-the-clock surveillance on the joint and were just waiting to apprehend the truck as it hit the road. An electrified shiver spread throughout my body. Of all the cases and detectives to work with, I'd struck undercover gold. I knew this shit like the back of my hand.

Barrett and Romano were fun to work with. They made me feel comfortable, asked about my past and freely swapped stories from the battlefield. Their welcoming nature put me at ease, and while they didn't ask me for advice or my opinion, they never halted my questions. I picked their brain, searching for different tactics. When they said something that was informative, I wrote it down. When they said something that I knew wouldn't work for me, I wrote it down. Though the detectives did things by the book, they were smart in their approach and tactics. I learned about their five-year history together, the cases they'd cracked and how they'd cracked them. The whole gig was going along swimmingly. Until the final night.

With two days of minimal activity coming from the warehouse, Barrett and Romano declared this night "the one." For two hours, I sat in the backseat of the cold car, waiting for something to happen. The detectives reported the activity as it went down: light in the rear of the warehouse went on, an unknown van parked beside the loading dock, three large men approached the warehouse, light went out.

"What the hell do you suppose they're doing?" Barrett questioned.

"Making sure no one sees what's going on, should someone be watching," Romano stated.

Barrett pulled out his binoculars and tried to get a better view. The warehouse, which was secreted behind a ten-foot-tall electric fence, posed multiple blind spots, and the 14-degree temperature outside kept causing the front window of our car to ice over.

An hour into the wait, Barrett caught something. The van, which was driving without any lights, pulled away from the loading dock. The eagerness I'd felt to sit back and observe suddenly slid down my body and landed in a puddle on the floor.

As the van made its way to the gate, I listened to Barrett and Romaro's plan. We were to follow the van, report where he went and then rush in and seize the vehicle with their secured warrant in hand.

"I've got a better idea," I said, pulling off my jacket. "Let me get in the truck with the driver and see what I can find out."

The detectives looked at me as if I'd lost my mind.

"And how does that work?" Barrett asked. "You just going to walk up and ask to take a look around?"

Romaro laughed.

"Why not?" I said, pulling off my shoes.

"This crazy newbie thinks he can just hop into the passenger seat while a criminal is hauling thousands of dollars of illegal products and have a chat." Barrett laughed. "That's not how this works, guy. Just sit back and take your notes like you're supposed to. Right now this is real police business, not a shadow operation."

"You doubt me," I stated, removing my socks.

The van approached the gate.

"Anyone ever tell you that you're an idiot?" Romaro joked.

"All my life." I laughed, removing my shirt and tossing it into the front seat.

Confused, Romano turned around, holding my shirt by the tip of his fingers as if it were diseased.

"What the fuck are you doing?"

Barrett now joined Romano, their jaws hanging as I sat there in my boxers.

"Gentlemen," I smiled, "you owe me a hot coffee if this shit works."

Before they could say anything, I bolted from the car and started running. The snow stung the bottoms of my feet, but my adrenaline and the hollering from the detectives behind me pushed me through each layer of rigid snow I ran over.

The secured gates opened, and the van began to drive out—his headlights still off. I sprinted into the road, just four feet ahead of him, flailing my arms and yelling. I prayed he'd notice me.

Three feet. Two feet. One foot.

The van took notice, stopped and turned on its lights.

"What the fuck are you doing, asshole?" the driver yelled, his head sticking out the driver's side window. He didn't sport a trucker's hat like I'd imagined he would. "Get the fuck out of the road."

I stepped closer to the van, pretending to hold my chest as if I were freezing.

"Please help me out, man. I'm fucking frozen out here. I need a ride."

"You've got no clothes on, idiot," he yelled.

"Man, I got caught with my buddy's girlfriend. He came home early and I had to jump out the window. I've been running, hoping to find someone. My feet are in serious pain."

The driver titled his head out the window, watching as I jostled from one foot to the next.

"Please man, can you give me a few minutes to warm up in your ride?"

"Women always get you in this much trouble?" the driver asked.

"Only about every other week," I responded, rubbing my arms. "Please man. I swear I'm a decent human being. Just a bit caught up with the ladies is all. Can you spare a ride?"

The driver hesitated. For a minute I thought he might say no, and that I'd be in some real shit when I arrived back at the detectives' car. Hell, if the guy said no I'd just fucked the case, let alone any chance I'd had of graduating and becoming an undercover. Then, like a ray of sunshine, the driver said those two magical words that erased the burden from my chest.

"Get in."

I ran my ass around the van and pulled myself inside as fast as I could. As cold as it was outside, my adrenaline was pumping so hard that I was actually sweating. I wiped the sweat from my brow so I could carry on with my frozen act.

"You turn out to be a crazy mother-fucker and I'll leave your cold ass in the woods, you hear me?" the driver said as I sat down.

"Man, you can do whatever you like," I said, throwing my hands in front of the heater. "I'm just grateful you saved my ass. If I didn't freeze to death, I'd probably be hunted and killed by my buddy any time now."

"You messed with his girl?" the driver inquired, shaking his head. "That's messed up. I should probably do your buddy a favor and leave you here for him to find."

"You wouldn't say that if you saw the girl," I grinned, rubbing my hands for warmth. "He should have known better, anyway. Girls like her aren't set to stay home and play wife for long. Girls like her get bored."

I studied the driver as I spoke. He was missing a tooth on his right side and had a small birthmark under his eye that resembled the state of Texas.

"How close are you two?" he asked.

"Close enough to have taken time in the slammer together."

"What jail you been in?"

"Clinton Correctional, two years. Forgery."

"Fuck me. I was there too. What year?"

"1990-1992. You were just a baby then. We weren't in together."

"'98-'99, smuggling."

"Shit. You don't look like you could smuggle my mother. What they'd get you on? Robbing baby formula?"

The driver laughed. "I ain't as young as you think," he smirked. "I've been pulling tricks since I was 16."

"Mom or dad issues?" I joked, pulling my chest up to the heater. "You got a blanket or something in here?"

"Dad. He left. Took the money. I had to support my mom and my three brothers. Stealing became second nature. Check behind your seat, there might be a sweatshirt."

I turned my body around, pretending to be stiff from the cold, and scanned the back of the open van. It was loaded from floor to ceiling with cigarettes.

"Wow," I called out. "You fucking rob a smoke shop?"

"Nah." The driver laughed, reaching behind my seat and pulling out the sweatshirt I was supposed to be seeking. "Just transporting some goods for a friend."

"Must be a pretty good friend," I said, draping the sweatshirt across my chest. Based on the driver's medium frame I didn't dare embarrass myself trying to put it on. "You allowed to smoke any of them?"

"Not these ones. They're for transport. But I do have my own stash that he hooks me up with."

"Shit," I said, turning my body to look at the amount of cigarettes again. "Why don't you just drive off and fucking sell them for a shit ton of money? I know people who would be interested."

"No fucking way," he stated. "This job is too good to mess with. Ain't no money your guys can give me that compares to the shit I get paid. Best gig of my career."

"How much money we talking about?"

"$10,000 a haul."

"$10,000 a haul!" I spat, whipping my body around to face his. "You make $10,000 for transporting cigarettes! What's inside them, gold?"

"Nah. They ain't real cigarettes per say. They're manufactured. Designed to look like the real shit. They fill them with a bunch of crap. Law says it's illegal, but what's the difference between the other shit they let people inhale? Fucking tobacco ain't no better and it sure as hell ain't pure. They've been lacing that shit with pesticides and wood chips and all kinds of crap to break down their costs. Law just wants their cut."

"Ten fucking thousand dollars," I repeated.

"Twice a month. Listen, where are you going anyway? I'm on a schedule here."

"I'm going anywhere you are," I shrugged. "Drop me when you're ready. I just need to get out of here quickly, if you know what I mean."

"Yeah, killer boyfriend on the loose. I got it."

The driver headed straight past the detectives, none the wiser.

"You're telling me you make $20,000 a month," I questioned, truly startled at what he was taking in. Maybe choosing the good way out was a bad decision after all. "That's $240,000 a year!"

"Yep. And your friends can't touch that shit. No one can make me waver from what this company can offer me."

I sat silent for a minute, calculating the numbers.

"You thinking about taking my rig now?"

"I'm thinking about what that money could do for my family and wondering how I can get a job like this."

"Well, running out in the snow with no clothes on is a start. Shows that you're one crazy motherfucker. You take risks and you're not scared of a little danger."

"All my life," I said.

The driver and I began sharing dangerous stories from our past. Deep down I couldn't help but think this story was already making the top of my list.

"Let me speak to your boss," I said after a few minutes. "I bet I can sway him to take me on board. Hell, maybe we could even double your load and be partners. That is if he has more material to sell."

"Oh, he's got it all right. But what makes you think I want your naked ass in my van all the time?"

"I'm a fun guy. And, unless you have a pretty lady you're trying to keep all to yourself, I'm fairly harmless."

"So you're admitting you're a poor judge of character when it comes to women."

"Just one. And she's history now. I got what I wanted."

"You're a sick son-of-a-bitch all right." The driver laughed, his Texas birthmark wrinkling into his skin.

"Come on, man. Let me talk to him. I bet I can persuade him. I need my life to turn around. Ain't nothing good waiting back home for me now anyway."

The driver sighed, looking straight ahead into the snow. "I've got a long drive, buddy. You will need to pick a spot, I can drop you at."

"I told you. I'm going wherever you're going. I'm with you now. I want a job."

"Guy, I'm headed two hours out. I ain't coming back this way for another two weeks. I can't get you home."

"Fuck home," I said, sitting back in the seat. "This is my new home."

"You are one insistent asshole," the driver said, smiling. "You think you really want this life?"

"I ain't got nothing else," I said. "Plus, I'm tapped out of new ladies to try."

"Well, you better buckle up then," he sighed. "Once you're in, you're in."

"I think it's fair to say that I already am. After all, I know what you're hauling."

"And I know about your intent to sell it," he smirked.

"So we're both on each other. Help me get a piece of the pie and I'll forever be indebted to you."

"First thing's for sure, you can't show up naked," the driver said, looking at me. "They'll toss you right on the street. You got any money?"

I pulled out my wallet with a big smile. "I wasn't stupid enough to leave the important shit behind."

The only shop that was open was a trucker stop ten miles up the road. I purchased a pair of shower sandals, a trucker hat, a sweatshirt that read, "I do it for the haul," a pair of oversized sweatpants, which I reckoned I'd still make use of after this night, and a turkey sandwich.

By the time we pulled into the driver's delivery spot I knew the names of everyone in charge, their set locations, where they shipped from, where their routes were and even the trucker's father's name: Chip. Chip the Dip, he called him.

I'd like to say I had the opportunity to meet them and obtain an interview, but the detectives had been too concerned. Not sure if my undercover had been blown or what was going on inside the van, but they called in a countywide backup. As soon as Bud, the driver who finally introduced himself after the first hour, pulled through the gates of an undisclosed garage, blue and red lights sprang from the darkness, lighting up the van like it was the fourth of July. Sirens flared and officers asked us to slowly step out of the vehicle on the loudspeaker. For a second, the activity caught me off guard, and my heart leapt into my throat.

"Fuck!" the driver screamed. "Fuck, Fuck."

Bud panicked, quickly turning his head left and right, searching for a way out.

"Pull the fuck over," I urged him.

"No fucking way. No fucking way," he yelled. "There has to be a way out of here."

"You're surrounded," I said. "Give up, man. Surrender so they'll take it easy on you."

"I can't," he said, gripping the wheel. "I can't let them get to me."

"Bud, offer up your people. You'll be out by tomorrow. It's easy man."

"I can't do that," he cried. "I can't rat them out."

"You already did," I said flatly.

"What the fuck do you mean" Bud said, wide eyed. "Huh? Tell me what the fuck you mean?"

"I mean my name is not Bob. I'm an officer with the PATB and you're under arrest for smuggling illegal cigarettes throughout the state."

Bud's Texas birthmark dropped like a confederate flag. "You're a cop. This whole time."

"Sorry, man. It was the only way we could crack the case," I said gently.

"The whole girlfriend and being naked in the snow. You made that all up?"

"I did," I said, holding my gaze. "Now stop the truck and surrender. Don't make it harder. They already know what you have. I had a wire in my pocket the whole time."

"A wire," the driver whined, sounding like my son at four years old. "Fuck!"

"I did enjoy our time together, for what it's worth. And $240,000 a year. I can't say I wouldn't have thought about taking the gig myself. That's a life changer."

Bud pulled the truck to a stop and handed me the keys. Together we raised our hands in surrender and stepped out of the truck. We were seized within seconds, both of us pulled apart and dragged to separate vehicles.

"Are you Billy?" an officer to my right questioned. Barrett could be heard broadcasting my description over the radio.

"I am," I said, taking in the amount of police and officers who were swarming the warehouse and surrounding area.

"Great job, Billy," the officer said, releasing my arm and leading me to the safety of his car. "You just cracked down an operation that we've been trying to break through for months."

I slid into the passenger seat of his car and continued to watch as the commotion outside gained momentum. It was like a scene out of the Wild West. I kept waiting for an officer to come running up to my window waving a scalping instrument and chanting.

"Your detectives are a little sore with you, but the rest of us are in awe," the officer said as he got into the driver's seat. "That's some crazy shit you pulled out there."

"You've got a pen and paper?" I inquired. "I need to write this shit down before I forget."

"Anything you need, Bud," he said, pulling his standard notepad from his front pocket.

The name Bud sent shivers down my spine. Poor guy. He was about to face a significant amount of jail time if he chose to protect his boss.

Since my imaginary recording device, which Bud believed lay inside a pocket I didn't have, didn't exist, I immediately wrote down everything Bud had told me. Barrett and Romaro's shadows lingered outside the passenger window as I wrote, so I took my time. I knew coffee was off the table.

∞

I graduated with flying colors the following week and received my official undercover certification, with Staton present.

"Bill," Sullivan said, shaking my hand for the last time. "I've got some high hopes for you. I want to see you deliver on them, you hear."

"Loud and clear, Mr. Sullivan."

Sullivan slapped me on the back and told me to stay safe.

"Nah," I said, smiling. "I plan to play it anything but safe."

I drove home with my certificate buckled into the passenger seat. After all these years, I had something I could be proud of and someone who saw what I'd seen in myself. As I walked around my backyard, picking up the dog shit the kids and my wife had left accumulating while I'd been gone, I couldn't feel anything other than pride.

CHAPTER FOUR

OP SPIRITS

"Operation Spirits," Staton said as I sat in his office. "That's what we're going under. I've set up a new team for you. Some guys you know, others you'll get to know quickly."

I turned to face a team of four other guys, all sitting around Staton's table.

Tony was to be my new partner. He was an instrumental investigator within the Albany unit. He was known for his business sense, was fluent in Spanish and Italian, and was good-looking and well-liked by everyone, including me.

"The operation will need a smart businessman. Tony will be your go-to. He will handle the sales, arrangements and meetings. He's been prepped and is knowledgeable on liquor prices, quality and brand names. Once you successfully make your pitch, Tony will step in to handle the money and sales transactions."

Jeff, also known as The Shoe, was to be our loader and surveillance assistant.

"Jeff is rumored to be able to drive anything, anywhere." Staton smiled. "Unfortunately, those rumors will more than likely be put to the test, should you boys do what we're expecting on this operation."

Jeff had a relaxed, calm demeanor that I picked up right away.

"You two are also the biggest guys on the team, so you'll be expected to load a lot of the liquor distribution once you get where I want you to be."

McNally was to be the leader of our unit. As our Chief of Operations he was to travel with us should we need to expand from our routed vicinity.

"I've worked with McNally for years, so I can assure you that he is the best guy for the job," Staton said. "He is not there to step on your toes, as I believe you're going to need a bit of creative freedom to get the job done. He's there to guide you, keep you out of harm's way, and will be responsible for reporting back to me and handling the red tape."

I'd met McNally once prior. He seemed stable and confident. Not at all like a Booth or Post. Then there was Docks, Tony's partner from the Albany office. I sensed his arrogance from across the room. He was a pretty boy thought highly of himself.

"Billy, you're going to love Docks. He's another pain in the ass, so you should get along."

I nodded my head and turned back to Staton.

"Now that we're all pleasantly introduced let's get down to the formalities," Staton said. "As of this afternoon, you five are all a part of Operation Spirits. You will work together as a unit. Your success will depend on one another. So, if you fail, it's on everyone's shoulders."

Operation Spirits was designed to uncover untaxed liquor sales happening around the Southern Tier of New York. A recent 40 percent drop in revenue had created a buzz within the Ivory Tower, something I was all too aware of. As an agent for the Petroleum, Alcohol, and Tobacco Bureau, I'd spent the past eight years investigating the distribution of untaxed cigarettes smuggled through Canada and distributed throughout the Native American reservations. It might sound small at first, but for those unaware of the true nature of the smuggling ring, let me explain.

In the 1700s, New York State made an agreement with the Native Americans granting them some of the land they'd been diligently pursuing. The land was split across the state, in what we know as the Six Nations; the Cayuga Gayohkohnyoh, Mohawk Kahnai'kehaka, Oneida Onyota'a:ka, Onondaga Ononda'ge, Seneca Onondawahgah, and Tuscarora Ska:ru:re. With these land claims came the loss of the state's jurisdiction on the reservations, which sounds just—until part of that unit goes rogue and wants more. For the Native Americans up near Massena, NY, that something regarded one of the few unpatrolled borders of Canada.

Under the Jay Treaty, which passed in 1794, the Native Americans were legally permitted to pass freely along the St. Lawrence River and the 45th parallel. Without New York State police or patrol borders allowed on the reservations, the border became prime opportunity for criminals looking for a way in. And by the 1980s that opportunity was happily filling the pockets of smuggling, bringing anything and everything into the United States. Think all cocaine routes were coming in through Mexico? Try again.

During this time, the government was sinking an alarming rate of taxpayer money into uncovering how all the drugs, guns and various illegal contraband were coming in. Yet, when the United States government finally discovered that the missing link had been under its nose the whole time, they made sure the public didn't catch wind of it. Why? Because alarming the country that we'd basically given a group of individuals a legal contract to smuggle anything they wanted into our country, and we technically couldn't do jack about it, wouldn't make for a very good political agenda, now would it?

In hopes of quietly resolving the problem, New York State developed a task force that operated under the law known as ATTEA, a class action lawsuit from New York State vs. Milhem ATTEA Bros. The United States Supreme Court had brought forth an injunction against the Native Americans, which gave them the right to purchase untaxed cigarettes for the people on their reservation. Seems like an easy case-closed situation. Yet, even with the law in hand, the Native Americans continued to receive 10,000 cases of cigarettes a week. With a ballpark of 2,500 people living on reservations, the number seemed ambiguous. Even if the reservation sold 10 cartons of cigarettes to each person, which would have to include children, they still wouldn't make a dent in sales. Therefore, it became the task force's job to spearhead finding out what was happening with all of the remaining untaxed cigarettes. Untaxed cigarettes might sound minimal to the untrained ear, but untaxed items created a large pay cut for New York State. And since the state needed money to repair and refund the loss it had created, our agency was placed on board.

The PATB had been a fairly quiet unit until then. But with Director Staton on the lead, and New York State willing to turn a blind eye in order to repair its ego, the PATB rose to an entirely new level. And boy was it heated.

Over the course of seven years, our task force worked with a premium multi-unit team, which included the Drug Task Force and ICE, who worked to uncover illegal immigration traffic. We were responsible for shutting down several motor fuel operations, untaxed cigarette rings, untagged tractor trailers, and ending hundreds of thousands of dollars in illegal sales. To say we were unstoppable would be right on—until Internal Affairs found fault with Staton and teamed up with Chief Booth to take us down.

"We're targeting the liquor stores," Staton proclaimed, to my surprise. "Billy's job is to see what stores are open to purchasing untaxed liquor. Once we get a go-ahead, I want Jeff and Docks to begin a full surveillance and background into the store and the owner. See what you can find. The deeper we can get into these sales, the more likely we are to connect with the distributors that are supplying the untaxed liquor out there."

I wasn't exactly sold on the liquor stores concept, but I was new and eager to start.

Our first two months produced miniscule results. Staton was frustrated to say the least. Time after time the doors closed in my face. I'd walk in, introduce myself as Billy, a former bar owner who'd been dealing in untaxed liquor since I left the business, here to let them know about a sweet deal I had. However, if I sold more than three bottles to the less than leery customers it was a miracle.

"They don't want to work with someone they don't know," I pleaded to Staton. "We have to try a different angle."

"So find the angle," he said, leaving my team and me stumped.

I changed my approach, reworded my scheme and sat for hours with my team discussing how we could change our tactics.

During the seventh week, with barely enough cases to floss our teeth, I took a shot on a large liquor chain, per Dock's advice.

"We've tried everything else," he said.

Leave it to my team to agree with this idiot. I wasn't in the store for ten minutes before the sheriff's department ran into the store, cuffing me and Tony and confiscating our van full of liquor. Those poor guys actually believed they'd landed a big case. It wasn't until we reached the station that Jeff and Docks explained who we were.

"You're undercover," the sheriff said.

"I am, sir," I replied.

"Well, why the fuck didn't you tell me in the first place?" he said, angrily unlocking the handcuffs, which were set a little too tight around my wrists.

"I was trying to protect my cover, sir."

The sheriff and his crew released Tony, me and our van without so much as a good luck. But who could blame them? If I'd walked into a liquor store and gotten my hands on a huge lead, only to watch it instantly dissolve, I would've been pissed too.

I went home from the arrest determined to convince Staton that the liquor stores were not the answer. To my surprise, he didn't disagree.

"When I began my career I was fortunate to have a boss that allowed me to trust my judgments and run with them. It was that freedom that I hold accountable for my success. If I'd been limited and stifled, I would have burned out and stayed at that level for God knows how long. That boss showed me that freedom, and a supportive unit, was the key to making things happen. Now I am going to give that to you."

"You're going to give me the key to freedom?" I questioned, somewhat confused about where he was going.

"If you'd like it," Staton said.

Quiet filled the line. I wasn't sure what to say or how to decipher what the fuck he was talking about.

"Billy," he finally interjected, "I don't think you've ever felt trusted in your life. You're someone people always watch. They're cautious of you because of your unconventional ways in the system. I think, given the freedom to take this operation into your own hands, you'll trust yourself. So if you want to go after the bars, I want you to give it a shot. Just let me know what you need."

"Are you fucking with me?" I laughed into the phone.

"No fucking on this end, just a belief in a promise that you can do better if you try it your way. Do try and report back."

Staton hung up the line. Dead air filtered through my brain. He trusted me. He was letting me do what I'd asked. Those two ideas were as confusing as they were liberating. After a few minutes I picked up the phone and called Tony.

"Get ready. We're about to go bar hopping."

Tony arrived on site with a smile as wide as a clown.

"You ready to make history?" I said, sliding into the passenger seat.

"Been ready for years," he said, putting the van into drive. "Where are we headed?"

"To the first bar we see."

We didn't sell to the first bar we stopped at. It was the second try that worked.

The bar we made our first sale to was old and run by an Italian guy named Mario. No joke, Mario was close to 250 pounds. I immediately branded him with the name Double-Wide.

Mario stepped out from a back room with an unlit cigar in mouth. His stomach hung so far over his pants that you couldn't tell where they began and where they ended.

I took a deep breath and tried to remain as calm as I could.

Talk to him like he's your uncle, I told myself. *You know this guy. He could be any one of your family members.*

Mario squinted as he approached me, his forehead frowning into the fat between his eyes.

I smiled and stuck out my hand like we were old pals.

"I've got something for you" I said in a soft voice. I leaned forward, "I think you'll be interested."

"What the fuck do you know what I'll be interested in?" he sneered, the cigar between his teeth.

"A friend of a friend referred me to you. Said you're always open to new business deals. Said you were smarter than shit when it came to fresh opportunities."

"What the fuck opportunity is that?" he questioned.

"How about a shit ton of untaxed liquor? That sound like an opportunity for you?"

Mario stood still for a minute, taking in his cigar and staring at me. I held my pose like I could give two shits if he believed me or not. It worked.

"Why the fuck would you think I would be interested in untaxed liquor?"

"Because word on the street is you're a smart businessman."

Mario puffed on his cigar, thinking.

"Listen, I've got a round of clients that I have to get to today. If you're not interested that's fine, but I think you should take a look at what I have before I leave. From the way people speak about you, I can't help but assume you'd be upset if you let this opportunity go by without exploring it."

"What type of liquor are you talking about?" he asked.

"Any type you want."

"Is this watered-down shit? I'm going to buy and find out you diluted half the bottle?"

"You can check the seals all yourself. They're all 100% authentic and on hand."

"You have them here?" he questioned.

"Out back in my van," I said smiling at him. "It's ready and waiting for you to come and have a look."

"Bobby!" Mario called someone in the back. "I need you to come check a delivery with me. Man here says he has something. Let's see if he's bluffing."

Another fat man, about half this guy's age, walked from the back of the bar, looking me up and down. There was a large brown stain on his white t-shirt. I couldn't tell if it was recent or pre-existing.

"Who the fuck is this?" he asked.

"Billy, Billy the Liquor Guy," I said, extending my hand.

"Billy the Liquor has something. I want you to see if it's legit."

"Fuck do we know about this guy?" Stain Boy said, ignoring my hand.

"Nothing. That's why you're here," Mario said, squinting at him. "Let's go see what he has."

I followed Mario and his sidekick through the kitchen and out a side door. I saw Tony's eyes widen as he spotted us.

"Open it up," I said, knocking on the back door.

Tony pulled open the doors from the inside and revealed what would be considered Disneyland to anyone in the bar industry. Tony turned on an overhead light, which Staton had installed, along with a camera, and revealed our treasure of liquor. Mario's mouth dropped.

"Gentlemen, this is Tony. He's my business partner and financial guru," I said.

"Nice to meet you, gentlemen." Tony smiled with a little salute. "You want to see anything, please let me know."

"Financial guru?" Stain Boy mocked. He folded his arms across his chest in defiance.

"Yeah. He can break down the cost of every bottle and order here, and he can show you how much you'll be saving, should you buy with us. He knows more about figures than I do. Hence the guru."

"So what's your job then, if he's handling all the money?" Mario grunted.

"To let smart business individuals like yourself know that we exist."

I pulled a bottle of Patron from the rack closest to me and let Mario check the label, the seal and everything in between.

"This isn't a gag," I said. "There's no switch fix, no gimmick. This is straight up liquor sold without the additional tax price tag."

Mario turned the bottle over, letting the golden liquid inside slush around.

"Tony, how much would this gentleman save on a case of Patron?" I asked while Mario passed the bottle to his partner to study.

"$139.68, to be exact," Tony said, not missing a beat.

Mario and Bobby looked up in surprise.

"See why he's my financial guru," I said. "He can do more, you know. Ask him about your vodka of choice."

"Kettle One," Mario said.

"$145."

"We can do this all day if you like. It's kind of a fun game when you get into it."

Mario turned to Bobby, looking for an answer. Bobby looked back at the van and then at Mario.

"It's your call, Bobby," Mario said. "Seems like a pretty good situation. If it's true."

"I'm pretty sure these aren't imaginary bottles you're seeing." I laughed. "You're seeing the deal with your own eyes. It's your choice if you take it or leave it."

Mario excused himself and pulled Bobby to the side. I didn't dare look at Tony as I was afraid my eyes might give it all away. Instead, I stood there, opening and closing my hands to quiet any shaking.

"Okay, here's what we're going to do," Mario said. "I'm going take some bottles today. If the price works out and all seems legit, I'll order some more. How often are you guys in town?"

"We hit our customers weekly," I responded. "Largest orders come first. Once we figure out our schedule, based on demand, we'll give you a heads up on when we'll be back."

Mario stood there taking in the bottles once again.

"One case of Patron, Kettle and a case of speed rack."

Tony put together his invoice on a three-tiered pad so we could keep track of sales as much as they could, while I gathered his order.

"I've got cash inside," Mario nodded to me. "Bobby will have it ready for you once all is delivered."

I expected Bobby to help me carry in the cases, but there I was loading up the liquor and hauling it in, while he stood back like a dainty woman, watching me work. This was my first insight into my new role. In the world of bad guys, I would have to play the peon.

The drive to the next bar was a fucking scene. Tony and I were like two little kids on Christmas morning. We couldn't believe what we'd just done. We were full of gusto and ready to take on bar after bar. And that's exactly what we did.

During the next five hours we secured four more bars, back to back. We set up weekly follow up visits and drove back to the office with one speed rack and two bottles of peppermint schnapps remaining. If Tony and I were the type for the sweet shit, I believe we would have walked into the office and cracked open a bottle to celebrate. Instead, we went back, filled out mounds of paperwork, and called Staton.

"We need more supplies," I said. "We're tapped out."

CHAPTER FIVE

BILLY THE LIQUOR GUY

Our operation expanded across the Binghamton/Vestal area when word of our business spread. One bar owner would talk to another bar owner, and we'd get a new lead. By the third month, our operation covered 40% of Broome County—and that was a huge deal when it came to the state and numbers.

Most of our bars were mainstream. Nothing too up and up, though we had a few middle-class joints and sports bars tossed into the mix. One sports bar in particular was run by a former college quarterback, once destined for the NFL. A national champion, the quarterback had retired after an injury and moved back to his hometown of Vestal, NY to try his hand in the bar business. He and I hit it off, as talking sports was second nature for me, and making small liquor deals was nature for him. His deals weren't anything noteworthy, but the connections he provided linked us to a long list of alcohol, tobacco, and eventually drug deals that transformed our investigation.

The former quarterback had two people interested in our products, but their bars were located in Elmira, NY, approximately 57 miles from where our current operation was set up. The jurisdiction wasn't a factor for Staton.

"If your guys are up for a bit of travel, then you have my blessing."

At first the expansion turned out to be a bust. We arrived at the recommended bar, ready to cash in on a big sale, only to find out the bar was closing.

"You're about a month too late," the landlord said as he swept the floor. "Owners bolted out of here without even paying the last month."

The second recommended bar didn't have much use for us either.

"I'm not getting mixed up in anything that goes against the state," the owner said. "I've already had my fair share of run-ins with inspectors. I don't want to give them any reason to step into my joint more than they already do."

"I understand," I said, leaning against his bar. "Do you know if any other bars in the area might be interested? We've come all this way and I'd like to save myself some fuel on the way home. Our load's pretty heavy."

The bartender took a hard look at me.

"I don't want to get in trouble, and I don't want anybody blowing me in," I told him, raising my hands up. "I'm just looking to get rid of my product."

At six feet tall, dressed in wind pants and a sloppy shirt, it was safe to assume I fit this guy's mold for another degenerate looking for business.

"There's a bar down the street. I don't know that they'll be interested in what you've got, but they run a lot of stolen things through there, so you've got a shot," he replied. "Now kindly finish your drink and leave my bar."

The Thirsty Bear was an older, one-floor, rectangular building on the corner of a main street. Behind the building was a large parking lot that everyone used to enter and exit, which would have been good to know at the time. Tony and I had been so busy looking for the joint that we nearly missed the turn to the front entranceway. Spotting it, Tony made an abrupt right-hand turn, causing the van to drive up over the curb almost on two wheels, making a large screeching sound as we halted in front of the door.

The turn captured the attention of an elderly biker, who happened to be sitting out front. It was only 11 a.m. but this guy was already stoned out of his mind.

"Are you guys drunk?" he said as we stumbled out of the van.

"No," we responded.

"Stoned?"

"No."

"Wow, then you guys are really fucked up!" He laughed.

You could already smell the liquor that was leaking out of the back door from the bottles we'd broke. We were fucked. We'd lost some of our product and probably lost our new lead since we arrived looking like morons. So far, it seemed as if expansion wasn't in the cards. But with every action comes a bit of levity. Our arrival had brought a few more patrons out of the bar, all assessing and laughing at the situation.

While Tony cleaned up the liquor and answered questions for the curious patrons, all half in the bag, I entered the bar hoping for a quick "no" so we could end the day.

The bar was like a dungeon. It had dark walls, old wooden bar stools and round wooden tables. There was one old TV mounted behind the bar, a dart board, and shuffleboard, which was already busy with activity. I counted twenty-five people, all of whom turned to stare at me as I entered the unused front door. Ten patrons sat at the bar, five played shuffleboard, three hard-looking women sat at the table with four other tired-looking bikers, and the rest just seemed to be straggling around. I didn't notice a bartender. I walked up to the bar beside a large motorcycle guy and tried to break the ice.

"So, is it open bar in this joint or what?"

The motorcycle guy didn't laugh.

"Because there's no bartender," I tried to explain. My attempt at breaking the ice was not going as planned. The other gentlemen at the bar inched forward, stopping their conversations to take me in.

"Do you happen to know if the owner's around?" I asked, not letting any more time linger.

The motorcycle guy grunted and turned his back from me, carrying on a conversation with the person on his right.

"What do you want and what are you selling?" a guy with a long brown ponytail barked from the kitchen window.

"I've got some liquor for sale. The guy down the road suggested I stop by."

"You're not from the liquor boards or a codes inspector are you?"

"Not today," I teased.

"I'm making lunch right now, so you got two minutes," he said.

The entire bar crowd turned and watched me. Someone turned down the music.

"Well, I used to own a bar, but now I'm in the business of selling cheap liquor to other bars."

"What do you mean cheap? Is it stolen?"

For taxation purposes we had to make sure everyone knew our liquor was untaxed, and that they were getting away from paying the state's costs through me.

"No, it's untaxed. When I had my bar I used to travel to New Hampshire to buy untaxed liquor for my bar. But now I sell it to my contacts. I've been doing business around Binghamton, but someone suggested I come out to Elmira to check out the bar down the street."

"They ain't open," he grunted.

"Yeah, I just found that out. Listen I don't want any trouble. I just want to sell my product. The guy from the bar down the street thought I could make a deal with you."

The gentleman stared at me through the open window. His eyes were dark, almost black, and large. Something about him put me on edge. After a few seconds of awkwardness, the guy called for someone to work the bar and walked out to greet me. He was taller than I'd estimated, a little above 6 feet, and thin, but not scrawny.

"I'm Nash," he said, wiping his hand down his apron and extending it to me. "This is my joint."

"Billy the Liquor guy," I said, shaking his hand. "Nice to meet you."

Up close I could see the gray wiry hair that surrounded Nash's face.

"Where's your shit?" he said, his voice raspy as if he'd smoked cigarettes all his life. "You've got two hard minutes."

I led him to the van out front, which Tony was still cleaning.

"What the fuck is this?" Nash said as he looked at the open back doors filled with liquor and a gentleman in a nice polo shirt bent over cleaning up broken bottles.

"We had an accident when we pulled in, and..."

"You idiots are parked in front of my bar with a van full of exposed liquor? Are you trying to get me busted?"

"Oh, shit. No," I said, realizing how stupid we looked. "We didn't know you had a back lot."

"Close the doors, for crying out loud," he yelled. "Pull around to the back for fuck sake!"

I heard Nash mutter choice obscenities as he stormed back into the bar, leaving us to discover the lot ourselves.

"Just pull the fuck around," I said nervously. "We've already irritated this guy enough."

Nash and two large men were waiting for us as we made the turn.

"You two fuckups trying to get me caught up in something?" Nash said as he approached the van.

"Nash, I swear that was just a stupid mistake. We're usually a bit more professional," I said.

Nash walked to the back of the van to see what we had. As Tony walked around, Nash stopped him.

"What the fuck were you doing in the van?" he questioned.

"Inventory. We got a lot of liquor that spilled in there. I've got to track our losses."

"Nash, this is Tony, my business partner," I interjected.

"He can fucking speak, can't he?" Nash sneered at me. "If he's your partner why didn't he come in the bar?"

"Told you. I was doing inventory. Plus I didn't want to leave all of our shit unattended," Tony stated.

I knew Tony had to be shitting his pants, and I knew he was going to chew me out for it once was all said and done. But, from the outside looking in, Tony handled himself like a champ.

"Is he carrying?" Nash asked me.

"I don't know you well enough to answer that, but what do you think?" I said. "We got thousands of dollars of liquor there. But I don't want to speak for him."

With those last words Nash cracked a smile.

"Open the fucking doors already," he said, looking back at Tony. "I've got customers waiting to eat. I can't be out here dicking around with you two morons all day."

Tony opened the back doors and, just like with the others, Nash's eyes lit up.

"How much for a case of JD?" he inquired.

"You buy one its $220 but you buy two and I'll cut it to $400," Tony stated.

"I don't really need that much, but that's a good price," Nash said, rubbing his chin. "Give me a couple cases of JD for now."

Nash called his guys over to carry in the cases, which was a nice change of pace. As I followed Nash in for payment, I visually tracked the two gentlemen as they delivered the products down the cellar, which was located to the left of the back door.

"Listen, is this a one-time deal or do you come out more often?" Nash inquired as he counted the money from the register. "I'll cut my regular liquor order back a bit if I know you're coming around again."

"Don't go crazy and cut back from your distributor," I advised him. "When I started going to New Hampshire I cut off a lot of sales and believe me it got noticed. They'll refer you right to the liquor board and then we'll both in jeopardy."

"I know that shit! I know what to do!"

"I gotcha buddy," I said, putting my arms up. "I just don't want you to start getting in trouble with the liquor board or tax bureau."

"I've been in this business for 20 years, so I know what to do," he said, handing me $400 in twenties. I had no doubt there were a few hundred- or fifty-dollar bills under his pile, yet he chose to pay me in small amounts. That was an old bar trick I knew too well. Pay small and people don't assume you're rolling in the dough, be that criminals or state officers. The small bills forced me to pay attention to how Nash carried himself. He was intelligent, spoke properly, and for as rough and tough as he looked, he seemed business savvy. He also handled the cooking, which told me he was a hard worker. My gut told me there was more going on here. So I agreed to take a chance and come back the following week. I wanted to see what I could find out.

Upon the return to Nash's I opted to dedicate a little more time inside bar. Normally we held a 30-minute policy, but I knew we needed to make an exception here. I spent an hour nestled up to the bar, watching sports on the old TV and making small talk with some of the patrons. By the time I left, with a larger order than the previous week, I'd learned that Nash was part of a well-known biker gang. His members came to the bar yet, oddly enough, so did other gang members. Nash had a policy that prohibited colors inside his bar, and he made sure his members led by example. He made it known that his bar was a safe haven. Therefore, if a fight broke out, both parties were banned for life. Thirsty Bear was essentially a sanctuary for all bikers—a place they came for a drink, brought a date or just relaxed. And somehow it worked.

On my third visit to Thirsty Bear, I was invited into the cellar, where Nash had been conducting business. The cellar was like an old cave, its exposed stone walls covered in white plaster spots from age or repair. As I made my way down the wooden rickety steps, I spotted stacks of beer and liquor that lined the right wall. This caught my attention as his supply base didn't seem to have a need for me, yet I had just delivered five cases of liquor.

The other half of the cellar was stocked with merchandise. There were flat screen TVs, power tools, clothes, and radios—all in their original boxes. As dingy as the cellar was, it was also clean. Nash had everything, including the beer and liquor, on raised pallets so they didn't touch the old, dirt floor. As I reached the last step, I noticed the same two guys Nash had brought outside with him the first time we met. Gunner and Bones, as I'd gotten to know them, were sitting around an old bar table. I noted the weapons that were protruding underneath their shirts. They merely grunted and nodded their heads towards Nash's office, which was tucked back in the corner.

"Well, that's quite an inventory," I joked as I stepped inside Nash's oasis. His office was larger than I had expected. The walls and floor were the same as outside, but he'd lined up shelves and filing cabinets so that everything was neatly organized.

"Yeah. I deal with a lot of stuff." Nash smiled.

"Strangest thing I ever sold over a bar was a quarter of a cow," I said, making myself comfortable in a chair across from his desk.

"Really?"

"Yep. One night some guy came in from a meat processing plant with a quarter of a cow cut up. I took it over the bar and put it in my freezer."

"Now that I've never done." He laughed.

"Well, I'd say that loot out there puts shame to a side of beef."

As we talked I noticed a bundle of cash laying on a shelf behind his chair. The money was wrapped in bank rolls. While Nash swapped stories I nonchalantly rattled the wrappers off in my head, estimating $20,000 to $30,000. My instincts were right, I assured myself. This guy was dealing in a lot more than liquor tax evasion.

I spent twenty minutes in Nash's office, shooting the shit about life, business and, my favorite topic, sports. I didn't comment on the money or inquire about any other business endeavors as I didn't want to break his trust. Too much curiosity from my end could have made me questionable. So I remained aloof talking about boring everyday shit.

I did find out that Nash had original stock in McDonalds and Harley Davidson, which had been set up by family members years ago. He also owned several apartment buildings in the area. This only validated that Nash was a smart businessman, be that criminal or not.

❧

"You're going to have to start wearing a wire," Staton stated over the line. "Your team needs to know what's going on when you're out of sight. If dangerous things are happening in the basement, surveillance can't tell. And from what it sounds like, you've got something bigger here that we need to explore."

I gave Staton a hard time about the wire but agreed on one stipulation.

"If I don't feel safe or comfortable, I have the right to remove it without worrying about the backlash."

"I trust you, Billy," Staton said. "Feel free to use your discretion. You're the one in there, not us. You need to do what you can to prove your case, while keeping yourself safe."

The next two visits to Thirsty Bear were uneventful, which was ironic since I had a wire, disguised inside a beeper, to record everything. I wasn't invited into the basement or able to have any long conversations with Nash due to the steady business that was rolling in.

One afternoon, I walked into the bar to find Nash in the kitchen, busy with lunch orders. I took a seat and shot the shit with a couple of guys, per usual.

"Billy," Nash called out. "Can you go around the bar and hand me a cup of seltzer?"

As I stepped behind the bar, happy to be chosen for a task, a large, angry man sitting at the opposite end of the bar began shouting at me.

"Who the fuck are you, and what the fuck do you think you're doing?" he sneered, rising from his seat.

"Nash asked me to grab him something from the bar," I said, holding up a red glass in defense.

"Well, not while I'm fucking sitting here he doesn't," he said, walking towards me.

The man's giant physique hovered over me. He was easily 6'5 "and stacked with muscles that I wanted to keep away from my face.

"Listen, I don't want a problem," I said, directing my voice towards the food service window.

"I don't give a fuck what you want," he grunted, less than a foot away from me. "This is my fucking bar and I don't know you from a hole in the wall."

I could tell he had had a few drinks from the stagger in his voice. He stopped an inch from my face, his shoulders pushed back and his chest pushed out—like a rooster preparing for a fight. I mentally scrambled as he backed me up against the bar. There was no way out. I braced for the impact of his fist, praying like hell Jeff and Docks didn't come storming in, when Nash stepped in.

"What the fuck are you doing yelling in my bar?" he shouted, pushing the guy away from me.

"What the fuck am I doing?" the angry man shouted at Nash. "You're questioning me? Who the fuck is this guy?"

"Are you questioning me?" Nash asked, stepping closer to the man who could send him flying through the wall. "Are you questioning my decisions in my bar? The bar that pays you to serve drinks?"

"That's exactly what I am doing!"

"I don't work well with people who question my judgment. Nor do I work well with people who interrupt my business, as you are."

"So, this guy just shows up and suddenly he's buddy, buddy with you? Your dumb ass doesn't even know who the fuck this guy is, yet you're protecting him? Over me?"

In actuality the angry muscleman was right. I was an undercover agent trying to get a lead on Nash's business. But because I was able to help Nash make money, my relationship became more important than his employee behind his bar. An employee who was paying attention and questioning things that Nash should have been. But, as I learned, money typically prevails over logic—especially when you're dealing with criminals.

"Number one, I like this guy," Nash said, his face tense. "Number two, he makes me money. Number three, all you do is steal my money."

Muscleman stood there, calm as ice, and stared at me with a large smile plastered across his face. He raised his hand over Nash's head and pointed his finger at me.

"The first time you fuck up I'm going to be there," he smirked. "And just when you're down, I'm gonna take your fucking head off. Understand?"

And that was it. Muscleman pushed his way past Nash and went back to his stool, angrily watching every move I made.

"Next person that questions my judgment is going to find their ass out of my establishment," Nash shouted.

I saw Muscleman a few more times, but he never said a word. He just stopped whatever he was doing and turned to watch me. Luckily for my crew and for Muscleman, his hostile presence dissolved a few weeks later when his bike hit a patch of gravel and landed him in a rehabilitation center for injuries to his back and left leg. Our operation would be complete without further interference from him, and he'd heal without taking part in the multiple arrests that would happen at Nash's bar.

Meanwhile, there had been a big to-do between Jeff, Docks and Tony while I was staring up the nostrils of Muscleman. Jeff and Docks wanted to run in and save me, while Tony urged them to hold back and let me take the hits. It sounded cold at the time, but Tony was ultimately right. As much as I didn't want Muscleman's fists hitting my face, I also didn't want my team to storm in and blow our undercover operation. Going forward, we decided that I would use the term "Black Smoke" to let my unit know if I needed backup should such an event arise in the future.

While the bar incident had put my team on edge, it confirmed I held Nash's trust. That was just what I needed to get him to divulge what else was going on inside the bar. Throughout the next few weeks I began staying for lunch at the Thirsty Bear. Nash was a pretty good cook and made a mean cheeseburger. I would wait for the lunch crowd to disperse, hang out with him for a bit and try to dig deeper.

"You know I can get you designer purses and scarves if you're interested," I suggested. "My buddy has a business."

"Does it look like I deal in fashion apparel?" he joked. "I only have time for larger ticket items. Get me some stolen TVs and we can talk business."

"All that shit is stolen?" I asked as I followed him to his office for his break.

"No, your mother gave it to us," he muttered. "Use your head. Where the fuck do you think it comes from? We got a guy at Sears. Hooks us up once a month."

Docks investigated the Sears connection and sent that case off to a separate division.

Once the weather became nice Nash invited me to his camp for one of his monthly biker parties. I knew the parties were significant because I would hear all the guys in the bar talking about them. However, excited as I may have been, the request and possibility to venture out there was immediately put to a stop by Staton.

"I don't deny you much, but this one is too secluded. Something happens, we can't get people out there to you fast enough. Sorry, Billy. This one is a no."

I pouted like a child at first. I knew the party would be loaded with criminal activity, and that we would be able to get our hands on some big shit. But eventually I rationalized that Staton had my best interest at heart. With no way for surveillance or backup to be on scene, I would have risked my life, and my team's life, in the hopes of some fast action. The upside of the scenario turned out to be a more manageable invitation to one of Nash's steak dinners. The only catch would be that he wanted Tony to come too.

"You're my guest. Come with your delivery and have a nice steak with us," he said. "And bring your partner. Tell him we would have robbed him by now if we wanted to. Polo shirts don't tend to scare us too easily. So there's no need for him to stay in the van any longer."

I knew Tony would be nervous. He talked to Nash and his bar keepers during liquor transactions all this time, but he never left the van. He'd grown comfortable in that role, so stepping outside of it was going to be a big deal.

⌘

"We'll go in, say hi, eat a steak, and go home," I told him. "It's just that easy."

I detected his nervousness, and for fear of Nash detecting it as well, I decided short visits would be best for both ends.

Tony was dressed in khaki pants and a polo shirt that had an alligator embroidered on the right side of his chest. His attire was far from appropriate for this crowd but I didn't want to make him nervous, so I left it alone.

The bar was packed with bikers dressed in chaps, leather vests and pants, and grungy t-shirts. Most of the guys, and some of the women, wore sleeveless shirts that advertised their heavily tattooed arms.

"Are you fucking kidding me?" Tony whispered as we made our way in, all eyes gleaming at Tony's unfamiliar presence.

"Just relax," I said, smiling and slapping my hand on his shoulder.

Nash came out to greet us. His handshake to Tony seemed to relax the crowd, who was standing on guard.

"I'm glad you finally came in," Nash said, gesturing for Tony to take a seat at the end of the bar. "Ryan's my numbers guy here. He likes to keep a low profile too, so I get your reluctance to be in the spotlight in here with us."

Nash had picked up on Tony's uncomfortableness, even after I thought we'd had him straight.

"What can I get you to drink?" Nash inquired, setting out silverware for Tony and myself.

Tony ordered a beer, while I tried to fill any voids.

"Tony has a business in Saratoga dealing with high end stuff. So he's always on the phone. Your cellphone range don't fucking work half the time we're down here, but he can get some shit from the parking lot. Now what kind of steak you got going tonight?"

The bantered helped put Tony at ease, but I knew I would pay for putting him in the middle of a lie. A lie Nash was excited to hear more about.

After a few minutes Tony's guard dropped. He joined in on a few jokes and laughs, but when Nash excused himself to grab our steaks Tony looked at me in a panic.

"I don't like steak!" he exclaimed.

"Seriously?" I questioned. "Who the fuck doesn't like steak?"

"I don't."

"Well, why the fuck didn't you say you didn't like steak before we came into the steak dinner?"

"I figured they'd have something else to eat!"

"Haven't you ever been to a spaghetti dinner or a chicken barbeque before? You know what they serve? They serve what the fuck is advertised: spaghetti or chicken. They're aren't other options."

Before Tony could respond, Nash arrived with two large beautiful pieces of prime rib, steaming hot baked potatoes, dripping with butter, blistered green beans and a fresh baked roll. My mouth watered.

"Eat your shit and slide pieces of your steak in your napkin," I whispered. "Don't let him see that you're not eating!"

I didn't wait to see if Tony agreed with my statement or not. Instead, I sliced into my juicy steak and indulged myself in one of the best slices of prime rib I'd ever had.

After dinner, Nash arrived with a box for Tony's leftover mashed potatoes, which he quickly slid his food into so Nash wouldn't catch his covered steak.

"You know, Tony, I can honestly say I would never see this guy as your partner," Nash said, leaning onto the bar.

"Ah, we get along pretty good. He makes the deals and I tend to the money. It's been working out well to this point."

"Yeah, I don't have a head for business, but he does," I added through a mouthful of potatoes.

To my surprise Nash and Tony ended up talking business and motorcycles for the remainder of the evening. Tony's riding knowledge and motorcycle history, something Staton had pegged from his file, drew in comments from fellow bikers around us. So everyone groaned when I thanked Nash for dinner and explained we had a delivery to get to.

"You deliver at night?" Nash questioned.

"Sometimes," I replied. "It depends on our order level and how fast we can get to all of them."

"Well, I might have to start placing larger orders then. Having you out here in the evening could be a whole new ballgame. You'd get to see what Thirsty Bear is really like."

Back in the van, Tony laid into me.

"Are you fucking crazy? Did you see the knives and things those guys all had? Every one of them was carrying!"

"I told you, they're real fucking bikers." I laughed, taking Tony's doggie bag away from him. If he wasn't going to eat the steak, I sure as hell wasn't going to let it go to waste.

"I can't believe that's what you've been dealing with this whole time!" he exclaimed.

"Yeah, well now you gotta start coming in with me."

"What?" Tony shouted. "I'm not fucking going back in there! They've got knives in their sleeves, and we're on our own!"

"I admit it's a stretch from liquor tax evasion, but we're on to something big here. Tell me you see that."

"What I fucking see is a dangerous situation we're not equipped to handle!" Tony stressed. "We could have fucking died in there. And for what, a something that we're not sure about?"

"Tony, no one is going to die at a steak dinner." I laughed. "I promise you're okay. I've been in and out of there for weeks now. They trust us."

"They trust you!" Tony huffed. "And now you're trying to pull me in on this shit."

"You were already in it," I said, perplexed by his statement. "Did you think if they killed me inside the bar that they weren't going to come out and shoot you just as quickly?"

"I guess I wasn't prepared for how rough it is in there," Tony shrugged. "And you've been in there the whole time."

"This was the evening," I reminded Tony. "Our route happens in the afternoon, when it's quiet. People are there for lunch. It's not like what you saw tonight. It's calmer."

Tony hemmed and hawed the rest of the drive back. I harassed him, trying to give him a hard time, but in the end I knew Tony was a family man. He had young kids at home that he wanted to be safe for. I had children and a wife at home too, yet in this moment the thrill and high from doing something big clouded that more than I cared to admit. By the time we arrived back at the station, Tony had agreed to go back inside Thirsty Bear. However, he insisted that his visits would be sporadic as he had no desire to become a fixed bar figure for the remainder of the operation. His request suited me just fine, since we needed to continue under the theory that Tony was a busy man consumed by phone calls and his mobile device.

CHAPTER SIX

TONY (MY MAN)

While my time with Nash grew so did our operation. Thanks to continual referrals and Staton's enthusiasm for expansion, Operation Spirits stretched across several regions of Upstate New York.

Tony, who was much more grounded when it came to time schedules, had mapped out our weekly route, which held deals in Binghamton, Elmira, Rochester, Syracuse, Albany and several other little towns in between. The strategically-arranged routes included days and times for each location. As tight and grounded as I thought it was, the schedule made us appear more legit to fellow criminals and kept us on track.

Once Nash got wind of our travel routes, he set up a meeting with his friends at the Polish Community Center in Albany. For two months we delivered a steady stream of untaxed liquor to them without a complaint or watchful eye. But by the third month we'd detected the attention of two large black gentlemen who monitored us from across the street. For three weeks, we would pull onto the scene and find the same two men, watching. Jeff and Docks looked into the men to see if they were harmful or just curious, but nothing turned up.

"I think they're just curious," Jeff said after the fifth week.

"I think they're waiting to rob us. They've been watching us for too long," Tony dug into Jeff.

I couldn't say if I thought those guys were going to rob us or if they were just bored. Yet I did have the sense that they were up to trouble. Either way, each week I got out of the van and nodded my head in their direction and the two would nod back.

On the eighth week we finally got some action.

"Hey," the heavyset guy yelled from the stoop he was sitting on. "You got a minute?"

Tony immediately grabbed my arm.

"No, Bill. We don't have time for this today."

He was nervous. All he saw was bad news. However, bad news is what I based my whole life around, so I couldn't let this opportunity pass me by.

"I've got two. Make it quick," I yelled back.

Both men stood up. The man on the right was tall, slender and dark. It was warm out, but he was sporting a long pair of pants and a flannel shirt. Unlike his partner, the heavyset guy wore shorts and sandals.

"For fuck sake, Billy," Tony sighed as the men crossed the street and walked toward us. "We've got a schedule."

"Tony, you want to keep pulling up to this spot wondering if these two assholes are going to rob us, or would you like to find out what the fuck they want?"

"I want to keep to the schedule and get the fuck out of here," he snapped.

Poor Tony wasn't going to win this one and he knew it.

"What you got in that van?" Heavyset asked as they approached us.

"What's it to you?"

"You got liquor in there?"

"Why do you need to know?" I asked, leaning back against the van to play my usual aloof routine.

"Is it stolen?" Tall One questioned.

"No, it's untaxed. You know the difference?" I asked, folding my arms across my chest.

"Means you got that from another state, right?"

"Yeah."

"We've been watching you," Heavyset said.

"So we noticed. You're not too discreet."

"Well, I've got a customer for you—if I can get a cut," Heavyset grinned.

"We're not into making deals. We've got enough business as it is."

"What if I told you that my cousin runs an underground club and needs a lot of liquor fast?"

Heavyset had my attention. An underground club sounded like a gold mine. I'd heard about them in the city, often set up in empty warehouses or two-story homes. They were constantly shut down due to safety regulations and city ordinances. More importantly, they were often littered with drugs and other criminal activity. So I wasn't about to let this one go.

"Who's this mysterious cousin?" I inquired. "And how soon does he need our products?"

A smile spread across Heavyset's face.

"If you've got a second, I can call him and have him come down."

"We don't have a second," Tony interjected. "We have other deliveries to make!"

"Tell you what," I said. "Why don't you give your cousin a call and see how far away he is."

Heavyset dialed, while I stood close enough to listen.

"Nah, it's the dude that's been making deliveries to the Polish Club," I heard him say. "They're the real deal. They want you to come look at their stuff. You're gonna be real interested in this one."

The cousin wanted us to drive to his pawn shop, which was five miles from our current location, but Tony wouldn't budge.

"I am not driving this van down there. We're already behind. If this guy wants to do business, then he has to coordinate a time for an actual deal instead of stalking us like a bunch of criminals."

Tony's frankness took me back. We were off schedule and a trip down to another shop, where we'd have to display our liquor and go through our whole spiel, would push us late into the evening. So, as much as I wanted to get this guy on board, I had to decline.

"Guys, I have to go with my partner here," I said. "If your guy wants to do business your cousin is going to have to arrange a time to meet up. We're on a tight delivery schedule today. Our customers that ordered products are waiting for us. And when we do business with someone they're always first priority."

"No doubt," Tall Man said. "That's some serious business shit right there."

Heavyset wrote his number on a piece of paper and handed it to me.

"Give me a call the next time you're coming in and I'll make sure he's here."

"Sounds good, partner," I said, shaking both guys' hands. "Looking forward to seeing you on this side of the street next time."

The two laughed and stepped aside as Tony and I drove off to our next destination. The ride wasn't ultra-pleasant, as Tony was pissed that I'd put us in another unpredictable situation. But my high of what was to come was enough to drive me through his heat and finish our remaining orders in record speed.

The rest of our week was typical. We sat through preliminary meetings, decided what bars and territories we needed to push into, calculated numbers and costs, and discussed a push for further connections from Nash. Meanwhile, I couldn't get my mind away from the possible meet up with the two gentlemen and their cousin.

Heavyset, whose name turned out to be Stump, solidified a date for the following week. By the time we reached the Polish Community Center I was running on pure adrenaline. I was so excited about this new prospect that I barely spoke to the old guys who always invited me to sit for coffee and a few stories. When we pulled up to the two-story location, just two blocks away from the community center, the cousin was already standing on his front porch, waiting for us. This guy was well above 6 feet tall, had a solid, strong build and was so large in stature that I hadn't noticed the guy who'd been standing behind him when we arrived.

Stump introduced us to his cousin, Steel.

"My cousin here tells me you got some really good shit," he said, all business.

"Your cousin is a smart man," I said, directing Steel towards the back of the van.

Tony opened the back doors and Steel followed the pattern we'd come to expect upon reveal.

"Dog, you got some good shit in here," he said, his eyes scouring the products.

"Yeah, we can get whatever you like. We deal in a lot of different items because we have a range of liquor customers. For example, I'm going to assume you aren't going to want the same stuff as the Polish center."

Steel laughed and listed off his typical inventory needs: Jack Daniel's, Hennessy, Evan Williams. With each name he listed Tony raised the bottle.

"You guys are the real deal." He smiled. Hitting his cousin on the back, he said to him, "You actually came through this time."

Steel took a few bottles of Hennessy and Evan but, despite his pleading, we couldn't sell him any Jack.

"We've got orders to fill today and our customers come first."

"I respect that," Steel replied, rubbing his hands together. "Let me place my order and become one of those customers then. I want some top priority here."

Steel put in a fair size order, which we agreed to deliver to the same location the following week. He wasn't comfortable giving his club's location yet, and I respected that. Keeping activity private was the sign of a true criminal. Low level criminals were proud to offer up their information in order to prove their worth. So his privacy was a sign that we'd hooked another big one.

Steel paid me for half of his order up front.

"The other half will be given upon delivery," he stated.

"Looks like you know a thing or two about the business."

"You can say that," he winked as he handed me his number, which he wrote on the back of someone else's business card. "If you need anything, this is my direct line. You don't need to go through Stump anymore. You and I will discuss business one-on-one from here on out."

Stump's face sunk. He had hoped for a share in this deal and clearly Steel wasn't going to allow that.

Tony and I ended our time-slotted session faster than I expected, which meant everyone walked away pleased. Tony didn't have to reconfigure our delivery times, Steel got a great score, and I was certain we had just landed a new case. Stump, however, just got a pat on the back.

CHAPTER SEVEN

BILLY THE BEAR

"Nash wants to see you in the basement," a new bartender stated as I walked into the bar.

Tony, who came inside with me, pretended to get an important phone call and headed to the van to alert the team.

As I walked down the stairs, three other bikers were coming up with merchandise. Two had small flat screen TVs, and the other had a box of something I couldn't quite make out. I suddenly wished Tony had stayed at the bar so he could figure out where they were going and what they had, but that wish was forgotten the second I spotted four shirtless bikers sitting around the table.

"So what we got going on here?" I teased, feeling uncomfortable as I walked past the table.

A red-headed guy covered in bad tattoos stood up to greet me.

"You're Billy the Liquor guy, right?" he asked.

"I am."

"Bones asked me to check you."

"Check me how?" I inquired, not sure if I was ready to hear the answer.

"Is that all you under there?" he asked, nodding to the oversized t-shirt I was wearing.

I instantly knew he was asking about a wire. I pulled my shirt over my head before he could say another word, and exposed my hairy chest. I emptied my pockets, throwing everything, including my beeper, onto the table.

"This is all me, brother. I'm all natural." I smiled, proudly displaying my bare chest.

"Billy, stop playing with those monkeys and get the hell in here!" Nash yelled from his office.

"Sorry, boys, but your boss is calling me," I said as I gathered my items from the table. "It was fun getting to know you all so well, though. Maybe next time you can buy me a drink before I have to see all your ghostly white chests."

"That's one hairy motherfucker," I heard the redhead say as I made my way to Nash's door. The rest of the guys roared in laughter.

Nash's office was filled with money again. Only this time it wasn't just stacked on a shelf behind his chair, it was spread across his desk for anyone to see. I estimated $40,000-$50,000 to be on the desk, and close to 50 packets of $100 bills wrapped and piled on the shelf behind him.

"Nash, don't you believe in a safe? Holy shit!" I exclaimed.

"Who's going to rob me?" he said, looking for something on his desk. "I've only had one employee steal a case of beer from me, and he's no longer around."

I realized why the men were shirtless. Nash might have told me that no one was going to rob him, but he wasn't stupid enough to give them a chance, either.

"I'm looking for this damn guy's number. One of my toilets is broken upstairs," he said, rummaging through his notes. I was tempted to make a crack about losing things in all his money, but I held off temporarily.

"You don't fix toilets? You seem to do everything else around here," I said, looking over at the shirtless men who appeared to be having a meeting.

"I used to. Now I own a contracting company that takes care of those things. Those assholes out there are part of that team. They're in charge of maintaining my properties and business."

"How many properties do you have?" I smirked.

"20."

Nash went on to list his properties and his business, while my beeper, which I'd placed on his desk, captured everything.

"I own the bar down the street, Soft Tail, too. I want you to stop down there and see what they're short on for liquor before you leave. Ask for Walt. He's leasing the place right now."

"So you own two bars?" I inquired, pretending to be impressed. "I couldn't handle one."

"This one's easy, because I'm here. The other one is a pain in the ass. I'm looking to get rid of it. Walt was supposed to buy it, but he's too much of a cokehead to figure his shit out right now."

I sat with Nash for a few more minutes discussing small matters, my chest-hair sticking out as we talked.

"You're always stopping in the day," he remarked in the middle of our conversation. "Why don't you stop by one night? I'll introduce you to a few of my property managers. It's a different scene at night."

"So I noticed from your steak night, which was excellent by the way." I smiled. "I'm not much of a night bar guy though. I enjoy my couch and baseball games in the evening, but for you, I'll make plans to pop in. Sound good?"

Nash was pleased with my answer. As I headed out of his office he found the number stuck to the bottom of a $500 bill. I kicked myself for not making the joke I intended.

જ

"We gotta hit up a new bar," I told Tony as I hopped into the van. "A place called Soft Tail. It's a few blocks down."

"You know we're not supposed to be adding any more joints to our list. We're maxed out!"

"Nash said this guy is a cokehead. Let's see what else he has."

"No. No more seeing. We're up to our eyeballs in seeing!"

"Tony, this is the last one, I swear."

Tony sighed and threw the van in drive while I radioed in our new stop.

The bar was set on the bottom floor of a three-story apartment complex. Unlike Thirsty Bear, Soft Tail was dark, dingy and had zero atmosphere. There was a pool and foosball table, a few dilapidated chairs and wooden tables, and one person, who turned out to be the bartender.

"Hey, I'm looking for Walt," I said, walking up to the gentleman.

He nodded behind me.

I almost had to look away. Walt was strangely deformed. His chin was elongated, and his lips hung in a diagonal line instead of across his face. He instantly reminded me of Cher's son in the movie *Mask*. His skin was also riddled in acne and his thinning hair was all over the place, making me question if that was how his hair always was or if he'd just woken up. I took a deep breath and pinched my thumb into my hand so I wouldn't stare. It took everything in me not to make a joke or react. I concentrated on being Billy the Liquor Guy, reached my hand out and introduced myself. Only, this guy didn't take it. I pulled my hand back with a sense of unease and went into my liquor spiel.

Walt didn't speak or move as I talked. He just stood there staring at me. For a moment I wondered if he could speak.

"How the fuck do I know Nash sent you?" Walt rudely interjected.

He can speak, I gathered, as the bartender turned around in his seat as if this were a daytime soap opera.

"Call him," I said, nonchalantly. "Ask him yourself."

Walt grunted and slowly walked toward the phone behind the bar. His conversation with Nash was short.

"Okay, so what'da ya got that I'm supposed to be so interested in?" Walt said as he put down the phone.

He was obnoxious and, I noted, not a professional bad guy. I took him to the van, introduced him to Tony, and showed him the liquor I had. He looked at it, unimpressed.

"If this shit is stolen, why isn't it cheaper?" he asked.

"It's not stolen, it's untaxed," I corrected him. "You ever been to New Hampshire?"

"Well I heard about it, but…"

"That state doesn't have tax, just like this here is untaxed," I said.

Walt stood there, looking at the bottles. Tony looked at me in confusion.

"Look," I said, irritated. "I got a bunch of other places to deliver to, so you want anything or not?"

Walt ended up purchasing two bottles of Jack and one bottle of well vodka. Up until now we'd only dealt in cases, but Nash had sent me to him, so I wanted to look cordial in his eyes—even if this guy was an idiot.

As I jumped back into the van, Tony gave me a wide-eyed stare.

"Waste of time," I said.

"Can you please start listening to me once and for all," Tony sighed. "We're an hour behind now. And that guy is going to make me have nightmares for days. His face is creepy!"

Walt, who had been standing there staring at us, suddenly darted back into the bar. I turned from Tony, attempting to figure out Walt's strange movement, when I noticed three black men approaching the rear of the van. Before I could say anything to Tony, they banged on the back hatch to let us know they were there.

"What the fuck!" Tony said, spotting the three men in his side window.

"Get ready to call for backup," I said, stepping out of the van.

I arched my back and puffed out my chest to over-emphasize my large stature as the men walked towards me. They were each about 5'8", fairly skinny and had dark complexions. They had a hard, street look to them too, so my radar was up.

"I hear you're selling cigarettes, man," one guy said in a thick Jamaican accident.

While it was posed as a question, the sentence came off in a demanding way, as if this guy was telling me what I had.

"What do you need?" I questioned, folding my arms across my chest.

"A couple of cartons if you got 'em," another guy answered, also in a Jamaican accent.

"You always just approach people on the street asking for items?" I inquired, holding my stance.

"Only if we know they got good stuff." The Jamaican smiled.

"We don't deal in cartons," I said.

"We can arrange for more." The Jamaican smiled again. "We do business better than your white folk in there."

The three Jamaicans laughed in unison.

"You know about that bar," I inquired.

"I know a little bit," he said, his white teeth gleaming.

"Doesn't seem to be too much business happening there."

"Maybe you're just not looking at the right kind of business."

With those words I was intrigued. I walked to the back of the van and pulled out three cartons of Salems.

"These are on the house," I said, handing them to the Jamaicans who were staring at all the liquor in the van.

"Holy shit, you white boys are the real deal!" the smiley one said, his eyes exploring the inventory.

"That we are," I said, closing the doors. "And unfortunately, we're on a schedule. So you'll have to excuse us as we're late."

"No problem." The Jamaican smiled, pleased with his free goods.

"Do me a favor, guys," I said, walking around to the front of the van. "Tell your friends about us. We're always looking for new business. And, that just might be the same business that goes on in there."

As Tony pulled away, he ranted about the time we'd just wasted.

"Tell Nash we're off that bar," Tony exclaimed. "We're stretched too thin as it is."

I agreed with Tony. I had little desire to return to Soft Tail anytime soon. Nash and Steel were our larger prospects and I needed to keep that in focus. Walt and his lonely bar were merely small potatoes.

"I'm on it," I said, pulling out our itinerary. "No more Soft Tail, or anything like it from now on. We've got bigger fish to fry."

At least, that was until the call from the Attorney General's office came through in the morning, informing us about just what we'd broken into.

CHAPTER EIGHT

THE TRANSITION

Stepping back into Thirsty Bear with different agendas now felt surreal. Here Tony and I were, two guys who'd dealt in liquor, about to break into the drug realm. Up until this moment, I'd been so excited about the chance to work a "real" undercover case that I hadn't considered the true emotions and stakes behind what we were about to embark on.

"You're the guy that my guys have been up against?" the Attorney General's words rang in my ear. "Let's see what you can really do."

They'd been impatient, quick to want me to dismiss my ways and jump into their case. But I'd held tight to what had gotten us this far. Now, I was ready to show them all I could do.

Tony, on the other hand, had already bitten his nails down to the bone. While I was ready to storm the bar, General style, he was worrying himself ragged about the new van and the deal with the General.

"Take a deep breath and just be cool," I said as we walked in the Thirsty Bear. "Let me do the talking."

"Aye, Billy," a familiar face from the bar yelled as we made our way in.

"What's up big guy?" I said, patting the loyal patron on the shoulder. "You remember my buddy, Tony?"

"Yeah, motorcycle guy," he said, sticking his hand out. "How are you?"

"Pretty good since I got a new van." Tony smiled.

My eyes sprang out of my head. Tony quickly backtracked.

"What I mean is we got a new van. The other day. Our other one broke down. It was time. For a new one, I mean."

"Okay," I said, pushing Tony down onto a bar stool. "My friend here's a little excited about his new ride. First one in a long time."

I could feel Tony's body shaking under the press of my firm palm.

"You got a new car," Nash yelled from the kitchen window.

"Ah," I said, brushing Nash's comment aside. "Tony here is a little excited about the payment is all. Thinks we went above and beyond what we can afford."

Nash immediately wanted to see the new ride. He tossed his apron off to another guy and walked us out back to take a look.

"Wow! Look at this fancy ride," he remarked, gliding his fingers across the black paint. "This is a pretty big upgrade from before. No wonder you're nervous, Tony, being the numbers guy and all. This must have cost you a pretty penny."

"Nah, we leased it," I said.

"Leased it?" Nash said, stepping back. "You idiots don't own this outright?"

"Who owns anything outright anymore? Lease is the best way to go nowadays," I replied. "Best option your money can get."

"You're dealing untaxed liquor out of a leased car?" he slowly repeated. "What are you guys, a bunch of idiots?"

"I tried to tell him," Tony interrupted. "Now you see why I am so bent out of shape about this."

"You two are some whiny bitches," I said. "You sound like an old bird who doesn't understand modern times and finance negotiations."

"Don't you have to pay per mileage on a lease?" Nash questioned.

"Nah, it comes with the deal."

"Tony, am I correct in believing that you only get so many miles on a lease before you have to pay?" Nash asked.

"That you are." Tony smiled at me.

"And don't you two drive all over creation transporting liquor?"

"That we do," Tony said, his smile morphing into an evil grin.

"Well, that confirms it then," Nash said, throwing his arms up in the air. "You're officially the world's biggest idiots."

"Who drive a nice car," I added.

Nash shook his head in disbelief.

"Listen, before I lose any more brain cells talking to you two idiots, show me what you got for me."

Tony opened the doors, showing Nash our spacious new layout.

"It does look nice, I'll admit. Much more room than before."

"Exactly." I smiled proudly at Nash. "You want anything new this week?"

"Add a few more cases of tequila in there, since I apparently need to help you pay your expenses now."

Tony added the order to his pad, which Nash happily signed under video surveillance.

"Listen, about your guy, Walt," I pushed in, while Tony arranged Nash's order. "He only bought a few bottles from me. He was a waste of time."

"That moron," Nash said. "He probably smoked too much crack that day. This here is the best fucking deal anybody can get. I'll call him again and hash it out. It shouldn't be a problem next time. You headed down there after this?"

"We weren't planning on it, but if you think it's worth it, we'll try again. I just don't like our time being wasted."

"Nor do I," Nash exclaimed, calling his bar back to carry in the liquor.

"Listen, I do need to talk to you about something else," I told Nash as Tony helped the bar back stack the cases on his pull cart. "But I'd like to keep it between you and me."

"Of course," Nash replied, stepping away from the van.

Once we appeared to be out of earshot of Tony, I hit Nash with my new spiel.

"Nash, she looks just like J.-Lo, I kid you not," I said, twisting my hands. "A fat old man like me can't expect to keep her around if I can't deliver. I know I've never asked you for anything like this before, but I'm hoping you know someone who can help me out."

Nash stared at me for a moment, leaving me to analyze everything I'd said.

"Walt should be able to hook you up. I'll give him a heads up when I call him about the liquor."

"That's it?" I said, standing there in disbelief. That's all I had to do to get into the drug ring with these guys? Just ask?

"What do you want a notarized letter?" he said, opening the back door. "I'll call him. Be there in an hour."

As Tony and I collected the money from Nash and enjoyed a refreshing beverage at the bar, I was bursting at the seams. I'd taken the first step, with Tony none the wiser, and possibly made our first coke exchange.

"He's all set for you," Nash yelled out from the kitchen. "Head down when you're ready."

Tony hesitated when we returned to the van.

"I didn't hear you say a fucking word to him," he questioned.

"It was that quick. I gave him my spiel about the girlfriend and he bought it. He called Walt himself."

"I gathered that," Tony said, nervously. "So what, you just walk in and pick it up?"

"I guess so," I said as we pulled in. "You staying in here?"

"Until you give me the go ahead, I think I'll let you hash it out without me. I don't want to mess up your sale. You saw how badly I almost fucked up Nash's shit. I couldn't stop blubbering about the van. Christ, it was the first thing I said!"

"Yeah, but you made us look like morons, so that was good."

Tony looked at me, confused.

"Morons aren't cops, remember. He just thinks we're two stupid salesmen."

Tony remained in the van, streaming my audio through the sound system, while I walked in. Walt and the smiley Jamaican were sitting at the bar, waiting for me, a liquor distributor's book laid out.

"You need a drink?" Walt asked hastily.

"I'll take a diet Coke, if you've got it," I said, leaning against the bar.

I nodded at the smiley Jamaican who was watching me.

"Cigarette guys, right?" I questioned, pretending to place him.

"Yeah, man." He smiled. "We were just talking about you. Think we can help you with your business."

"That is one conversation I always like to have," I said, extending my hand to him. "I'm Billy. Billy the Liquor guy, as they call me. I don't believe we had a chance to introduce ourselves last time."

"Nice to meet you, Billy the Liquor Guy. People call me Double J."

"Double J," I said, frowning. "You got a lot of J's in your name?"

"Nah, man." He smiled again. "It's for my love of the Jack Daniel's."

"Ah, so you really are talking about me," I said, retrieving the soda from Walt. "That's my main point of business."

Walt slammed the liquor book in front of me and pointed to a bottle of well vodka, which was set at the same price I sold him.

"Why the fuck would I buy this shit from you when I can buy it from the distributor at the same price, without worrying about problems from the liquor board?" Walt spit out.

I concentrated on his right eye.

"Because I'm here," I replied.

Walt gave me a quizzical look.

"Because I'm here," I reiterated.

"You're not making any sense."

"Walt, look at me. Is your liquor salesman here right now?" I asked, spreading my arms out and looking around the room. "No, he's not. But I am."

"Yeah, but…"

"No buts! I'm here. Therefore, I can sell you the products you need right now."

"But it's not at a price that makes it worthwhile for me," Walt exclaimed.

"Any half ass bar owner knows that product you obtain illegally doesn't get claimed on your sales receipt," I said, forcing myself to stay on his eye. "That right there saves you more money."

"Well I know that," Walt stumbled.

"It doesn't appear so," I said, aware that Double J was watching me. "You call me and I'm here the next day. Does your liquor salesman do that? No. I've dealt with those morons for years. And you want to talk about money? Walt, you buy such cheap shit there's no room for me to cut cost. When you start buying more expensive stuff I can sell it to you at a cheaper price."

Since Jack Daniel's is Double J's favorite drink, I quote a case.

"I can sell you JD for $60 cheaper than the listed price here."

"That's not that much of a difference."

"Walt, you can't be that stupid," I said, growing irritated. "Look, you get 30 shots out of each bottle. You charge three bucks a shot. That equals $90 a bottle. Minus the tax you won't pay. Do you get that?"

My tone is strained. While I'm there to sell Walt liquor for my agency, I really wanted to cut to the chase and make the coke deal.

"I'll tell you what, when you actually get $234 together you call me and then we'll talk about price differences."

"This man does seem to know what he's talking about," Double J said to Walt. "I think you should consider making a few transactions so you don't take the heat. You don't want your bosses getting mad that you lost an opportunity to make money for the bar."

"Nash should have already called you and explained all of this," I sighed. "You should have been ready to go before I even got down here. This is a lot of wasted time on my end, and that was something Nash assured me wouldn't happen again."

"Fuck does Nash want to do with this man's business, anyway?" Double J asked, his smile dropping. "He pays his fucking lease, and that's all Nash needs to know. The rest of the shit ain't for him to concern himself with."

I stared at Double J, confused by his defensiveness.

"Man, get a couple of cases of Jack from this man and a decent case of vodka. People be tired of tasting all your shitty alcohol over here anyway," Double J directed Walt.

Without a word Walt headed towards the cash register.

"Take it out of the back. I'll count it," Double J informed him.

Walt scrambled to the back and returned with a large yellow envelope, which he handed to Double J. As the three of us walked to the van and scanned Walt's liquor order, Double J turned to Tony, paying for the order with a wad of cash from the envelope.

"See you two gents next week," Double J said as he walked back towards the bar.

"Walt," I whispered, catching his arm. "I was supposed to pick me up a small amount of cocaine from you. Nash said you could hook me up with an eight ball."

Walt eyed Double J, who was standing in the doorway waiting for Walt to wheel in the cases he'd just bought.

"I don't have anything right now. Come back next week."

Without an explanation Walt quickly turned away and wheeled his liquor into the bar. I stepped back into our fancy van, disappointed. I'd lost our first potential drug sale.

CHAPTER NINE

ROLEX WATCHES

Between the stress of the new details and the extra tales we had to incorporate everything we did, Tony continued to grow antsy.

During our time with Steel, we'd heard stories of things that came into his pawn shop or people he had to fire for stealing or taking in shitty pieces. Tony, who collected watches, always inquired about what brands he had.

"You should stop by and see for yourself," Steel would exclaim. "I've got cases full."

"You have any Rolexes?"

"What kind of pawn shop do you think I run? Of course I have Rolexes. Come down and I'll give you a good price."

While Tony talked about visiting the shop, he never gave himself time to make that happen. Now, as I tried to look for little ways to keep Tony happy, I approached the idea.

"Let's hit up Steel's shop this week and see what's on the up and up."

"How on earth do you assume we do that?"

"Easy. We get there 40 minutes before our delivery to the Polish Center. You check for your watches and we head back to the center. No big deal."

Tony sat, considering my plan.

"Think about it. We take it as our 'lunch break.' Even undercover operatives can shop on their lunchtime, right?"

Tony looked at me.

"Plus, it gives us more credibility with Steel. Especially if we buy something from his store," I smirked.

"What if Steel is there?"

"Then he offers you a good deal."

"What if he's there and he wants his liquor?"

"We tell him he can't have it. Besides, he doesn't work in the mornings, so we'll be good."

"This whole thing sounds stupid," Tony exclaimed.

"Well, it's the best I can do. Think about it, your coveted watch could be waiting in there right now."

Two days later Tony bought into the plan and we were in action.

The shop was in a sketchy neighborhood. Therefore, leaving a van loaded with liquor unattended wasn't the smartest move. So I agreed to stay inside and monitor the area, while Tony perused the shop.

"Tony, you're going in, getting your watches and leaving. That's all you're doing."

Tony gave me a quick head nod before entering Steel's shop. There was a large window in front of the shop that left a clear view of Tony. I watched as he headed to the glass window, requested to see the Rolex watches and examined what the attendant put out as display. Just as Tony was clasping a gold watch around his wrist I heard a familiar voice ring out.

"Is that Tony I see?"

It was Steel. Unlike my previous theory, Steel was in fact in the shop. Murphy's Law struck again!

I jumped out of the van, said hello to Steel and, as calm as I could contain myself, walked beside him into the shop.

Tony's face went white when he saw me walking through the door with Steel.

"Yo," I called out, my eyes bulging at Tony. "Look who's here!"

"What the hell are you guys doing here!" Steel said, slapping Tony on the shoulder. "You two should have called me so I knew you were coming."

"Ah, another day. We're short on time, but I wanted to pop in and see those watches you were talking about," Tony stated.

"My man ain't going nowhere. Keep looking. I'll go back out with Billy and collect my order while you're shopping."

"Unfortunately, Tony's right and we have to get going. We've got an order we've got to fill before the Polish Center. Tony just wanted to pop in."

"Well I'll grab my stuff from you while you're here. I have a busy day, so this actually works out best for me."

Our team was miles away, with no knowledge of where we were, and per protocol our van surveillance had yet to be turned on. If we sold Steel the liquor without our crew or feed on, we'd have to answer to Staton and the Attorney General's unit. That would look bad for business, especially since they'd yet to spend a full week on board with us.

Before I came up with anything, Tony broke in.

"No, we can't do that! We have another order and we have to go there now!"

Steel looked at Tony like he was insane.

"But my order is here and I'm here. It will take five minutes. I'll even help you unload it if you're that worried."

"We can't lose another customer," I chimed in. "We've already lost two this week due to timing. We can't afford to take another loss. We'll be back to get you in an hour."

"I am your customer and I am here now," Steel stated, looking between Tony and myself. "You should be worried about losing me."

Tony and I started walking towards the door.

"Listen, we were supposed to be there 20 minutes ago and he's 15 minutes away. We'll be back as soon as we can," Tony replied as we stepped outside.

Steel continued to follow us.

"Are you guys serious?" he yelled, as we hopped into the van. "It will take two minutes. You're right here!"

Tony pulled out of the parking lot.

"I'm sorry man, it just can't happen," I yelled out the window. "We'll be back in an hour. We appreciate your business."

"You guys are some of the most fucked up crooks I know," Steel yelled back.

I rolled up the window, watching as Steel stood there, dazed by what just went down. We were getting pretty good at being stupid and it was working for us.

"Call the guys and see if they can change the meetup spot to Steel's location," Tony responded. "Let them know we bumped into Steel while checking out his pawn shop and we need to move up his time slot. Tell them we're already here and can proceed with the sale if they're ready."

Sweat rolled down Tony's forehead as I dialed. To our relief the crew was ten minutes out.

"Perfect," I said, giving them the address to the pawn shop.

"Now call Steel and tell him we're on our way back. Tell him we called our customer because we want him to have top priority."

Steel was apprehensive by the call, but pleased.

Tony and I drove around the area until our team confirmed they were in position. When we rolled onto the scene again, Tony honked the horn for Steel to come out while I jumped out and began stacking his order beside his car.

"You want these in your trunk?" I asked as he cautiously approached us.

"That'd be great," he responded. His voice was tense.

Tony and I worked fast, before Steel could comment and tell us we were the dumbest crooks again.

"All set," I said, shutting his truck and wiping my hands on my pants. "See you next week?"

"See you next week," Steel said, handing me a stack of cash.

Tony and I left Steel in the driveway again, shaking his head. If looking stupid helped seal our relationship with Nash, I only prayed this episode did the same for Steel.

CHAPTER TEN

AG'S IMPATIENCE

Over the next week Tony and I did a lot of back and forth with Nash, Walt, Steel and all the joints in between. The Attorney General's office was growing impatient with our lack of product, and Staton pushed us to try harder.

Walt had been playing coy, promising me cocaine and showing up empty handed every week. So far, the closest attempt we'd had to a buy was when Walt handed me less than a line of coke.

"What the fuck is my girlfriend supposed to do with this? Sprinkle it in her coffee?"

"It's all I got, man," Walt said. "You want more you're going to have to wait."

I stormed out of there, making Tony turn back to Thirsty Bear.

"Your man is pulling some shit," I said to Nash as I stormed inside. "He keeps playing me week after week. Now I know he's your friend and all, but I don't like being dicked around. If he doesn't have any product I need to go to someone else who does."

Nash got on the line and called Walt.

"This is a business deal! You don't keep up your end of the deal and you look bad for business," Nash yelled into the phone. "And when I'm referring someone to you and you don't do business, that makes me and my crew look bad for business. I don't appreciate that!"

I heard Walt apologizing as Nash hung up.

"He snorted your shit," Nash said, looking at me. "He's a cokehead. That's what he does."

"So what the fuck am I supposed to do? Wait by his bar so I can purchase it before he gets his hands on it?"

"Let me send someone else down," Nash stated. "I assure you he'll have your stuff next week."

"He better," I said, breathless. "I'm going crazy over here. I haven't gotten laid in over two weeks. That's not good for my head."

"That ain't good for anyone's head," Nash sighed. "What are you and Tony doing tonight anyway? Why don't you come back down? I'm having a closed party. You can relax and meet some more of my friends. Maybe someone here will even be able to help you out."

※

Tony had a family function, so no matter how I chose to spin it, Tony turned Nash's option down flat. Jeff, however, was game. Old quiet boy had grown tired of sitting in the van, listening to hours of tapes, so it was agreed that he would act as a stand in for Tony.

The night of the party we had surveillance covering the block, as well as the pole cameras the narcotics unit had installed months ago. Mike, our firearms instructor, happily stepped into Jeff's position in the surveillance van, while Jeff took his wheels. While my ego had led me to believe I was safe with these guys, Mike's presence did offer me a bit more confidence as he was one of the best shots in the agency. If I decided to push this evening or found myself in any trouble, Mike had my back, and I felt that.

We arrived at the party a little past 8 p.m. to a fairly heavy crowd. Nash had the back door open and tables spread along the parking lot to make way for dancing inside. Half of the tables were already littered with beer cups and gentlemen busy in card games. A band was rolling as we walked in. The music was loud and the air was thick with cigarette smoke and marijuana. Jeff started to cough and I gave him a soft elbow to the ribs.

"Take small breaths," I muttered.

Guys I knew from the daytime scene greeted me as we walked in. Though they all kept calling me Bear and slapping me on the back.

"Why are they calling you Bear?" Jeff asked as we took a spot at the bar.

"I have no fucking idea," I said, glancing around, confused.

While I knew a handful of people from my day to day operations there were several more that I'd never met. All of whom glanced our way.

"There he is," Gunner shouted as he walked over to greet me, with Bones by his side. "The Bear."

"What the fuck is this shit, 'The Bear'?" I questioned. "Everyone's saying that to me."

Gunner and Bones broke into hysterics. Jeff and I looked at each other perplexed, waiting for them to share in the hilarity of the moment.

"Nash's guys decided we should change your name to Bear once they saw how hairy you were," Gunner said between spits of laughter.

"You got the whole fucking place calling me that?" I said, throwing my hands up.

"According to them, you are one hairy motherfucker," Bones said, laughing. "Just like a bear."

"We played the video the other night," Gunner stated. "The place was roaring."

With that the two started howling like banshees. I silently wondered if they'd think our video was as funny.

I turned from my seat, unimpressed, and began looking for Nash, who didn't appear to be around.

"He's downstairs," Gunner said, still laughing. "Important meetings."

"Let him know we're here when you get a chance."

"Yes, sir, Bear," Bones said, cracking himself up.

I felt a headache coming on. This wasn't my scene. Between the band, these two idiots and all the smoke, I wasn't sure how long this evening would last.

"I say we give this a solid thirty for appearance sake and jet," I told Jeff.

Jeff, who was looking around like a kid in Disneyland, didn't listen to me.

"Jeff," I repeated, nudging him in the side. "You hear me?"

"Do you know those guys?" Jeff said, gesturing to two skinny gentlemen, both covered in tattoos and sporting leather vests.

I didn't recognize them, but as they caught Jeff and I looking they waved us over.

"Think they're gay?" Jeff asked, pulling himself off the stool.

"No, I don't think they're gay! Stop being stupid. I think they're looking for something. Play it cool."

As we walked over, the two gentlemen rose from their seats and invited us to sit at their table. It was the only one remaining in the bar. Both seemed familiar, but I couldn't tell if I'd seen them before or if they just blended in with the others—long hair in a ponytail, beard, blue jeans, motorcycle boots and yellow-tinged fingers.

"You're Billy, right? Nash's guy," the man on the right said. He was missing a front tooth.

"I used to be. Apparently I'm known as Bear now."

The two looked confused, causing me to assume they weren't part of the viewing crowd.

"I'm Earl," Toothless said. "This is my friend, Jack."

"Nice to meet you," I said. Jack had all of his teeth. "This is my partner, Jeff. My other guy, Tony, is at his own business meeting tonight."

The two made small talk about the band, the crowd and Nash's no color or name policy.

My head thumped in line with the music, so I wasn't interested in making small talk.

"Guys, I don't want to be rude, but we're heading out shortly," I yelled over the band. "Was there something you wanted to talk to us about?"

"We heard you sell liquor," Toothless said. "We've got a joint you should check out. Its twenty minutes outside of here. A gentlemen's club. We frequent there quite a bit. We want you to tell him we sent you."

"Sorry guys, but we're not looking at bringing in any new business," I said. "We're pretty busy at the moment."

As the men tried to make their case, Gunner approached the table.

"Nash will be right up. He doesn't want you to leave yet. Come outside with me."

Jeff and I excused ourselves from the table and followed Gunner through the crowd. Bones was outside with the card group we'd seen earlier, flagging us over.

"Nash has something for you," Bones said, holding up a bag of marijuana. "It's from his buddy downstairs. Says this might be able to tide over your woman while Walt comes through."

Jeff's eyes lit up as he saw the bag, which clearly held quite a few ounces.

"First rule of thumb when purchasing weed is to try that shit out first," Gunner said, eyeing the bag. "You've got enough customers here. You should let us help you."

Six wide-eyed faces grinned back at me.

"Don't be selfish, man," one card guy said. "It's always good to share the wealth."

Never one to pass up a fair amount of peer pressure, I turned to Gunner.

"I don't have anything to roll it with right now. My papers are at home."

Gunner promptly pulled out a roll of papers from his back pocket.

"Good thing I'm always prepared."

"Your papers, so you do the honors," I said, tossing the bag to Gunner. "Don't be too greedy, though. I have a purpose for that shit."

I couldn't look in Jeff's direction as I knew I'd just put us in a bad spot. I should have just said no, like Barbara Bush taught us, but my mouth worked before my brain could catch up.

Gunner began rolling two joints just as Nash emerged from the back door.

"There you are," he said, slapping me on the shoulder. "I see you're testing the stuff before heading home. Smart man."

"Isn't that the first rule of thumb?" I joked, glancing at Gunner.

I introduced Nash to Jeff, who had remained quiet throughout the evening. I suddenly wondered if his excitement to be on the front line had worn off.

"Any friend of Billy's is a friend of mine," Nash said, shaking Jeff's hand. "Thanks for getting this guy down here. He's not much of a night person, is he?"

"Depends on how you look at it," Jeff said. "If your night consists of baseball and some dip, then he's in."

"And ladies, I'm guessing." Nash smiled. "Maybe I need to get more women his speed down here."

"I'm still going to go with the dip," Jeff joked.

"You got a funny guy here." Nash laughed.

Gunner handed a joint to me.

"Do the honors. Bear."

"Nah, it's your shit," I said. "I don't want to be greedy."

"Greedy. Fuck that, Billy. This is your shit. You shouldn't be sharing it with these dimwits in the first place. Now test the shit I got you and tell me I didn't do good," Nash said, standing behind me.

I held the joint up to my lips and took a slight inhale. My lungs immediately gasped for clean air as Gunner took the joint from my hand and passed it around. I doubled over, my lungs screaming for air, while everyone around laughed.

"I told you it was good shit," Nash said, slapping me on the back and passing the joint back my way. "Take another hit to calm yourself down."

I waved away the joint, but Nash insisted.

"Take a hit. You'll calm down."

I grabbed the joint and took a tiny puff. I expected the coughing fit to continue, but instead a warm trickle made its way down my burning lungs.

"What did I tell you?" Nash said, hitting me on the back again. Either I was high or that was getting annoying as hell. "Feels better, right?"

"What the hell is that?" I questioned, pretending as if that wasn't the first round of dope I'd smoked in over twenty years.

"Comes straight from my Cuban dealer. They're meticulous about their shit."

"I'd say so," I replied, pulling the night air into my lungs. "Fucking air tastes like cotton candy."

Nash and the guys started laughing as I took another deep breath.

"It seriously fucking does. Everybody try this," I said, breathing in the air.

More laughter erupted. I turned to look at Jeff.

"Can you taste it?" I asked.

Jeff shook his head.

"I think you've had a bit too much of the Cuban fun," he said. "Might be time to call it a night."

"No way!" I exclaimed. "There's still so much to do here. Just try the air. I swear you'll like it."

The guys were laughing so hard they'd begun holding onto their sides. Apparently I was a very funny man.

"Guys, watch this one," I said, sucking in the air. "Oh my god that's so good!"

Jeff grabbed me by the elbow.

"Okay, fun air is over. We gotta get going now, Billy."

"Just one more breath," I said, squatting down and standing up as I inhaled.

Everyone roared in laughter again.

"Okay, you did it. Time to go now," Jeff tensed, pulling my arm.

"Come on, don't go home yet," Nash exclaimed, tears rolling down his face as he fought to speak between his laughing fits. "The night is just getting started."

"True, but Billy isn't the lightest person to carry home," Jeff said, pulling me away. "Trust me, I've had the experience before.

Ended up leaving him to sleep on his front porch because nobody could move him."

I started making faces, mocking Jeff behind his back, while he dragged me back to the van, shoved me in, and threw the weed onto my lap.

"You're one stupid motherfucker," Jeff said as he closed his door. "You're going to be in deep shit tomorrow morning."

I rolled down the window to take in the cotton candy air.

"Enjoy it now," Jeff muttered. "I can promise this high is going to make you fall flat on your face tomorrow."

CHAPTER ELEVEN

DIDN'T INHALE

I wasn't home less than ten minutes before Staton rang to let me know the higher ups weren't happy.

"They want a meeting tomorrow, Billy. Clear your schedule," Staton said. "My office. 9am."

"It was just a setup," I stated. "I didn't even inhale."

"Clinton jokes aside, they want to see you in person. They've got some questions. Just arrive a few minutes early so we can go over your shit before they get here."

Any high I might have had ended with Staton's call. However, the paranoia seemed to set in for life. I roamed the halls of the tiny studio apartment I was set up in while away from home, worried about my job. I couldn't imagine they'd shut me down for something so small, but there are always the what-ifs that roll around in your head. And this one might have been the ultimate what-if.

"You're smoking marijuana. On camera!" San yelled at me as we sat down.

"I didn't inhale," I exclaimed. "What you saw was me putting the joint to my mouth. I didn't go any further."

"You're coughing all over the fucking surveillance," San said, leaning his fists on the table. "We couldn't even hear half your conversation because of your hacking! You expect us to believe that was acting?"

"You think I'm dumb enough to try any of their shit?" I questioned through a pounding headache. "I don't know where it came from or if it's laced with anything. It was all show. You should know me better by now. I wouldn't do anything to risk my health or my job. This is the number one thing for me."

Staton had coached me on what to say before we'd entered the room. So far his lines seemed to be working.

"Well, tell me how the hell I'm going to explain this tape to the Governor, should he come across it?" San's cheeks were as red as a pile of beets.

"How about with the truth?" I said, looking straight at San. "In all seriousness, the Attorney General sent me there to take down a major drug operation. You can't tell me he didn't expect drugs to come about? If he did, then we have a problem."

San held my gaze, allowing me to finish.

"As soon as we get over this hump, my team and I will be surrounded by drugs. So I need to know that I have the Attorney General's support. I don't want to walk into a room and feel like I need to leave because they're doing drugs in front of me and you're afraid the evidence will make me look incriminating."

"Let's discuss moving forward, while we're on the subject," he interrupted. "The Attorney General is paying you to produce a closed case. He wants a major breakthrough here, and so far we're not seeing any movement."

"Like I originally said, this is a process. We move too fast and everything will blow up in our faces. Give me two more weeks and you'll have something."

"Two more weeks!" San exclaimed.

"Two weeks and you'll have a buy on the table."

"And the possible backlash of drug interaction?"

"Again, I can't promise drugs won't come up. All I can ask is for your support moving forward. I'll try my best to keep things on the screen clean, but I need to know if you have my back if things end up looking tricky."

San stared at me from across the table. And then, just as quickly as the meeting had begun, it was over. San had agreed to show his support and put his faith in our team, and I'd agreed to take myself out of as many incriminating situations as possible.

❧

Ready to show the Attorney General who they were dealing with, I tossed Tony's schedule out the window and advised him to take me straight to Soft Tail.

Double J was already seated at the bar, watching soccer.

"Walt here?" I demanded as I stormed in.

"He's around back, man," Double J replied. "He'll be back soon. Have a seat."

Double J pulled out a stool and gestured for me to sit.

"Everything okay, man? You seemed less like you today," he said, glancing over at me.

"Ah, I'm just frustrated. Walt's been promising me a deal he hasn't been delivering on."

"That doesn't sound good for business," Double J said.

"I don't think anything Walt does is good for business. Kid can't even get a liquor order straight."

"Well, if that be the case then you need to talk to me."

I looked at Double J who was sporting his large smile once again.

"Walt don't own this bar. I do," he said coyly.

"You do?" I asked, confused.

"Walt is the front man. Ain't no way Nash going to sell this bar to a Jamaican. So Walt acts as if he's buying it. But I am the man whose name the bar will be in."

"Oh man," I said, knowing how mad this would make Nash.

"Oh man is right." Double J smiled. "Your man down there going to shit his pants when he hears that news. But for now we keep it quiet, ey? I don't want any of them messing up my plans."

"Your secret is safe with me," I said, looking up at the screen. "You really love this soccer shit, huh?"

"Man, this is the sport to be. All that bat and base shit you be watching is bull. Have those guys run around the field chasing a ball. That's a real man's sport."

"If you say so," I sighed, looking at the door once again.

"Man, why Walt have you crawling out of your skin anyway? You in a hurry or something?"

"I am today," I said, taking a hard look at the colorful hat Double J was wearing. "Let me ask you something," I said. "You're always wearing that hat. Even if it's hot outside. You gotta be dying underneath there, right? It looks hot."

"Hell yes that hat is hot sometimes. We're not animals, man. But it's a significant piece of our culture," Double J explained. "Every color means something different. We wear it to show our pride."

I listened as Double J explained the meanings behind the colors on his hat. Green stood for the fertile land that fed their families, yellow was for their religious freedom, and red for the blood that had been shed in defending their country. Double J's eyes lit up as he explained the colors, his voice rising as he shared stories of the war his family had fought in.

"We don't get these hats here," he stated. "Stores don't have them, and we don't travel out of the area for lots of reasons. So we hold on tight to what we have."

My instincts perked up.

"Shit, I can get you a hat if you want," I replied.

"Whatch you know about hats?"

"Nothing, but I have an ex-brother-in-law who is Jamaican so I know a few spots where I can pick some up for you."

"You're pulling my leg." Double J laughed. "You don't have an ex-brother-in-law from Jamaica."

"True. But I am in the city a lot. I can easily stop on the corner and pick one up for you."

"You'd have to get some for my guys too. I can't ask for just me."

"No problem. I'll bring you a box full if you want." The words flew from my mouth before my brain could stop them.

"Man, that would be golden if you could do that. My guys would love it."

"Let me see what I can do," I said, standing up from my seat.

"You not gonna wait for Walt?" Double J said, looking around.

"I've waited long enough," I said. "I have work to do and it's clear he's not the right man for the job."

"You're always busy." He laughed. "Never in one place too long."

"Hey, we all gotta make money, right?" I said, walking out the door. "I'll be in touch."

I pulled myself back into the van and looked at Tony, who was deeply involved in a crossword puzzle.

"We gotta take a drive to the city and pick up some Jamaican hats."

"Now?" Tony questioned, annoyed by his puzzle interruption.

"Not now, you ass," I said. "I've gotta make a few phone calls first to see where to go. I don't want to be wandering around the city all night shopping for these guys."

"We have that Jamaican investigator in the city," Tony mentioned. "Cart, Clark something. Give him a call and see if he knows a place."

"I knew I kept you around for something." I smiled, pulling out my phone.

I contacted our surveillance crew, requesting the name and number of the investigator Tony was referring to, and within ten minutes I was on the phone with Investigator Blarke, arranging a meet-up in the city.

"I gotta ask, though," Blarke said. "What's an old white guy need with a bunch of Jamaican hats?"

"The confidence to close a fairly big case."

�ै

I met Blarke at a coffee shop two blocks away from Chelsea Piers. The shop was busy, as Carter expected, so I ordered a medium iced coffee with a touch of skim milk and settled up to the window seat, watching all the foot traffic go by. I'd never meet Blarke before, but I picked him out of the crowd within seconds.

He didn't look like a cop. In fact, he struck me as more of a professor. He was clean shaven, his hair freshly cut, and he had on a pair of dark jeans, a crisp white dress shirt and brown dress shoes.

I guess I stood out as much as he did, as he entered the shop and walked straight towards me, hand outstretched.

"The Billy," he said. "I hear you're starting to make a name for yourself up there."

"Ah, well, I'm hoping you can help me push that name even further," I said, standing up to shake his hand.

"Well, I have to admit I'm a little curious about what trouble Jamaicans can be getting into up there. Other than learning how to shovel snow."

"They're doing more than their fair share, that much I can say."

"Word is they've got you working with the Attorney General now, so it must be some big shit."

I gave Blarke the gist of what we were working with, without giving too much away. I'd just met him, and while he was helping me, I'd been burnt by too many to fully trust him.

Blarke pulled up a chair beside me and gave me an inside look into his long career with the NYPD. As an investigator set in the Bronx, Blarke's jurisdiction dealt directly with the Jamaican population. He'd been involved in a large undercover operation for five years that worked to break down Jamaican gang activity.

"Your best option is to befriend them," Blarke explained. "Though, due to their cultural bond, I doubt that a few hats can gain a white man like yourself acceptance."

"Well, let's get those hats first and then see what happens." I smiled.

"I like a man with brass balls." Blarke laughed.

Blarke walked me down to the piers.

"This is primarily a Jamaican market," Blarke told me as we approached the tents. "They come here to sell their wares every day from 9 a.m. to noon. They typically shut down and get out of here before anybody bothers them."

I strolled through the market, examining the tables and small, tented areas. People were already lined up for fresh fruits and vegetables, questionable meat, clothing and Jamaican trinkets.

Blarke tugged my arm and gestured towards a large Jamaican woman dressed in a long, colorful dress.

"That's Carlita," Blarke said. "She'll have your hats."

Carlita's heavy demeanor, covered by her dress, was highlighted by her thick braids, which she wrapped at the top of her head.

As Blarke and I approached her table I could tell she was analyzing me.

"Good morning, Carlita. How are you today?" Blarke asked.

"And, what do you two want?" she asked, not moving from her chair.

"Carlita, my man here needs some hats. Can you hook him up?"

"What would this old white man need with my hats?" she asked, glaring at me.

"What everyone else does, Carlita. He wants to make money."

"Make money, how?"

"He works Upstate with the Jamaican community. He says there aren't any hats up there."

Carlita grunted, her arms folded across her chest.

"If you don't have enough we can head down to Jimmy's cart," Blarke said. "I'm sure he won't have a problem selling 100 hats. I just wanted to show you the respect of offering you the sale first."

"One hundred hats," Carlita said, uncRossong her arms. "Your man here needs one hundred hats? Well why didn't you say so in the first place? Of course Carlita can help him out."

Carlita stuck her hand out for payment, which I happily added an extra twenty to, before she rummaged through her boxes, stored behind her table. In that moment I couldn't tell who was more excited; Carlita for the unexpected sale, or me for the quick score.

I pulled up to Double J's the next day and placed the box of fine Jamaican hats on the bar.

"What's this?" Double J said, peeking into the box. "You got the hats!"

"Of course I did," I said, taking a seat next to him. "Did you think I was bullshitting you?"

"Oh man!" Double J exclaimed, pulling the hats from the box. "This is amazing, Billy! There are so many!"

"You said you needed to take care of your guys. So take care of them and sell the rest."

"Holy shit," he repeated, rummaging through the box.

Double J headed to the back door and yelled for his guys to come inside. For thirty minutes Soft Tail was like a scene from Christmas morning. Double J's tossed hats to everyone and they thanked me like I was Santa Claus.

Once everything settled down, Double J thanked me again and asked if there was anything he could do for me in return.

"Actually, I've got this girl," I said. "She's a little young for me, but she's good looking as hell. Double J, she has this J. Lo ass you could rest a drink on while you're fucking her from behind."

Double J's wide grin emerged.

"Only problem is she's a bit of a coke whore. This guy ain't getting none until she gets some. My dealer in Binghamton got caught up a few weeks ago. Walt's supposed to have been hooking me up these past weeks, but he keeps bullshitting me. I need help man. I've got to get laid tonight or I'm going to go out of my mind."

As nervous as I should have been, the conversation flowed effortlessly.

"How much you need, man?" Double J smiled.

"An eight ball will do, but I'll take anything at this point."

"Tell you what, man. You come back in an hour and I'll have it ready for you. You won't be disappointed either. I've got some good shit. Trust me, she's going to fall in love with you after she has this."

Tony and I popped into Nash's to kill time. We made small talk, had a bowl of soup and counted down the minutes until we made our first buy. By the time we met up with the surveillance crew, my adrenaline was in overdrive. They adhered a camera to the top button of my Thurman Munson jersey and helped prep me for the sale. I took a few deep breaths, closed my eyes and exited the van, ready to over-deliver on my two-week promise. And I did just that.

After weeks of back and forth and failed transactions, Double J happily greeted me at the door, slipped an eight ball in my hand and sent me on my way with well wishes.

It was one of the happiest moments of my life.

�

"You're spending a lot of time with the Jamaicans," Nash stated. "I don't like it."

Nash had been busy selling his monthly wares from the basement. Shoppers were leaving with televisions large and small, and one patron even purchased a stainless-steel hood-range oven.

"My girl would love that," I said as I watched Nash's men haul it upstairs. "Can you get another one of those?"

"The next time my guy swipes a truck with one I'll save it for you," Nash said, counting his money. "But are you listening to what I'm telling you about those guys? They're not good for business, Billy."

"I can barely understand what the fuck they're saying. You think I'm interested in making them my next customer?"

"They'll shoot a man square in the face for five dollars. They have no regard and no cares, and that's what makes them truly dangerous."

Nash had forbidden the Jamaicans from even stepping foot in his bar. Though I was fairly certain any man of color wasn't welcomed there, Nash made sure the Jamaicans knew it.

Once, when a Jamaican entered his bar, all the bikers stopped what they were doing, rose to their feet, cut the music and switched on the lights. According to Nash, the Jamaican put his hands in the air, apologized and ran out of there faster than a rabbit being chased by a fox. There were rumors as to why the Jamaican had come there in the first place. Some people claimed he was there to rat on his fellow brothers, others claimed he was sent as a lookout to rob Nash's joint, and even more said he'd been looking for a certain biker chick who was known to offer sexual favors to darker men. According to Double J, the Jamaican had just been sent to the bar from Walt who needed some change.

"How you doing with your girl, anyway? Walt hook you up?"

I felt my throat tense as I lied to Nash, for what felt like the first time.

"Yeah. He took good care of me."

As our case heated up with Double J, the narcotics unit began pushing. They wanted more coke, frequent sales and more insight.

By the second week I'd asked Double J for two eight balls.

"Man, your woman's really into it, huh? I expect you to come in here walking all hunched over next time I see you," Double J said as he slipped me what I needed.

∾

"This shit is too easy," Tony said one day. "It's going to fall apart soon. I see it."

"It's not going to do anything of the sort," I assured him. "We're in and out. It's quick business. That's it."

"And when Nash finds out you're dealing directly with Double J?"

"Then we figure that out when it occurs. But for now let's just ride the wave and see where we wind up. Okay?"

"And if we spent all our time building a case for the narcotics unit and lose our own?"

"We can expand on our deliveries, if that concerns you. Jeff and I got an offer on that gentlemen's club a few weeks ago. We could try that if it will make you feel better. Get back onto our scene for a bit."

"I don't know. Maybe I just need a break from the drugs for a minute, ya know. Things are going too fast."

"So let's do that then. Let's go check out the joint and see what we find. It'll be like old times."

"Four weeks ago old times." Tony smiled.

"Exactly," I said, phoning in our new deal to Staton and the crew. For some reason I didn't think anyone would have a problem examining this club for one night.

The Gentlemen's Club looked like every other club. The windows were blacked out, the room was dark and there was a stage set with shiny, silver poles and, of course, a handful of female dancers. The stale smell of beer and sweat permeated my nose as soon as I walked through the door.

"This place look alright to you?" I turned to ask Tony as we entered the club.

Tony's eyes focused on the pole, a big fucking smile plastered across his face.

"I'm good," he replied.

We made our way to the bar, ordered a drink and asked for the owner.

"He expecting you?" the bartender asked. He was a fairly large guy, who I assumed acted as security when needed.

"No, but his friends sent me down. I've got some items he's supposed to be interested in."

The bartender picked up the phone and called his boss, while Tony and I paced the joint, taking in the women and the surroundings.

Entranced by the blonde who'd made her way to the pole, I failed to see the owner who stood beside me.

"You like her?" he asked. "She's new."

"She's okay," I replied. "A little too young for my liking."

The gentleman eyed me suspiciously. He was about six inches shorter than me, so I got a clear view of the hair that was thinning on top of his head.

"That's one complaint we've never heard," he shrugged. "Too fat, too old, that we've heard. Too young, not too much."

"Are you the owner?" I inquired. "Guy at the bar told me you'd find me."

"Jack," he said, sticking out his hand. "What can I do for you?"

I introduced myself as Billy the Liquor Guy and began my story of untaxed liquor sales. I made sure to mention the two men I met in the bar.

"Names don't ring a bell," he replied. "I'll have to check in with the bartender, Anthony. Anyway, what type of product you talking here?"

"I've got an overstocked supply right now," I told him. "Come out and take a look."

I dragged Tony from his luxury seat by the stage. Clearly my plan had worked and Tony was finally starting to relax.

Jack was in awe when we showed him our product. Right off the bat he ran an order for multiple speed rack units, as his customers weren't known to spend their money on top shelf liquor. As we made our way inside, each carrying two cases, Jack offered to buy us a drink. I wanted to keep Tony as engaged as possible, so despite my desire to head out of there and make more time with Double J and his crew, I took him up on his offer.

Within 20 minutes this guy and I were best friends. He told me about his lazy liquor distributor, complained about his business and talked about the difficulties of working with women all day.

"I don't think that would sound like a problem to a lot of guys." I laughed.

"That's because they've never worked with a lot of broads before."

Tony was caught up with a brunette who'd taken the stage. While he was watching her, I was watching the gentlemen who kept walking into a back room with the dancers.

"I've got a golf tournament coming up next week," Jack told me. "You guys should come as my guests. There will be all sorts of bar owners coming. It can be a good business introduction for you."

"I appreciate the offer, but we're pretty good on business at the moment. Can't really afford to take any other new clients on. But if you're looking to purchase some extra liquor for the day we'd be happy to help you out."

"Just trying to help you out is all," Jack stated, gesturing for another round of drinks. "How about girls? See any you like?"

"You've got a nice group here," I responded, accepting another drink. "Best club of women I've been to in a while."

"I work hard to keep it like that." He smiled. "You see anyone you like for yourself? They're all available, you know."

"Does that one over there look like Catherine Zeta Jones?" I questioned.

Jack called over the dark-haired woman and introduced her to Tony and me. My initial response was correct, the girl looked just like the Hollywood talent.

"It's something we're known for." He smiled proudly. "We've got a makeup artist in the back. I pay her a good chunk to help the girls favor different personalities."

"Well, that's pretty good," I said, taking another look.

"She's for Tony," he said, brushing her off on him.

Jack gestured over to a larger girl.

"What? No," I exclaimed as I saw her approach. "She looks like Kathy Bates!"

"You said you didn't like the young ones," Jack backtracked. "She's older!"

"I don't want a young girl dancing in front of me, but I also don't want that. Who the hell fantasizes about Kathy Bates?"

"You'd be surprised." Jack smiled, gesturing for the girl to go back. "We get a lot of requests for her."

"Well, on that note I'm going to excuse myself to go take a piss," I informed Jack. "I'll be back."

It was our first time here, which let me plead ignorance should I be caught snooping around. I easily made way around back to "look" for a bathroom and began checking out the rooms I'd watched people go into. At first I counted five, but as I looked harder I noticed that the back room had another room attached to it. I stepped in for a closer look to discover the rooms were designed to entice further pleasure for the customers.

"You a watcher," the blonde from earlier asked as she stepped out from a room.

"I'm all kinds of things," I responded. "Out of curiosity, how much does something like that go for?"

"Well, peeping is illegal, I'm pretty sure," she teased. "However, for the real deal it ranges from $50 to $200, depending on what you want."

The blonde stepped closer to me, making me uncomfortable in my role.

Tony and the crew were out of sight. Should anything go down or the girl accuse me of anything, there was no one to back me up.

"That's good to know," I said, stepping away from her. "I'll let Jack know you were very good about offering."

The blonde sent me off with a wave and a bright smile. By the time I was back in the bar, I was running numbers through my head. I calculated seven rooms, ten working girls, that I could see, and thirty gentlemen. I quickly add up a large number of untaxed transactions that were happening every day, just as Jack was waving me back over.

"Where's Tony?" I asked, spotting the lovely Catherine seated on Jack's lap.

"He got an important call and had to head back out to the van. Something about his reception not working right in here."

Shit, I thought! I didn't give Tony a heads up before I went exploring. Being apart was a big no-no when it came to the surveillance crew, who was awaiting us out front.

"What the fuck do you mean you don't know!" the crew screamed at Tony. "How can you not know where he is? You were in there together, right?"

"Yeah," Tony replied as they stood there glaring at him.

"You made liquor sales with him?"

"Yeah."

"THEN HOW THE FUCK DO YOU NOT KNOW WHERE HE IS?!" Jeff hollered.

Docks being Docks attempted to throw me under the bus, claiming I was with a girl.

"Billy ain't like that," Tony said, shutting down Dock's idiotic response. "He's probably in the bathroom."

"Suddenly you know where your partner is," Dock said sarcastically.

"You need to go back in there," Jeff yelled. "We can't have something happen and not know what he was doing."

"They're trying to get me to hook up with one of the dancers," Tony said. "I can't go back in there."

"But Billy's in there!" Jeff cried. "You have to go back in and find him!"

"Fuck!" Dock shouted. "Billy is always putting us in these situations. He's going to fuck our whole team!"

"What team am I going to fuck?" I said as I walked up.

Everyone turned to look at me, their faces flushed.

"Where were you?!" Jeff shouted, angrily approaching me.

"I was in the back seeing what's going on," I said. "Wait until you hear this."

"I don't want to hear anything from you," Dock spat out. "You've got the whole team in disarray. You didn't communicate jack shit with your partner. We were about to bombard the place, looking for you."

"Well, I'm here." I smiled, extending my arms. "And I've got some good shit on this place. Man is turning over a whole sex operation back there. We hit another jackpot."

The team didn't care what I found. They were so pissed at Tony and me that they headed back to their van without another word.

Tony and I documented what we'd found and tracked our liquor order. But, thanks to my missing time and Tony's questionable knowledge about my whereabouts, Staton and all the powers-that-be made a written documentation informing all case workers that we were not allowed to go inside any type of gentlemen's club again. Even though Tony worried that the ban made us look questionable, I was happy I'd gotten Tony back to his old self for the night. If anything, we had one hell of a story to tell. Kathy Bates and all.

CHAPTER TWELVE

DOUBLE J

As my time with Double J increased, we developed a friendly relationship. Like most bad guys, I saw through the criminal and took a liking to the person behind the element. Double J was a typical guy, like you or I, only with different circumstances. He had a humorous side, and when he wasn't running his crew, his tough façade melted into a relaxed individual who was somewhat fun to be around. I felt like this understanding is what made me a better undercover. A lot of others disagreed, but they'd never worked a day undercover.

Double J had a family he was providing for. He had an apartment that needed water, utilities, cable, and children who needed to eat. He didn't want to take from the system, because he felt he could do better. Unfortunately for Double J and his family, better didn't equal going to school to become a doctor or lawyer. Instead, like most street youth, better was becoming the head of the family, be that with the mob, drugs or stolen goods. In those regards, Double J had succeeded. And thus far there had yet to be anything to slow him down.

From the beginning Double J seemed to like my laid-back motif. I acted like I didn't give a shit. I dressed in what some would call sloppy, but what I considered comfortable. I kept the guys at the bar and my surrounding clientele busy with small talk. I'd spend an hour shooting the shit about the Yankees game and then turn around and spend five minutes discussing untaxed liquor sales and other criminal activity. And it worked. Double J would be so relaxed by the end of the conversation that he didn't mind asking for more or telling me about other illegal elements that I could get involved in. To him I was just an everyday thief, quick to make my money and leave.

As I walked into Soft Tail the next afternoon, prepared to make another deal, Double J was nowhere to be found. I sat at the bar, chatting with two other patrons and Walt, before I inquired about his absence.

"He's out back," Walt said. "He's had a tough day."

I walked out back to find Double J seated on the back steps, smoking a joint. He looked solemn and there was no smile to be found when he looked up at me.

"You alright buddy?" I said, taking a seat next to him.

"I lost my nephew yesterday," Double J replied, taking a hit from his joint. "He was stabbed to death outside of a nightclub. Some sort of misunderstanding about a girl."

"Shit," I said. "I'm so sorry, Double J. When are the arrangements?"

My sick mind already spun with how I could make this development work for our operation. The obvious answer was to attend the funeral.

"I think they're going to be in the next few days. The police still have to release the body. My poor sister. I don't know how I can help her."

"You can't," I said. "All you can do is be there."

Double J took a long drag.

"I'd like to come to the services if that's okay. Show you and your family how sorry I am."

Double J looked at me as if I'd just set the bar on fire.

"If it's too much, let me know. But back home, that's what we do. We come to pay respect."

Double J nodded as if he understood and then passed me the joint. I wasn't prepared to smoke. Unlike my time with Nash, I'd promised my crew and the Attorney General that I'd stay out of hazardous situations. Now, here I was, a camera hanging off my jersey, smack in the middle of one again.

Double J nudged my leg, referencing the joint he had waiting for me. Without hesitation, I took the joint from his hand and took a hit. I tried to block the camera with my arm and suppress my cough, but I wasn't anywhere ready for what Double J passed me than I was with Nash.

With one hit my lungs were gasping for fresh air again. My body contracted with each forceful cough, so much that I thought my temples might burst.

Just like Nash and his team, Double J laughed at me.

"That's some heavy stuff for an old white guy," I choked out.

"Yeah, white people usually don't like this stuff. It's too harsh for you guys, but this is the shit we grew up on. This is the quality stuff."

Double J rambled on about weed quality and its cultural differences, while I scrambled to pull myself together, thinking of a way I could back track this situation on tape. Instinctively I bent over with the joint, so it was in full view for the camera, and pretended to take a drag and then choke again. Double J was so busy talking that he didn't catch on to my supreme acting performance. Deep down I hoped everyone behind the scenes would buy it as well.

"I never even asked if you needed anything from me," Double J said, taking another hit.

"No, I'm good for a bit. I just have a shitload of Jameson that I need to get rid of, but I'll bother you with that later."

"I'll take that shit, man. Fucking bar's always full of Jameson drinkers. Business is still business, even when someone dies. Life still goes on."

"I'll give you a good price, for your nephew's sake. You'll be happy."

"Man, I'm always happy with your shit. You're always full of surprises."

"You ain't seen nothing yet." I laughed, feeling the effects of the weed I couldn't handle.

∽

"That's how long you were in there," Tony said, holding up a completed crossword puzzle. "And you can bet I am not attending any funeral service with you, so you better find yourself another undercover to accompany you on that one."

Tony wasn't the only one convinced that I had no business attending the funeral. The entire agency went around and around, discussing surveillance costs, crew members and liability.

"You have no business there," San said. "It doesn't offer any headway in our operation."

"Only it does, because this will make Double J and I closer," I interjected.

"I don't give a fuck about you and Double J," San sighed. "You've got to get your head out of your ass, and his ass for that matter. You're too concerned with this guy. It's cRossong a line and I'm beginning to wonder if you're taking this too far."

"How do you expect me to get deeper into the drug trade with this guy without obtaining his trust? Your boss wants a big fucking deal on the table, right? Well, here's your chance. Attending this funeral will make Double J feel closer to me. And, as we all learned from our diligent studies, the more he feels like we have a valid trusting relationship, the more he will confide in me for bigger prospects."

"Even if I said yes and agreed to this crazy idea of yours I don't have a partner that I can send with you. Frankly, Bill, no one feels comfortable working with you anymore. You're too unpredictable. Making one of my guys go with you now puts me in a bad light."

"I'll go," DEA Dave said, raising his hand. "I've been dying to work alongside Billy."

DEA Dave was an untamed agent. He was 5'8, 150 pounds and looked like a UPS driver. He had thick, shaggy hair that was always in his eyes and a thin mustache. He was in his mid-40s and had spent a lot of time working with biker gangs, since he had an extreme amount of motorcycle knowledge. DEA Dave was known for being wild and crazy, as he took risky chances, but he was also an agent who held a strong position in the Blue Knights, a private police officer motorcycle group.

"You're buying this shit, Dave?" San asked. "You want in on this?"

"I do," he said, stepping forward. He'd yet to let go of the metal chain that connected his jean belt to his wallet, a trait he'd sported while undercover with bikers. "I've been waiting for another chance like this for a long time."

"These guys don't deal in motorcycles," San said, running his fingers through his thinning hair.

"As I am aware."

"Well," San said, after a moment. "You two have one chance. You fuck this up, or take any risky moves that puts our team in danger, and you're out. Attorney General or not, Billy. Are we clear?"

"Can you define risky before I agree?" I said, hoping to gain some levity.

DEA Dave burst out laughing.

"You crazy assholes can get yourselves killed however you like," San yelled. "But don't you think you're getting a special funeral with a fuckin' bugle. We don't cater to suicides. Now get the fuck out of my office before I kick your intolerable asses out myself."

DEA Dave and I escorted ourselves out, with San's pygmies right behind.

"Well, Dave," I said, shaking his hand. "You own a suit?"

"Hell no," he said. "Do you?"

"Nope. I just wanted to make sure we were on the same page."

∾

Two days later DEA Dave and I were on our way to Rochester, NY for the funeral. The weather had begun to turn, transforming the thruway into a blanket of red and orange.

"Pretty enough to almost make you forget the day to day shit you're dealing with," DEA Dave said as we drove along.

I looked out at the changing leaves. Years ago I would have been accompanying my wife and kids to pick out pumpkins and pick apples. Now here I was far away from home, mentally as much as physically, attending a funeral to score points with a bad guy.

The line for the funeral was longer than I expected. Apparently Double J's nephew was fairly well known in the community as people from all over were waiting to pay their respects.

"Good luck," DEA Dave said as I stepped out of the van. "I'll be listening in."

Wearing a wire to the funeral seemed somewhat invasive, but I knew my boss had already bent enough. Asking him to forgo the wire would've pushed him over the limit. Plus, deep down, I was hoping I might catch a thing or two while I was there. And, if I happened to catch that thing or two on audio, the opportunity to prove myself and rub it into San's face would be well worth it.

I made my way to the back of the line, which I'd noted hadn't moved since we'd pulled in. Automatically I knew the wait time was going to be the worst for me due to my apparel. Sporting pressed khaki pants and a pastel polo shirt, I was far from my everyday comfort clothes. My feet had already begun to swell and sweat inside my brown dress shoes.

Within thirty minutes I'd only moved from the outside to the inside. The extra bodies crammed inside did little to curb my sweat and discomfort. As the line edged closer to the parlor I could hear rap music playing. It was the first time I'd been to a funeral without the traditional sad music.

Young kids were running in and out of the line, and somewhere in the crowd I could hear their relatives telling them to go back inside and sit down.

I'd always hated funerals as a kid. I never understood why my brother, sister and I had to go. It was boring and full of crying people, and if we didn't sit still we'd take a smack to the back of the head. I used to tell my siblings that all dressed up events were merely a stage set up for children to fail in front of their family members.

Most of the funerals I had attended also had police escorts. There was always a cousin or uncle who'd gotten released from prison for the day so he could attend the funeral. I never understood this to be abnormal until I was older. Imagine that. A kid watching his uncle arrive to the funeral parlor dressed in an orange jumpsuit, his feet and hands shackled together, while police officers stood by his side.

The last funeral I attended had been my aunt's. My cousin Larry had arrived in shackles, and cried like a baby beside his mother's casket. I remember watching in horror as this tough-ass cousin of mine, who'd been in and out of jail for as long as I could remember, had to be pulled from his mother's casket and dragged back to the police car kicking and screaming for his mom.

"Mom," his words filled my ears. "My mom. Mom I am so sorry. I'm so sorry mom. MOMMMM!"

I shook the thought from my head just in time to see Double J approaching me.

"You came," he said, placing his hand on my shoulder. "My brother, thank you."

"Of course," I said. "It's a tough time. I wanted you to know I was here for you."

"None of my guys came. They couldn't get here. No cars."

"Well, I'm sure they would have come if they could have. They're here with you in spirit."

"Umm, they're here with me as long as the money is—and don't think I don't know different."

Double J pulled me out of the line and walked me into the parlor, ahead of everyone, to the casket.

It was closed.

"His face was too messed up to show," Double J whispered.

"That's too bad," I said, bending down to say a little prayer.

Dear God, watch over this boy and his family. Keep me safe while I am here, and never let me know the pain of having to bury one of my own children like this.

After I stood up, Double J led me around the room introducing me to his friends and family.

"This is Billy, my brother from another mother," he'd say.

I met Double J's entire family, his business partners, and his girlfriend, who was about eight months pregnant.

"I didn't know you had a baby coming," I said as we walked away from his woman.

"Yeah, my sixth baby. It's a girl. I'm thinking of naming her after my mama."

"Six kids. God Bless. I don't know if I could handle one."

I spent an hour inside the parlor. By the time I left I'd met so many people I couldn't remember one of their names.

"You were quicker than I expected," DEA Dave said as I reentered the vehicle. "Tony told me horror stories about you and your chatty escapades."

I laughed at DEA Dave's words.

"I needed that," I said, fastening my seatbelt. "That was intense."

"I think it was a little more than intense," DEA Dave smirked. "Deine already called. She wants you in the Syracuse office first thing in the morning."

Deine was the Senior Investigator for the Drug Task Force. She'd been working beside us throughout the operation, but she'd been fairly low key—allowing San to run the show. Her need to see me meant one of two things: I'd crossed the line attending the funeral and she was going to take matters into her own hands, or I'd just discovered something that she needed to address.

"You think it's good?" I questioned.

"Can't be anything worse than what San has said and done to you."

"Point taken," I said.

DEA Dave and I spent the next two hours discussing funeral stories. Turns out I was right—I was the only fucked up individual who grew up thinking that family members arriving handcuffed from prison at a funeral was normal.

CHAPTER THIRTEEN

CRIMINAL'S PYRAMID

Tony and I walked into the Drug Task Force's office at 9:30 the following morning, wondering if I was about to get my ass handed to me.

Deine's assistant escorted us into a large office where several top drug task force investigators were already meeting. I recognized most of the gentlemen straight away. Some I'd been introduced to through fellow colleagues, and others I'd heard about, read about or seen from afar. They were in the middle of a heated discussion. Paperwork, large banded printouts and yellow notepads filled the tables and laps of the investigators.

"Welcome, William. You're just in time," Deine said, interrupting their conversation at hand. "Please, take a seat."

The assistant pointed to an open seat beside Deine's empty chair in the center of the room. I hiked up my khaki pants—I'd been smart enough to arrive somewhat refined this time—and casually nodded to the gentlemen who were staring at me.

"Mr. William and Mr. Anthony," Deine addressed us, "I want to thank you for taking the time to come here this morning. As you can see, my team and I have been up all night unfolding everything that you brought to light yesterday."

As I looked around the room, I now noticed the hair that was sticking up in the back of some of their heads, the red eyes and the five o'clock shadows.

"Before we go any further and dive into our findings, I want to congratulate you on thinking outside of the box and taking a chance several agents would not," she said, her hands clasped together in front of her chest. "You stood up against all the naysayers and went after something you knew would be better for the job—even when others didn't. For that we say kudos to you."

Everyone around the table nodded their heads and smiled in approval.

"Yesterday, you pieced together one of the largest puzzles that we've been trying to put together for months," Deine said, walking to a whiteboard. "We wanted to invite you here so that you can see what your hard work did."

A young, strong agent, seated to Deine's left, popped out of his seat and flipped the whiteboard around, revealing a giant pyramid of faces. Over thirty pictures, all strung and linked together, stared back at me. On top of the pyramid sat one familiar face who seemed to look directly into my soul. Double J.

"William, what you're looking at is the largest trail of drug lords in the Upstate, New York region. When we got word that you would be attending the funeral we had a backup team follow with surveillance for our own curiosity. What we captured was amazing."

My mind wandered away from what Deine was saying and back to the board, where I attempted to process Double J's face taped on top.

"…is the head of the traffic ring," my mind heard her say. "… over seventy connected individuals running underneath him… even linked to your contact in Albany."

There, next to several of the faces I recognized from the funeral, was Steel. Several other offshoots were strung from Steel's picture, including the cousin from the stoop.

Then I heard Deine say, "Without intending to, you just tied together one of the largest drug trafficking cases in history."

I sat there, gobsmacked. I wasn't sure what to say or what to do.

"We received an order from the judge last night allowing us to tap all of their phones. We'll be busy monitoring everyone's conversations from this end. That we can handle. What we need from you is to keep pushing. Keep them on the line and see what else you can get."

"How far are you asking me to go?" I inquired, my eyes still glued to the numerous faces on the board.

"As far as you can." She smiled. "You've proven that you can go beyond expectations for the job. We simply want you to continue on that path."

"I'm not sure how much more our boss will allow us to continue to explore here, if I'm being honest. We're tied to our agency first," I added, trying to unravel the connection between Steel and Double J in my mind.

"We don't need you to do anything different than what you're doing already," Deine stated. "All we need is for you to try and strike up a conversation about these guys, see if you can't help our team link them together even further."

"He can't," Tony spoke up. For a minute, I almost forgot he was there. "He's already in too deep. He's on an assignment with the PATB unit and the Attorney General. You can't stretch this man any further than he already is."

Deine smiled at Tony, baring a sweet, mothering regard.

"I'm touched by your concern, Tony. You two work incredibly well together, which is what we believe makes you such a success. But I would like to hear Bill's response."

Deine and Tony turned to look at me.

"Well," I said, wiping my sweaty palms on my pants. "Tony is correct about our obligations. I don't want to say no and toss this aside, because I might be able to help bring some things up that would be helpful for you. However, I'm not looking to be held to any more promises or additional work."

Deine leaned in, looking directly at me.

"William, you are an incredible agent. You've proven to everyone that you're a valuable commodity to this case. And, if this goes down how we want it, you will go down as one of the most influential agents in history."

"For walking into a funeral." I laughed. It was the same stroke I'd gotten from others who wanted in, just under a different agency's name this time.

"No," Deine said, standing up straight, her eyes still locked on mine. "For taking the chances other small-minded agents have been too afraid to do."

The table grunted with several "uh-huhs" and head nods. All eyes were on me, and the attention made me feel drunk.

"I don't like to promise anything I can't deliver on. That's not in my nature," I said.

"I respect that."

"I can try and bring a few things up. If conversation flies, then it's yours to run with. But other than that, my guys and I will be out."

"We come as a unit," Tony reminded Deine. "Those guys were up until 3 a.m. uncovering notes from the funeral. So this is as much extra work for them as it is for Billy."

"Which is why we'd like to add our own guy onto your surveillance crew. He'll only be there to gather information for our purpose. This way your crew isn't responsible for anything other than what they're currently assigned to."

"That seems right by me," I said, looking at Tony. "How does it sit with you?"

"I don't think it matters at this point."

"Alright," I said, standing from my seat. "We'll let you guys hash out the details with the General's office."

Tony threw a cutting look my way and rose from his seat, ending the meeting.

Deine thanked us for our time, did a round of handshakes, and ended with a few more appreciation mentions. As shitty as it was to admit, that had yet to grow old.

"Billy, remember we're here if you need help with anything. Including San."

"Is he aware of this meeting?" I asked.

"He's is. However, he's currently taking all the kudos at the Attorney General's office as we speak." She smiled again. "You are aware that's how this line will go, aren't you? San will ride your ass and step on your toes, but when it comes down to a win, he'll happily collect your recognition and still give you shit."

"That, I'm well aware of. It's the nature of the business. Luckily, I'm okay with that. My face isn't one that tends to shine on the news."

℘

Back in the van Tony laid into me for what seemed like the hundredth time.

"When I said it didn't matter, I meant it didn't matter what I said, not that it didn't matter to the case."

"How the hell was I supposed to know that?" I said. "I'm not a speech interpreter."

"We've been partners for almost a year. You should know what the fuck I mean by now."

I apologized to Tony, but he didn't seem ready to let it go.

"You saw Steel up there, right?" I remarked after a few minutes of silence. "That one got me."

Tony didn't answer.

"We've been dealing with him for months and now here he is with his face linked to Double J and guys in Pennsylvania."

Tony drummed his thumb on the steering wheel.

"You thinking I should try my spiel on him? See where it gets us?"

"You're going to do what you want, so go ahead," Tony sighed. "See where it gets you. We're already over our heads as it is. What does one more matter?"

"Now, when you say 'what does one more matter,' am I to think that it really doesn't matter, or should I think that it does? I'm obviously not good at this shit."

"I don't know how the fuck I got assigned to you!" Tony said. "You drive me absolutely crazy. You know that, right?"

"Tony, I drive everyone crazy. That's the beauty of me."

"You're a beauty alright."

"So, you're cool with it?"

"Just get it the hell done. At this rate it feels like these cases are never going to end."

∽

I laid in bed that night, tossing and turning. I kept visualizing Double J's picture at the top of the drug pyramid and Steel's face at the bottom right. In all my findings with Steel, be it with liquor sales, cigarettes, stolen property, money laundering through the pawn shop, and underground club exposure, I'd never thought about venturing into the drug realm. We had so much on him that that avenue somehow slipped my mind. Yet now I couldn't escape it.

As we drove to Steel's house the next morning, I felt Tony's unease. His jaw was tight and his knuckles were white as he gripped the steering wheel.

"I won't bring you in," I told him. "Stay in the van and distribute liquor like normal. I'll keep this as a side business."

I wondered if I was being selfish. If I was putting Tony directly in the lane he was trying to avoid. Yet, at the same time, I knew that if I was going to break into Steel's drug ring, I needed my partner. Introducing a drug proposition without Tony and/or a liquor delivery didn't seem to mesh too well.

By the time we pulled up to Steel's home the color had faded from Tony's face.

"Trust me," I said. "You won't even know it's going down. I wouldn't do that to you."

Tony stepped out of the van, slamming the door behind him. He was pissed, I knew. But this was more important at the time. I figured I could mend him and me. However, a drug trade that never happened, I couldn't.

Steel had two guys in their mid-twenties with him.

"This is Antwane and Hersal," Steele said as they approached the van alongside him.

Antwane and Hersal, my mind repeated, wondering if their faces were on Deine's board. The new helpers didn't say much. They lifted the liquor from the truck so Tony and I didn't have to, and loaded it into the back of Steel's shiny Cadillac.

"Steel, you got a sec?" I asked, motioning for him to walk with me.

Steel followed me to the front of the van.

"Listen, I don't want Tony to know what I'm talking to you about," I said. "But I'm looking for some help."

"You in trouble, Billy?"

"No, nothing like that. I need help with my lady."

Steel stepped back and looked at me, his forehead creasing above his eyes.

I quickly ran into the same J. Lo girlfriend routine that I'd won Double J over with.

"This old guy isn't getting laid without and my guy from Binghamton has shown up empty-handed for two weeks now. You know someone who could hook me up?"

"Man," Steel said, laughing. "You had me going there for a minute. I was afraid to know what kind of help you needed with a lady. How much you looking for, man?"

"An eight ball if I can get one. But I'll take whatever. I just really need to get laid tonight."

"I can't let your love life affect my sales." Steel smiled. "I'll get you what you need."

Steel turned and walked over to the two gentlemen, who were finishing their final haul. He whispered something to them and then turned and gestured towards me. The tall guy to his right nodded and walked into the house. I stood there, hands in my pockets, anxious as hell.

It can't be this easy, I thought.

But it was.

Steel's guy walked up to him, slipped something in his hand, and headed back to the car.

"Write the cost off with the liquor," Steel said as he handed me an eight ball. "The less cash rendering the better."

ℂ

"No way," Tony said, as I showed him the cocaine. "You just fucking bought drugs from him. Just now?"

"Fucking crazy, right?" I smiled.

"Billy, at this point everything seems fucking crazy to me."

And just like that we'd delivered what we promised. At least, we thought we did.

CHAPTER FOURTEEN

MARX BROTHER ROUTINE

"You can't exchange liquor for drugs," San said the following afternoon. "It's considered null and void. You have to pay cash."

"But they're buying liquor at the same time that we're buying drugs," Tony interjected. "That makes it a tad conspicuous, don't you think?"

"I hate to put you boys in another sticky situation, but unfortunately this is out of my control. For the DA to successfully prosecute Steel we must eliminate any factors that can make the state's case less credible. Exchanging liquor for drugs could be considered entrapment."

I ran my fingers through my hair, tugging at my scalp in frustration.

"Fine," I sighed. "We'll figure a way around it."

Tony glanced at me.

"What do you want?" I snapped. "We've got nothing else, so obviously we have no choice but to figure it out."

"That seems to be our answer for everything," Tony snapped back. "We're in charge of running the cases and figuring out everything along the way. What the fuck do you guys do?"

Tony looked at San, whose face had turned red like a beet again.

"I know this seems like a stretch…"

"A stretch my ass. This is fucking draining. Every step forward is two steps back with you guys."

"Again, I understand your complaint."

"I want off," Tony interrupted. "Find someone else to replace me."

Tony crossed his arms over his chest and sat back in his seat. It was the first time I'd seen him so angry.

"Look, San, we're tired. We worked until 9 p.m. last night and now you've got us back down here for another meeting. That puts us behind—again. All these meetings just make more work for us."

"We can increase your overtime pay, if that would help," San said.

"Increase by how much?"

"Triple."

I turned to face Tony and Staton, who was quietly seated beside us. Staton raised his eyebrows.

"We know how hard you guys are working and the last thing we want is for you to get burnt out. Hopefully, this can help in some way. Think of it as money you can use to take your family on vacation after all this is over."

That was exactly what Tony needed to hear. I knew part of his aggravation stemmed from not being able to go home at night. He was missing his kids and his family life.

"That's a good start," I said, looking at Tony for reassurance. He nodded.

"While that's on the table we need to discuss something else with you." San folded his hands together. "The Attorney General would like you to consider wrapping up your case on Thirsty Bear. He thinks it would help speed everything else along if you spent less time there."

Panic shot throughout my body. No way was I letting go of Nash's case. I'd spent too much time gaining his trust. I'd formed a business relationship with him and, as fucked up as it sounds, I wasn't ready to give that up.

"What's the General's theory behind closing this particular case?" Staton questioned.

"He believes Bill hasn't uncovered anything significant there. He sees it as poor time management at this point. We've calculated his visits. Billy spends approximately an hour and a half there every week. This is a concern for the General."

"Billy has obtained significant liquor sales inside that bar."

"I'm not so sure the General sees it that way."

"You idiots have no idea what I've uncovered with Nash," I broke in angrily. "That man has hundreds of thousands of dollars of illegal material coming in and out of his bar."

"Illegal material isn't going to make the front page. Nobody is going to care about a few televisions or stereos hidden in a basement. We're dealing with real shit that people care about, Billy. People want drugs off their street. They want to feel safe in their neighborhood. Ask them to choose between uncovering an illegal drug ring or a stolen television operation that's hurting corporations already bankrolling on their consumers and I'm going to guess you know what their answer will be."

"Everyone has their own way of saying potato," I replied. "And your agency is no different. You believe it's all about the headlines and recognition. A little more calculating on your end might show that untaxed liquor sales creates a million-dollar revenue loss for New York State every year. I think the taxpayer might be a little interested in that. Especially since their taxes go towards that loss."

"Gentlemen," Staton interrupted. "Before this meeting gets out of hand, I'm going to stop you. Billy is not going to end his running operations to focus on your cases. You asked him and his team to be under your wing to help push along your sting. Now he'll most certainly continue to get you what you need, but our agency isn't going to get fucked as a result. At the end of the day we still need to maintain the presence and liquor sales that we've built our operation on. If that's not clear, then Billy walks away from your case today."

San sat back in his chair, defeated.

"I'll inform the General," he sighed. "But, please take into consideration what we discussed."

"I already have," I said, rising from my seat. "We'll handle the drugs in cash, and we'll take the increased overtime."

❧

From that moment on, my job became a matter of balance. One minute I was wheeling and dealing drugs for the Attorney General, while helping infiltrate Diene's case, and the next I was selling untaxed liquor for the PATB. It became a tricky role to balance, but I had no choice other than to find my bearings—and to find them quickly.

As for Steel, that was a little more tricky.

❧

"Listen, Tony isn't comfortable with the drugs sales," I told Steel upon our next visit. "I'm not going to be able to exchange liquor for any purchases. That has to be on my own from now on. I want Tony happy."

Steel and I stood inside the small 4x4 entrance of his two-story home. It seemed a little awkward, but Steel didn't seem put out so I stood there, anxiously discussing my new proposition.

"Whatever makes your man comfortable." Steel shrugged. "That's cool with me."

"Can I get two eight balls this time then? Since we're cool and all," I teased.

"Shit, I'll give you all my inventory if you want." Steel laughed. "Always happy to get this shit off my hands."

"Don't joke with me," I said, aloof. "I make several deliveries a week. It would be too easy for me to add some of your special shit to my load and sell it off as incentive."

Tony walked up the driveway with the liquor bill and squeezed his way into the hall with us. Steel counted his money and handed it over to Tony. Tony in turn counted out the money and handed it to me, to which I turned and passed it back to Steel.

"For the double eight balls." I smiled.

Steel looked at us as if we were the biggest morons on the planet.

"You two are really fucked up. You know that, right?"

Tony and I smiled in unison.

"So we've been told," I said, happily pocketing the eight balls. "See you next week."

As we walked out of the cramped entrance, feeling like the biggest bunch of idiots, Steel called out to me.

"Hey, if you're serious about more give me a call. Might be worth a chance."

I saluted Steel, and Deine's phone tap's validation, and stepped into the van.

"Think that was good for the assholes Upstate?" I said to Tony, knowing the camera and audio equipment were still rolling.

"I think it'll show the court system how clueless the state is when it comes to undercover operations, that's for sure." Tony smiled, putting the van in drive.

"Bunch of pristine desk boys." I laughed, happily knowing that our hallway interaction looked as foolish as we could make it. "I can't wait to see the confused faces on the jury when they show that tape."

CHAPTER FIFTEEN

A GIFT

With Steel taken care of, my next act of business was getting Nash into the scene. I figured if I could get him on board, I'd be able to show the General just cause. But I had no such luck.

"Word on the street is you're getting more than your share of cocaine from the Jamaicans," Nash said, wiping down the bar. "I think it's safe to assume my guys and I don't need to be a part of that."

To my surprise Nash's response made me happy. Even though I wanted him to stay on course, in that moment I realized what I was asking him to get into. This would be major jail time for Nash. And when it came down to it, I liked him. He was a businessman. Yes, he was running some illegal shit through there, but he worked hard, and I respected that. Serious prison time wasn't what I wanted for him, bad guy or not.

"You don't fuck with blacks or Jamaicans, do you understand that? It's bad for business," Nash instructed me.

"Nash, I know these guys aren't like you or I, but they have money. And right now, I'm just trying to make a little extra side business. I'm not looking to be their best friend."

"Sooner or later they're going to bite you in the ass," he said, pointing his finger at me. "You're right about these guys not being like you or I. They have major criminal records, and they're involved in a lot of heavy shit that we're too smart to be a part of. Hell, we've made it this long averting police. You're smart enough to realize that those idiots are being watched. They're targeted from the moment they walk down the street, guilty or not guilty. And if they're being watched, that means you're being watched too."

"Well, let me ask you something," I said, leaning across the bar. "You rent the bar to that fucking moron for face value when you know Double J's running it, right? You're using Walt as a front man to make sure no one else knows that a Jamaican is running your shit. So why aren't you complaining about the extra business or fucking worried about being watched?"

"What the fuck do you know?" Nash sneered through yellow teeth. "You fucking think you can come in here and tell me shit about my bars and my business?"

I immediately knew I'd pushed Nash too far. The veins in his forehead were turning purple. I needed to backtrack quickly.

"Look, Nash. I apologize," I said, lifting up my hands and leaning back from the bar. "I don't mean any ill-intent. I guess my emotions are running high because you're questioning my business. I'm just trying to make some extra money, and I thought you'd understand that part. I mean, you may not be directly working with those guys, but you're still making money off them. Maybe I'm being greedy, but I want part of that too."

As strange as it sounds, the look upon Nash's face was crushing. Just like that, I watched all the respect I'd worked hard to gain drain from his face.

"Listen, Nash. It's just another customer to me. You and I know these guys won't be in business long because they're idiots," I said.

"You're right about that," Nash mumbled under his breath.

"So why not take the credit now?" I pleaded. "Dive into that shit and make some extra cash before they ruin it for themselves and get locked down."

"What the fuck do you think I've been doing?" he said, his voice tense and low so others couldn't hear. "You've got a lot to learn about business yet, Billy, and about keeping your mouth shut with it."

"Now that one you might have me on." I smiled. "But you gotta hold yourself a little accountable. You sent me down there to that idiot, Walt. You didn't even give me a heads up on his face, for crying out loud!"

Despite his anger, Nash couldn't suppress the smile that spread across his face.

"I wondered when you were going to say something about that." Nash laughed. "Fucked up ain't it."

"He's like the real-life Elephant Man," I exclaimed. "Wait, you think we could make money off that? Maybe instead of celebrity bartender nights you could advertise an Elephant Man bartender night and bring people from all over to come and see him?"

"You really are trying to make more business, aren't you?" Nash laughed. "You're one money hungry son of a bitch."

"Yes sir, I am," I said, raising my glass in a toast. "Money and women are what move me, and I'm not ashamed to admit it."

"Ain't that most men?" Nash said, pouring himself of a shot of Jack Daniel's and tossing it back.

❦

"Billy," Nash called out as I reached the door. "I still don't want those motherfuckers coming to my bar. Got it?"

"I wouldn't think otherwise," I said, stepping out of the dark bar and into the welcomed sunshine of a spring day.

❦

Despite Nash's misgivings about my time with the Jamaicans, I found myself heading straight over there to grieve the inevitable decline in partnership with Nash.

"I don't want to be here all night, Billy," Tony said as I stepped out of the van with a baby gift in hand, compliments of a savvy coworker. "I'd like to get a solid night's sleep for once."

I felt like an average guy who'd just come in from a hard day. I walked over to my stool, grabbed a handful of bar pretzels and ordered a Jack and Coke from the usual bartender.

"You here to see Walt or Double J?" Butch, the tattooed bartender, asked.

I let out a small laugh when he said Walt's name. I'd been coming into the bar for months now, and Walt was the furthest thing from a successful criminal I could have imagined. How ironic is it that Nash had sent me to one of the most underwhelming individuals, thinking he had access to drugs and profitable shit, when lo and behold it was the Jamaicans he hated who were running the operation all along?

"Who do you think?" I said in a joking manner.

"I'll get Double J for you." He smiled. "He's right out back."

Double J walked into the bar with his arms spread open and a big fucking smile on his face.

"Billy," he said, his accent dragging out the y. "You bringing me something good?"

"Not this time," I said, staring into my drink. "I'm just here to tell you I got into it with Nash."

"Hold on," Double J said, taking the stool next to mine. "Whatch you mean you got into it with Nash? You two have a fight?"

"Not really a fight, but a business misunderstanding."

"Oh, Billy. Don't say you screwed Nash out of something. Him and his motorcycle guys will be all over your shit."

"No. Nothing like that," I said. "Nash didn't want me doing business with you anymore. He can't see us working together if I kept ties with you and this bar."

Double J waved the bartender over to pour him a drink.

"I can't let someone's racist views get in the way of my business and my life."

Double J sipped his drink and continued to listen.

"He wanted me to choose between business with you and business with him. I choose you. And I'm not telling you this because I want a pat on the back. I'm here because I want you to hear what happened from my mouth. My business with Nash is ending. Thirsty Bear is going to be dropped from my route soon. So from now on I will come directly to you with my scores. If you like them, fine. If you don't, I have other people I can go to. I just want you to know that I've been giving you priority over Nash for a few weeks now and after today it remains that way."

"You know I have never been inside The Thirsty Bear?" Double J said. "Even though those guys buy drugs from me outside of the joint, I know if I stepped foot in that bar there would be problems for me. Only because I am Jamaican. Not because of something I did to them. That I can't understand. But for the safety of my family and my guys, I don't fight that. It's not worth a war and it's bad for business. So I am respectful. I stay away and do not enter his space. But he should have no problem with you just because you work with me."

"Which is why I can't do business with him any longer. I respect Nash and his business, but I can't work with someone whose views I don't respect. You are my main guy now."

Double J and I sat at that same spot for an hour, talking about life, war, racism and family.

"What if we merged together?" I finally asked. "I've got customers across the board. What if I began selling your shit to them? We could become partners. You said before you don't drive. Tony and I could be your exporters. Help you get to larger destinations."

"I've got a lot of partners right now," Double J remarked.

I encouraged the conversation and slowly Double J began to list his partners names and where and how they helped him in the cocaine trade. I did a mental high five with each name and location he gave up.

"What about the Albany area?" I continued. "We're down there a lot. You can't have guys out there too."

Double J smiled while he fed Deine a fresh trail of breadcrumbs that glanced over Steel. I almost spilled my beans about working with him, but I wasn't sure if that was a good thing or not. So I held back.

"But I am always open to more possibilities," Double J finally revealed. "I can help you grow your business, if that's what you need."

"I think it might be," I said, finishing my second drink. "Especially since I'm wrapping up Nash's end. He dealt in a lot of products for me."

"You and everyone else. Bars across the board will be upset to hear his news. They waited on his deliveries."

"What deliveries?" I inquired.

"You knew he was selling your shit, right? You didn't think he needed that much liquor every week for just his bar?"

The stacks of liquor in the basement suddenly popped in my mind. In that moment, despite how in control I felt over my undercover work, I realized I'd let something slip. In all my excitement to work with Nash and build a big case, I missed the giant fact that he wasn't buying liquor for his bar alone. I missed my big case with him. Selling untaxed liquor to other establishments was a whole different ball game when it came to the state.

"Wow, you learn something new every day," I told Double J.

"Yep. Your man was stealing from you right under your nose. Didn't even give you a chance to work with other bars, because he had them in the bag."

I slammed my fist on the bar, not sure if I was frustrated or playing the part. My head was too scrambled in the moment.

Nash isn't really your friend, I reminded myself. *This is all an act. You played him, remember.*

"Let's do a deal then. You good to start next week?" I asked Double J, shoving back from my stool.

"I've got a guy coming this Thursday. Come here around 8 and I'll set you up with a trial run," Double J said, patting me on the back. "We'll get you back in shape. You don't need Nash any longer."

His last sentence was a truth serum. I didn't need Nash anymore. It was time to put his case to bed.

"I got you a little something," I said, pulling the pretty pink box from the floor. "For your little one."

Double J looked at me as if I had two heads.

"Man, you really are something," he said, tearing into the gift.

Double J held up the pink frilly dress. Tears welled in Double J's eyes as he pulled me in for a hug.

I gave him a hard pat on the back.

"None of my guys ever gave a gift for my child before," he said. "Thank you."

CHAPTER SIXTEEN

OFFER I HAD TO REFUSE

The deal I established with Double J was for a kilo of cocaine. The product was arranged to be at Soft Tail, but other factors slowed Double J's driver, forcing Tony and me to hang inside the bar.

Over the past few weeks Tony had grown comfortable inside Soft Tail. This isn't to say he was as comfortable as he'd been in Thirsty Bear, but it was a start. As an avid dart player, Tony took to showing the Jamaicans a thing or two on the old machine they'd pushed into the corner. To Double J and Tony's surprise, his guys took to it quickly.

"Look at you bringing your white boy here, corrupting my men," Double J joked as I sat at the bar discussing sales.

"Hey, he's doing you a favor. You know what they say about idle hands, right? He's keeping your men busy."

Double J's supplier was coming up from Pennsylvania and was already two hours late. Two hours inside a bar was more time than I ever planned to do. I grew antsy in my seat, checking my watch and cellphone several times with each hour.

"Man, let me hook you up with one of the girls," Double J said, gesturing to a group of prostitutes at the far end of the bar. "To make up for your time."

"Nah, I'm good," I said, stirring my drink. Butch had poured this one a little strong.

"I'm serious, Billy," he said, dragging out the y in my name again. "What do you want? They'll take care of you. And they don't even need any coke like your woman at home."

"Thanks, but I'm good." I laughed, hoping to deflect the situation. "All that gets me off in the moment is a whole lot of cash. I'm fine waiting."

"Billy, I'm not going to take no for an answer," Double J said. "It's disrespectful for a man to refuse a gift from another man in my country."

"Well, we're not in your country," I teased him. "Besides those girls look young enough to be my daughter. I can't do that."

"Okay, so we get you a blow job. Keep her head under the table so you don't see her face."

Double J was serious. I looked at Tony, but he was lost in his own world. The one time he was actually enjoying himself among the criminal element.

"Double J, I appreciate your offer, but I'm not going to take any of these girls," I said matter-of-factly. "If you're concerned about how I feel I'd much rather have you pick up the phone and find out how far out your guy is. We planned to bring our first delivery tonight."

Double J stared at me.

"You really mean to tell me that a big man like you, running around buying eight balls for coke for some mama at home, doesn't care about getting laid? Am I supposed to believe this? That you're only interested in business?"

"It's the only way I can get off anymore, man. Plus," I said, leaning forward. "I don't have any little blue pills."

A light bulb went off in Double J's head.

"Ah, man. I'm sorry. I didn't know. I thought only old fogies had that problem, but I guess big men can have them too, right?" He laughed.

"You don't have to laugh about it!"

"No, man. I'm sorry," he continued, trying to suppress the chuckles that were still emerging. "I don't mean no disrespect. I just didn't expect that."

"Well, now you know," I said, looking back up at the television. Soccer was on again. "But you do need to either call your man or change the channel. I can't sit here and watch this shit much longer."

"I'll call and I'll see if I can get you one of those blue pills too."

I wiped my sweaty palms on my pants. If Double J were to find a pill, I was fucked. There was no way I could get out of this, yet there was no way that I was willing to take a woman for the team.

"Aye," Double J yelled from across the bar. "You've got thirty more minutes."

I nodded at Double J and watched as he made a few more calls. I prayed that they were business calls from his end, but deep down I knew he was searching for that pill. I slid off the stool and headed over to Tony, pretending to be engrossed in their game.

"We have to go," I whispered as he walked by.

Tony looked at me, mid-throw.

"Now?"

"As soon as the sale arrives, understand."

"Of course I'll get a bullseye," he stated, loud enough for the other guys to hear.

"Good. So be on point. I'll get the sale and you get us the fuck out."

Tony's body went tense. I didn't have time to tell him what was going on, but he knew enough to understand that danger was involved.

After a few minutes of boring throws, I made my way back to the bar and waited. I had to use every ounce of strength within me to bind myself to the stool. Deep down I wanted to call it a night and bolt.

"I've got one guy looking for you," Double J said as he walked over to my seat. "Thinks he might have something."

"Double J, business comes first. Are we clear on that?"

"Man, no need to get your whites in a bunch. We'll get to your business, no worries."

"Listen, can you just sit and have a drink with me already?" I asked, pulling out the stool beside me. "You're making me antsy with all your girl bullshit."

I convinced Double J to have a drink with me. One drink turned into two. Just before Double J could pour a third his guy pulled in. Double J excused himself and headed out back with three of his men, while I turned and nodded at Tony. Double J returned, a smile plastered across his face, and proudly set sixteen eight balls (enough for a Class A felony) and a little blue pill in front of me.

"Did I tell you my guy would come through for you or what." He smiled.

The blue pill seemed to grow in front of me as my mind raced.

"Go on, Billy," Double J prodded me with his elbow. "Take the pill. Enjoy yourself, business is done."

"Billy, we gotta go. Something's wrong with the liquor," Tony rushed over with his phone out. "Shit tipped on a delivery. Bottles are all over the highway. We gotta help the guys clean it up before the cops get there."

"Shit," I exclaimed, jumping up from my seat. "Those idiots are always fucking up! Goddamnit!"

Pretending to be enraged, I shoved the coke and blue pill into my pocket and headed towards the door.

"Sorry, man," I turned to Double J. "Next time."

"Go, take care of business!" Double J said. "The pill was a fake anyway. We hoped it still might work for you."

I looked back, perplexed, while Double J laughed. That asshole was going to give me a fake pill!

Consumed with the fake pill and the crisis I'd just averted, I neglected to feel the eight ball slide out of a large hole in my pocket. Tony and I jumped into the van, quick to hightail it out of there, just as Jeff and Docks tapped into our speakers.

"You dropped some fucking coke in the road, you moron. Go back!"

I reached into my pocket, sure that they didn't know what the fuck they were talking about, and discovered the bag was missing.

"They're right," I said, jumping back out of the van. "Fuck, I don't see it."

Tony joined me in our search as we looked under the van and around the curb. Two of Double J's men were outside watching us.

"To the left," they called. Tony stepped to the right.

"Your other left." They laughed.

Tony took two more steps to his other left and stepped on the bag.

"Got it," he yelled to the guys. "Thank you."

Tony and I jumped back into the van, our hearts racing. So far, looking like idiots was a working trait we seemed destined to follow.

CHAPTER SEVENTEEN

TONY'S WARNING

By the time Tony and I returned to unplug for the evening, the team was in awe. Tony smiled and stood next to me, sharing and laughing in our street search story, but I could tell something was off. His laughter and smile felt forced. As we wrapped up the evening, I made sure to walk out with him.

"What's wrong?" I asked out of earshot from our crew.

"What do you mean?"

"You're leery. I can feel it. What's wrong?"

"I'm just tired," Tony said as we reached his car. "I'll see you in the morning."

I knew Tony's absence was coming, but I had no idea the grandeur we'd just put in the General's hand would also be the one that sealed my partner's fate.

ℰↅ

Tony and I had three deliveries the next morning. A fluke snowstorm had decided to hit the area, which wasn't unusual for Upstate, but it put a damper on our schedule.

"Let's move it out early," Tony said back in the office the next morning. "I don't want to get caught up in this today. Not after last night."

The way Tony said "last night" as if it were a poison solidified any thoughts I had on Tony's apprehension. Once we got on the road and he began an awaited discussion, I was ready.

"We've been partners for a long time, Billy," Tony said. "We've done some crazy shit and uncovered some pretty bad guys."

"And?"

"And I have a family," he replied, looking at me. "This shit is getting to be too much. I'm not comfortable walking into this anymore. Especially after last night. What if you had really needed me? What if you'd gotten into a situation with Double J and those girls that you couldn't talk your way out of for once? This is some pretty big shit, Billy. I have to think about my family."

"So you're saying you want out?"

"Not entirely," Tony said. "I still want to remain on board, but not as your partner. I'm going to talk to Staton today and see if he'll move me to surveillance or set up. But I wanted to talk to you first. I'm not saying I'm out tomorrow. I know what comes with the job. I know I can't just be replaced."

"I get it. And I don't blame you," I said. "My stomach dropped about two feet when Double J placed that pill in front of me. To tell you the truth, I was scared that I wasn't going to be able to talk myself out of that one either. I know I got lucky. You saved my ass."

"For the hundredth time." Tony smiled.

"I did think about everything last night, too. It must have been the high from the night because I barely slept. I kept thinking about how we're just two guys who've been running on instincts this whole time, and somehow it's worked for us."

"Correction, you run on instincts. I just travel along because you drag me into those instincts."

"This is somewhat true." I laughed. "But seriously, you and I are responsible for this whole thing. It seems crazy when you sit back and think about it, doesn't it?"

"Not at all," Tony stated matter-of-factly. "Billy, you've gone in every bar we've entered—hungry. You can't wait to get in there, go deep and get the grit. You have no fear. And that proves valid in your work. You're an authentic day to day bullshitter who's become one of the hardest working undercovers out there. Don't ever sell yourself short. You worked hard for every drop of what we have. We may not have known we were uncovering a giant ring of drug lords, but we did it anyway. Sometimes going into something not knowing what it really is can be the result of an amazing journey."

"And when you learn how intense that something is, and your partner tells you he wants out, well, you just have to reflect on all the good you've had and happily let him go."

Tony smiled with my last words.

"Thank you for understanding, Billy."

"Yeah, yeah," I said, looking at the snow outside the window. "Let's get to that schedule of yours. Any more gibbering and you're going to slow us down by our third delivery."

Our final delivery together was at Steel's residence, which seemed fitting. We'd arrived an hour ahead of schedule, pulled in and waited. The snow fell around us. To tell someone outside of Upstate, New York that it was the middle of spring seemed like a joke within itself.

When Steel arrived he pulled his Cadillac approximately 50 feet behind us. I stepped out of the van to unload our cases and quickly realized we'd have to transport them over large snow piles. I was afraid we'd slip on the icy terrain, shattering his order.

"Just back the van up a little," Steel said, pointing to a clear opening.

For whatever fucked up reason Tony decided I should move the van while he directed me. With only Steel's order in the rear, we no longer held the weight we typically had. So I took my time backing up.

"A little bit more. You've got room," Tony hollered, flagging his hands to come back. "Come on."

I'm inching like a sloth. Steel is shaking his head and Tony's yelling for me to move.

"Give it some gas or we're going to be here until tomorrow," Steel called out.

I applied a little more pressure only to hit a solid patch of ice. The rear of the van began to swerve and, before I could stop it, I slammed the trailer hitch right through the grill of Steel's car.

My stomach dropped as Steel ran over to access the damage.

"You wrecked my fucking car! You wrecked my car!" he began screaming.

I walked to the back of the van to see a gaping hole in the front of Steel's shiny black Cadillac. I'd destroyed the front grill.

Out of nowhere Tony, the man who'd always been on point, always been stern and diligent, began laughing.

"Why is this funny? He wrecked my car. He wrecked my fucking car!" Steel yelled.

For whatever reason this made Tony laugh even harder. Steel started jumping up and down, pacing over the snow-covered payment, yelling.

"Don't worry, we'll whack it up," I told him, hoping to calm him down.

"Whack what up? You ruined my fucking car! You ruined my fucking car!"

Just as he's yelling a State Trooper happened to slowly drive by the cRossong street. This became my saving grace.

"Listen, calm the fuck down or you're going to bring that fucking police car over here," I told Steel.

"I don't give a fuck! You wrecked my fucking car!"

"Okay, let's call the police then," I exclaimed, pulling out my phone. "We got thousands of dollars' worth of stolen products in the van, but let's focus on your fucking Cadillac and go to jail."

Steel stopped, realizing the seriousness of the situation.

"Hurry up and help us unload this shit before he comes back," I ordered, opening the back door.

Steel just looked at me, unimpressed.

"At least pop your trunk while you stand there glaring at us."

Steel did as I asked, and Tony and I quickly began tossing cases into his trunk, while Tony giggled under his breath.

"You two are a bunch of assholes," Steel replied as I closed his trunk. "I don't know why I keep working with you."

"We're a bunch of assholes saving you from not going to jail tonight," I said, holding my hand out for payment.

"Are you serious? You guys fucking owe me!" Steel shouted, pointing to the front of his car again.

"We'll whack it up!" I said. "We're good for it. Trust us."

"Whack it up. I don't even know what the fuck you white boys are talking about. What the fuck is whack it up?"

"It means we'll take care of the grill," I said, opening and closing my hand in a hurry. "Now pay us so we can go. I see headlights coming again."

Docks and Jeff had caught on to what I was trying to do, so they used the surveillance car to appear as if it were crawling down the street.

"Fuck," Steel yelled, quickly reaching in his pocket for our payment. "You two better come back ready to pay for this shit."

"Let us know what it is," I said, shoving the money in my pocket. I made sure this pair of pants didn't have any holes.

"Damn right I'll let you know," Steel mumbled, studying the approaching lights. "Fucking cops trying to mess with me tonight."

His choice of words seemed ironic.

"We'll see you next week." I waved as we pulled into the snowy evening. "We'll take care of it."

We did pay for Steel's grill a few days later, as promised. However, Tony wouldn't be there when I delivered payment. Instead, he'd moved behind the scenes, per Staton's approval, three days after the incident. It was a hard transition, both for Tony and me, but I never lost track of that final night. We ended our undercover just as we'd ended every other—laughing, carrying on and finding the levity in the craziness that was all around us.

CHAPTER EIGHTEEN

DEA DAVE

While my feelings were unsettled about Tony's departure, I knew right away who I wanted in his spot. DEA Dave had left a strong impression on me. I felt relaxed around him, which was important. Some days you're together for countless hours, you smell, you're irritated, you're scared, you're tired or you're all amped up and ready to take on an entire bar. No matter what your mood, you have to like, trust and feel confident in who you're working with. DEA Dave, I was certain, had those traits.

Aside from the rounds of drugs I was buying with Double J, we were still running a heavy untaxed cigarette sale with him. Every two weeks I'd show up with his normal liquor order and three cases of untaxed cigarettes. So it made sense to introduce DEA Dave during our next cigarette transaction, which happened to be a week away.

Tony was on board.

"The only thing you're going to have to be careful of is your craziness together," Tony instructed. "I work to hold you back and keep you in line. You need to make sure he is able to do the same."

"You think they'll take to him?" I asked, still seeking Tony's guidance and approval.

"I think if you introduce him as one of your guys they will," Tony said. "They trust you. Therefore, they'll trust him. Just remember slow is better. You've always known that, so continue to follow what works."

The following week, as we pulled up to the office, DEA Dave stood outside the garage doors, coat on, ready to go.

"Gentlemen," he shouted, his arms spread out in a welcoming gesture.

"Dave," Tony said, stepping out of the van. "You got your shit ready?"

"Only for over a week now."

"Good," Tony exclaimed. "We have a lot to get through today. The first thing I'm going to teach you about is the schedule. You're already on time, so that's a great start."

Tony and DEA Dave jabbered about schedules, morning routines, invoices and stocking the van, while I quietly stepped away to grab some coffee and bagels from the small mom and pop shop next door. When I returned the van was stocked and DEA Dave and Tony were already inside waiting for me.

"Hurry your ass up," DEA Dave yelled from the window. "We're on a tight schedule today."

I could see Tony's white teeth from outside the van's exterior, proud of the protégé he'd just created.

The van was only equipped with two bucket seats in the front, so Tony sat in the fold down seat in the back, happily navigating while DEA Dave drove.

"So, what we've been working on with Double J, beside the drugs and liquor," I expressed, "is a large supply of untaxed cigarettes. We have a different task unit who tracks where Double J's supply goes after we sell it to him, but that's out of our jurisdiction and not our concern. Double J has a standing order that we deliver every week. It's a simple drop, actually. So I'm going to have you work as my loader today. I'll introduce you and show you around, but I want you to stay low."

"Remember to walk in with your head up," Tony interjected.

"Good point. Walk in confident. Don't walk in trying to be invisible and get in and out. Walk in like you own the fucking joint, like you're there watching my back."

"But don't walk in cocky," Tony interjected again.

"Right. Play it smooth, like you've been doing this all day. This is just another bar for you."

"Got it," DEA Dave said, taking a right turn.

"Easy!" Tony told him. "You've got thousands of dollars of liquor back here that you're responsible for."

"Noted," DEA Dave replied.

If he was nervous we sure as hell weren't able to tell.

❧

Tony and I continued to give DEA Dave a breakdown of all we'd been doing. As we talked, I studied him. I watched his moves to see if I noticed anything out of the ordinary, like a twitch or an inability to sit still. I also paid attention to how he spoke and how he gripped the wheel. Small signals like these told me a lot about a person. By the time we pulled the van into the back entrance of Soft Tail I was confident DEA Dave was as calm as he projected.

"Time to work," I said, opening the door. "Any problems and the code word is Black Smoke. Got it?"

"Got it," DEA Dave responded, stepping out of the van.

We headed to the back of the van, grabbing the extra bottles of Hennessey Double J had requested, while Tony secreted himself in the back of the van.

"Remember what we told you," Tony said, his face growing hot. "And remember the schedule!"

DEA Dave closed the van door and pulled the liquor, which we'd stacked on our pulley, in behind me.

It was 10:30 in the morning and the bar was quiet. Butch, the usual bartender, was wiping the bar down as we walked in.

"Billy," he said, looking up from his dirty wash rag. "Usual delivery today?"

"Nah, today's our two-week delivery. We need Double J to sign off on this one."

"Grab a seat," Butch instructed, gesturing to the open bar stools with his dirty rag. "Double J is in a conference with Walt at the moment."

"Oh boy," I exclaimed, careful not to touch the counter he'd just washed. "Another one of those days, huh."

"I don't think Walt would know it was daytime if you showed him. Double J came in to find him still high and partying from last night."

"Ouch," I said, shaking off the thought of Walt's punishment. DEA Dave parked his pulley and took a seat next to me.

"Dave, this is Butch," I said, gesturing to the bartender. "Butch, this is my driver today. He's helping me out while Tony's busy."

"Everything okay with you and Tony?" he inquired.

"Yeah, he just has some family shit going on at the moment. Dave's been with me for a while. He's my warehouse guy. He normally stocks the van and runs across the state to pick up orders for me."

"Ah, well it's nice to meet you, Dave."

"Likewise."

"How about a drink while you two gentlemen wait?"

I ordered a diet Coke and DEA Dave ordered an iced tea.

"What do you think this is, a restaurant?" Butch joked. "We don't got no fucking iced tea here."

"Well how the hell do you make a Long Island iced tea if you ain't got no tea?"

"Does this look like a place where people come and order a fucking Long Island iced tea?"

"Mark my words," DEA Dave stated. "One day someone is going to ask for that drink and you're going to have to scramble to make it."

"Do I look like a scrambler to you, Dave?" Butch's smile revealed a missing eye tooth. I wonder if it had rotted or if it had been knocked out.

"You look like a man who would go out of his way to please a pretty woman."

"Now that you have me on, sir."

"How about a Sprite," DEA Dave asked.

"A Sprite I can do."

As Butch turned to walk away a hand fell on my shoulder.

"Billy," Double J said, slapping my on the back, "why didn't you tell me you were down a man? You know I have plenty for you."

"Double J," I sighed, "you know how quick business is. You make do with what you have. And I couldn't take your guys anyway."

"Why not?" Double J asked. "I can spare some for you."

"It's not you I'm worried about." I laughed. "It's the fact that nobody would fucking understand them."

Double J laughed and turned to DEA Dave.

"So you're Dave?" he asked. "You think you know enough about the bar business to instruct my bartenders?"

My stomach went tight.

"Not at all, sir," DEA Dave backtracked. "Just merely suggesting a drink alternative."

"Well, lucky for you I think you're right. In fact, I think we should have a ladies night special with these Long Island drinks you're talking about. We know the more ladies, the happier the gents. Am I right?"

"That you are." DEA Dave smiled.

"Butch, see if we have some fucking tea bags in the back and start brewing up some of this lady drink Billy's friend here suggests."

Butch nodded at Double J, placed our drinks down, and stepped to the back.

"Rumor is Walt has you all worked up this morning," I inquired, taking a sip of my drink. The bubbles hit my nose before the soda touched my lips.

"Ah, that man. He is a mess. I told him one more time and I have to make him leave. Nash will freeze hell before he gives me this bar though. It's a fucking situation."

Double J took a seat next to us.

"What we got today anyways, boys?"

DEA Dave hauled the liquor onto the bar in front of Double J, and then wheeled the pulley beside him while we talked.

"If this shit keeps moving this fast I might have to order something bigger next time," Double J said, checking out the cases of cigarettes.

"You let me know. Whatever you need."

"How about you?" Double J asked. "Are you good?"

I nodded my head towards DEA Dave, insinuating that I didn't want him to know what we're talking about.

"I'm always in need." I smiled. "You know that. I'm a man."

Double J laughed.

"You know, you crack me up. Isn't he funny?" he asked DEA Dave.

"About as funny as my dad."

"Ah, you hear that, Billy? Your man is insulting you."

"I can take it," I said. "I just don't know if the cut in his check can."

Double J laughed and DEA Dave put his hands up admitting defeat.

"I guess he is somewhat funny," he shrugged.

"That's what I'm talking about," Double J said, clapping his hands. "Respect for your boss and the funny shit he says."

"Where would you like me to load these?" DEA Dave asked, changing the subject.

"Right around the back bar there. Butch will show you," Double J said, calling out for Butch.

As DEA Dave walked around the bar, Double J leaned in.

"How much you need?"

"A kilo," I said, pulling money out of my pocket.

"Man, you sold out already? I'm gonna start hooking you up with the smack I got next." Double J laughed.

"What the fuck is smack?"

"Ah, man. Tell me you are joking. Smack's the shit really putting us in business."

"It's like cocaine?"

"It's crack. You never heard of crack before?"

"Like crack is wack? I've heard of that. I thought it was a low-level drug."

"Nah. It's been hitting the streets pretty hard now. I'll let you try some next time."

"Double J, you know my heart can't handle that shit."

"Well, you give it to your girl then. Shit, you two will be having sex hanging from the ceiling on my stuff."

"Your shit?" I questioned, quickly catching what he said.

"Yeah, been making my own for a little bit now. Can't fuck with it, man. It's pretty high quality."

"How the hell do you have time to make crack when you're always here?" I inquired. "You're not making it in the basement, are you? I don't want to be one of those people who blows up with the lab!"

"Billy, calm down. It's not here."

"You had me going for a minute there," I said, holding my chest. "You really think this crack is something I could sell? If it's your product I'd like to help you sell it."

"You know Tony ain't going to be down with all that," Double J said, raising his eyebrows.

"What Tony don't know won't hurt him. And besides, Tony's having some family issues at home. I'm wondering if he's on his way out."

Double J leaned forward, his chin resting on his hand. He looked funny. This dark Jamaican man in a bright colored fluorescent shirt, posing like the famous Thinker statue.

"It's not a bad opportunity," Double J said. "For you and for me. However, I'm not sure you're ready to get into this type of business."

"Ready for what?" I said, throwing my arms out wide. "I'm not in any type of business other than my own. It's no different than now. I take my order, deliver my order and go home. It's as simple as that."

"Until it ain't," Double J said.

"Well, when it ain't I'll call you and we go from there," I told him. "Look, Double J, I'm not looking to get into any big shit. You know that. Just a little side business is all, and if I can help you promote through my travels, I'm happy to do so."

Double J sat looking at me. His head moved back and forth in a slight nod.

"Okay," he said just as DEA Dave came around the corner. "Let's start next week. I'll give you a small order. You sell it and we'll continue this talk."

"Sounds good, boss," I replied as DEA Dave walked over.

"So, I was talking to Butch back there and he might have some work for us," DEA Dave boasted.

"What's that?" I smiled, giving a sideways wink to Double J.

"Walt back there wants us to steal a guy's bike for him."

"Oh for Christ's sake!" Double J yelled. "Walt, get your ass out here."

Walt looked like a wounded dog as he stepped around the corner.

"What's up, Double J?"

"Whose bike are you over here trying to get this new guy to rob?"

"Manfredo's. You know that bastard owes us lots of money. I saw him riding by last night on a brand-new Harley. That's our fucking money he's riding!" Walt exclaimed.

"And what do you think this dude is going to do?" he said, pointing to DEA Dave.

"I told Walt that I would take the bike, chop it up and spread all the parts around in his driveway so we could enjoy watching him pick them all up."

Double J stepped back.

"Billy, you didn't tell me this guy was a hustler. Shit, you left Tony and brought along a crazy motherfucker."

"I only roll with crazy motherfuckers. You should know that, Double J." I laughed. "Dave here is no joke. He'll chop up that bike if that's what you want."

"That's what we want," Walt stated.

"I'll tell you what then. Give us a week. Let Dave here get all his deliveries done and get used to the route. I've got enough shit to handle while Tony is out right now. Give Dave this guy's information next week and he'll handle it then. Right now, he's on strict orders not to touch anything other than those liquor bottles in the back of the van."

"Wow, look at boss man over here." Double J smiled. "Billy getting all serious."

"It's making me cranky too," I said, standing up from my stool. "Now I have to be in charge of my schedule. It's too much responsibility."

Double J, Walt and Butch made a few jokes at my expense before I headed out.

"Double J, next week. I'll be ready to go," I said, heading out the door.

As we hopped back in the van Tony was ecstatic.

"That went great," he whispered as DEA Dave started up the van. "He's fucking in."

"We're both in!" I exclaimed as DEA Dave pulled out of the parking lot and headed down the road. "I just got us into part of Double J's crack ring."

"I heard," Tony said indifferently. "Just use your judgment."

"Yeah," I said, my mind wandering with the old buildings we passed.

"Dave, I heard you bump into Walt. I thought you were going to scream."

"That asshole scared the shit out of me!" DEA Dave said. "Were none of you motherfuckers going to tell me his face was that messed up?"

"Nope." Tony laughed. "We thought it would be best if you discovered that on your own."

"You're an asshole," DEA Dave countered. "I could have blown my whole cover right there. I couldn't even think when I saw him. My mind just oozed into a puddle right on the floor in front of him."

Tony and I laughed as DEA Dave continued to go into detail about his unexpected encounter.

"Listen, you've got bigger things on your hands now." I laughed.

"What's that?" DEA Dave inquired.

"You've got to figure out how the fuck you're going to get out of stealing some guy's bike and chopping it up. No way is the agency approving that. But it was some good shit though."

"It's all I thought of in the moment. Elephant Man over there was breathing on me, Butch was mumbling about the iced tea he had to make, and it just came out. I just wanted Elephant Man to shut up and for Butch to step aside so I could get away from them. Solving the problem they were ranting over just seemed right."

"Well, you better seem right yourself a new idea," I told him. "Otherwise I'm really going to let Elephant Boy breathe all over you next time."

Tony and I took jabs at DEA Dave throughout the rest of our deliveries. We didn't run into one glitch. No matter what bar we went into, DEA Dave kept his cool and blended in naturally. It was almost as if he'd been part of our crew all along, which was a good thing because things were about to really heat up.

CHAPTER NINETEEN

"STAY SAFE"

Just as my time with Tony came to an end, so did my time with Nash. Two weeks after Tony's departure, Nash began avoiding me. DEA Dave and I would arrive to find him busy in the kitchen, or in the basement. He'd have his guys carry in the delivery, pay us and leave us at the bar, without so much as an offer of soup or a sandwich.

"We've got to wrap up Thirsty Bear," Staton said. "You're not making any headway, and something seems to be up."

I couldn't disagree with Staton's decision. As much as I hated to give San any credit, he was right. With all that was going on in our undercover right now, Nash had become time ill-spent.

"I'll take it from here," I said to DEA Dave as we pulled in with our weekly delivery.

My intention was to tell Nash that I was ending sales and moving on to something bigger. But whatever dialog I planned flew straight out the window as I walked in.

"Word is you've got a good cocaine thing happening at Soft Tail," Nash said, standing up from his seat to greet me. "Looks like you got what you wanted, huh."

This was the first time Nash had made a physical appearance at our sales in two weeks, yet it seemed like months since I'd last saw him.

"Well, my lady friend is happy," I joked, walking over to greet Nash.

Nash put out his hands, signalling for me to stay where I was. Gunner and Bones stepped beside Nash, their arms folded across their chest.

"I don't want drugs in my bar, and I don't want a guy working to sell drugs in here either."

"Nash," I said. "It's not like that."

"Well, while you're fooling around with that shit it is like that and you're not welcome here."

"I understand," I said, knowing it wasn't wise to push the issue any further. "I'm wrapping up the liquor business. Heading out of the area. I just wanted to let you know."

Nash let out a grunt and nodded his head. He wasn't going to give. His conversation and time with me was over.

"For what it's worth, I enjoyed our time together," I said before I turned to leave. "You guys stay safe."

The moment "stay safe" came out of my mouth my body went tight. "Stay safe" was a term law enforcement uses when they leave each other. I couldn't believe I'd just made such an obvious mistake. I kept waiting for him to turn around, realizing that I'd just exposed myself as a cop, and come rushing at me.

But that never happened. He never caught on.

I pulled myself into the van, my emotions running high. I'd just said goodbye to the head of our biggest liquor case at the agency and I'd put myself and my team in jeopardy. All within a matter of minutes.

"It's over?" DEA Dave questioned. "Just like that?"

He'd heard everything that was said over the wire.

"Our work here was done anyway," I sighed, still wrapping my head around my slip. "He's got nothing left for us to uncover. He's already showed us everything he's got going on."

"So, what now?" DEA Dave asked.

"Let's go to Soft Tail," I said, staring at the curb Tony ran over on our first visit. "It's time to wrap this one up too."

To this day I've often wondered if my slip with Nash was intentional, due to the feelings and respect I had for him, or if "stay safe" was just what it was—a slip. A large fucking Freudian slip.

Soft Tail was busy when we arrived, which was odd. It was mid-day, when it barely saw the light of two patrons, let alone the twenty now inside. DEA Dave and I took a spot at the bar, where he immediately got into discussing the motorcycle setup with Butch. Walt was ready with the guy's name, address and motorcycle make and model.

"First time he's been prepared for anything," Double J said, taking a seat next to me. "How'd it go with Nash?"

"Not too good, which I expected," I said. "I think it's safe to say that's the last time I'll ever see the inside of his bar again."

I wouldn't be allowed inside when the raid went down, so my statement to Double J was bittersweet as it was lined with the truth.

"Come on, I want to show you something," Double J said, nodding to the front door. "My shop. I'll show you how I make my shit."

"Where?" I inquired, turning around in my seat.

Double J pointed outside the front window to a three-story apartment building across the street.

"Second and third floor are mine," he said, proudly.

I tapped my foot against DEA Dave's so he could zero in on the conversation.

"You're making crack right across the street!" I exclaimed, feeling DEA Dave's body shift towards me.

"Yep. I want to show you."

Double J rose from his seat. I turned to look at DEA Dave who stood up as well.

"Care if Dave comes?" I casually threw in.

"Makes no difference. I'm always up for schooling some white folks."

My mind bounced to a previous meeting with San and Staton.

"Find out more about his crack location," San told me. "But in no way are you to leave that bar and venture off on your own. Understand? We're not putting everyone's lives in danger for this shit. You're getting into some thick stuff now that others need to handle."

Now here I was about to do exactly what he told me not to. But how was I to say no? I was curious. I'd never been in a crack house. Never seen a drug lab or watched how they made things. And, as bad as it sounded, I wanted that. In fact, I wanted all of it. I wasn't ready for another unit to step in and handle this part, and by the looks of it, DEA Dave wasn't either. Besides, I told myself as we walked out the door, it's right across the street. How they hell was I expected to talk my way out of that one?

We arrived at the faded yellow building in a matter of seconds. We were so close to the bar that I could still hear the music playing. I followed Double J down the long driveway, its pavement cracked and broken, to the back door.

"You boys ready to see some shit?" he said as we followed him up the old skinny stairway.

Double J stopped at the second level, knocked on the door four times and then turned his key. A large Jamaican man, who he called Tom Tom, greeted him straight away. If business had been slacking without the boss around, there was no sign of it. Women, wearing only their bras and underwear, were working at three large tables. There were scales, baggies, tweezers and all sorts of metal junk. Next to them, in the kitchen, was another team of women, about five to be precise, who were cooking, though Double J laughed when I asked if they were making macaroni.

"They're making the crack, dog," he stated.

As we walked through the kitchen, Double J described what each woman was doing.

"Crack is delicate," he told us. "To get the quality just right it takes time. Sheri and Vernice have to cook the cocaine down."

Sheri and Vernice glanced up at us from their boiling pots. They were wearing sunglasses to protect their eyes.

"Girls gotta come with their own gear. I've lost too many goggles and shit already. If they come with their own, they remember to leave with their own. It's been working out that way."

It was 11 o'clock in the afternoon, but the apartment was dark. As Double J talked, I kept moving around, trying to get the right angle so the footage was clear.

"Denise and Patricia take the rocks once they're formed and leave them to cool," Double J said, gesturing to the collection of rocks the girls were sifting through with tweezers.

"Bigger rocks get bigger money. However, Gina here is in charge of breaking down the rocks that are too big."

Gina looked up and smiled at us. Unlike the other girls, she covered her exposed body with an apron. Double J explained that Gina had been with him for three years. She knew the quality and style he was looking for. She also knew when the girls had substituted too much baking soda in the mixture.

"Color comes out all cloudy," Double J stated.

"You add baking soda?" I said. It felt odd to hear my voice bounce around the busy apartment.

"Helps cut the cost and calm the cocaine when we boil it down," he replied.

Double J took us through the living room, where three large men were sitting. Lines of cocaine were spread across a coffee table and one woman was curled up on the couch, sound asleep. We reached another door and Double J gave the same knock before turning the key. What was once someone's light blue bedroom was now storage for Double J's enterprise. There were metal shelves along the walls filled with piles of cocaine, crack, marijuana and some pills, which resembled the one Double J had placed on the bar a few weeks ago. Beside the door were two men with pistols strapped to their sides. Double J gave the two men our names but didn't reciprocate theirs.

"So, what do you think?" Double J said, his smile so broad it covered his face.

"Holy shit is what I think."

"You proud of your man, or what? Nash don't have shit like this going down."

"Double J," I said, making sure the audio had no confusion on who I was talking to. "I don't think anyone has anything like this going down. How the hell did you put this shit together?"

"Took a while, Billy," he said, looking around at his own creation. "I started small in my own home three years ago. Gina over there is my girl's sister. We all got to work and played around until it got good. Now it's just too big to be in my place. Plus, my lady don't want all these girls in and out, especially with another baby coming."

"She sounds like a good mom," I said, turning around the room to capture the magnitude of what was inside.

"That she is. You gotta pick good ones to raise the kids, ya know. The others you leave on the side for fun."

Double J gave me a friendly pat on the back.

"How much product are you pushing a week?" I asked.

"About half of this room," he gestured. "We have people working around the clock now. We're supplying all the way to Baltimore."

"I thought your crew didn't drive?"

"Aye, but we have other means of getting it down. You met some of my drivers at the funeral."

Another mental high five for Deine.

"The stocky guy, right? What was his name?"

"Dennis. Dennis and Big T are my main guys. They come and distribute it to my suppliers. I've got a nice crew here. Everyone's been on since we began. I don't work with anyone I don't know."

"Maybe that's what I should start doing," I said, elbowing DEA Dave.

"Shit, there goes my chance of leaving you and working for him," DEA Dave exclaimed.

"Aye, I could never take you on, newbie," Double J said to DEA Dave. "I'd make your man look small once you saw how well I paid you."

"Alright, let's not give Double J a bigger head than he already has," I joked. "Man's got the biggest business here I know, and to think all this time I thought I was the one running the enterprise."

"I told you when I met you, Billy. You came to the bar with the wrong business. Good thing for you that you finally found it."

Good thing for me is right, I said to myself.

DEA Dave and I made small talk, asking about instruments and scales and crap, hoping to bore Double J out of the place.

"Do we get a sample to take home?" DEA Dave asked. I noted the quick thinking on his part. The narcotics unit would need to test the authenticity of the material Double J was selling.

"Look at your man, all curious," Double J said. "You ever do this shit before?"

"I haven't."

"Go slow," he said, placing a small rock in his hand. "This shit isn't like anything you've had."

DEA Dave nodded as I headed for the door.

"You got more to show us?" I asked.

"What more you want?" Double J questioned. "You two are some hard to impress motherfuckers."

"Nah, I'm just getting a little freaked out is all. I feel like the floor is going to fall underneath me."

"This floor," Double J said, jumping up and down. "This floor is solid as shit."

"Don't do that!" I hollered. "I've got a thing with old floors. I'm always afraid they can't hold me."

DEA Dave and Double J started laughing as the two guards stood there, emotionless.

Pretending to be freaked out by my weight and the old floor, I headed outside the storage unit and began walking towards the front door.

"Billy, don't go!" Double J laughed behind me. "It's just a joke. We'll quit."

"You two keep playing games and it'll be the last time I follow you anywhere."

DEA Dave and Double J were still laughing as Double J signaled for the large Jamaican man to open the door so we could exit.

I walked through, stepping aside to make sure DEA Dave was leaving with me.

"You scared of the steps too?" he asked, walking past me.

Unfortunately it wasn't me who should have been scared of the steps. DEA Dave was so busy laughing and carrying on with

Double J that he missed the first step. Double J and I stood there watching as DEA Dave's body bounced down each stair. By the time he reached the bottom, he was sprawled out, moaning in pain.

"Well, I guess I should have been scared of the stairs, after all," I joked as I tried to lift him up.

"Fuck me for laughing," DEA Dave cried as he placed his foot on the floor.

"Shit! Help me take this asshole to the van, will you? He's going to fuck up the rest of my deliveries today!" I told Double J.

"Wait!" DEA Dave hollered, reaching in his pocket. "Okay, we can go. I still have the rock."

"This motherfucker is more concerned about getting his smack on than what bones he just broke," Double J stated, balancing DEA Dave on the left side.

The three of us slowly made our way across the street, cameras glaring at us from all angles. By the time we reached the van, DEA Dave was moaning so loud that my ears hurt.

CHAPTER TWENTY

THEY'RE ARRESTING EVERYBODY

DEA Dave's leg was broken in two spots. It took a metal rod and a lengthy surgery to set it back in place. The doctor said he would be out for a few months, but the General and Staton weren't concerned about his timeline.

"Because it's over!" San yelled, back at the office. "You have put yourself and your partners in too many dangerous situations for the last time!"

I turned to Staton, who failed to look my way.

"You are selfish! We tell you no and you break away and do what you like anyway. You're lucky all DEA Dave got was a broken leg. You two could have gotten shot in there. Did you ever stop to think that maybe your undercover wasn't as good as you thought and they'd made you? They made you and were bringing you up to there to kill you?"

"I don't think they'd take me to their crack house to kill me. Especially if they thought I was a cop."

"THAT'S IT!" San yelled, spit flying from his mouth. "I'm done with the back and forth, the quick replies and the disregard for authority."

"For the record I never went against what you said. The orders just didn't come from my boss's mouth, so…"

Staton turned to me, his eyebrows raised, while San stood there, foaming at the mouth.

"I'm sorry, guys," I said. "I didn't mean to put anyone in harm's way. I just couldn't think of another option out. The lab was right there, directly across the street. I knew I could get you what you wanted without bringing in another team of guys. It was too close to say no, and I just didn't sense the danger with Double J. We have a tight relationship. He trusts me."

"Billy, it's over," Staton said, breaking my apologetic rant. "We've got what we need."

"What do you mean over? Everything is over or just Double J?"

"Everything," Staton replied. "You did an awesome job. You were an asset for Deine and the General and the PATB. But Sans and I feel that the cases, on all sides, are ready to be put to rest."

It sounds strange but, in that moment, I felt like they were punishing me.

"Guys, I made a bad call."

"Billy," Staton said, placing his hand on my arm, "you made a great call. That call just gave us everything we needed. It's done. We can reel them all in now. You can go home."

I drove to my house that afternoon feeling as if I'd just buried my dog. I received congratulations around the board, Staton was proud of me, the crew was ecstatic to go home, and yet, there I was, driving with my heart in my throat.

How could it be over? Just like that? I kept wondering.

For two days I sat on the couch, absently strolling through channels, and ultimately deciding upon any police show, movie or documentary I could find. I'd get lost in the moment, seize the adrenaline, figure out the criminal and wait to see if my theory was right. Nine out of 10 times I wasn't. When I wasn't sleeping, or searching for another episode of *Law and Order,* I was checking in on the details.

The first bar to go down was Thirsty Bear. They arrested Nash, along with Gunner and Bones. Even as they handcuffed him, Nash was calm and collected. Steel, on the other hand, thrashed and swore and carried on.

During the raid, Double J called my phone. I was nervous that he'd found me out, so I let the call drop to voicemail. Then, with shaky hands, I pressed the replay button, ready to take the beating I deserved.

"Billy," he said over the line, "wherever you're at turn around. The police are raiding everything. They're arresting everyone! Don't come down or you'll get caught too."

The police had to firebomb Double J's house to get him to come out. I often wondered if he had been in that very home calling me as they threw the cans through his windows. Double J had trusted me, right down to the very second.

In the end, the General took credit for 18 major arrests that day, while the PATB took a total of 22 bars from Binghamton to Albany, including our original guy, Mario. I'd see Nash one final time after his sentencing, when he arrived at our office to retrieve his files. He looked old, tired and his hair was cut short and white. He never noticed me as I sat back watching him from my office, but I often wondered what he would have done if he had. In my fantasy, he'd simply nod his head in my direction and walk away. No hard feelings.

CHAPTER TWENTY-ONE

KEY WEST

It took a few weeks for us to close the remaining details of the cases. It was boring as shit. Day after day, I dragged myself to the office, plopped in front of the computer and wrapped up any notes or documents that needed to be tended to.

"You've got to have something else for me," I pleaded to Staton. "I'm not office material. How about that operation you've got going on in Virginia? You must need someone down there?"

"Billy," Staton replied. "I want you to take it easy. You need to decompress before I can put you on something new. Things will come, I swear. But, for now, take some time off. Be you again."

"This is your chance to sit back and enjoy what's around you," my wife reiterated. "You need to decompress from all you've been through the past year."

Their words didn't even scratch the surface. I'd return to the office, pacing around the room, looking for a new case I could break into. I wasn't ready to let Billy the Liquor Guy go. I wasn't close to being done and I sure as hell didn't think I needed a break to be me. I didn't want to be me. I wanted anything else. My life was on the field with the bad guys. That was where I felt at home, where I related and, as far as I could tell, no one understood that besides myself.

Thank God it only took me a week to convince Staton to see it my way.

"I have something lined up right now. I'm ironing out the details and I want you on board. It will be completely different this time. Less running around and more customers coming to you."

I was intrigued before he even told me what the new undercover operation involved.

"They've just established that the terrorists from 9/11 obtained their funds from dealing in untaxed cigarettes. The FBI has asked us to put together a cigarette sting to see who turns up."

"So we're looking to uncover terrorists?" I questioned.

"Terrorists and anyone else who arrives. It's a link they definitely want to dive into, and since it runs in line with the tobacco industry, we're the top agency for the job."

Any sadness or uneasiness I had been coping with immediately dissolved.

"I think you'd be one of the best guys for the case," Staton said, "but I need some time to finish the details."

"I can help with details too, if you need. I'll take anything to get out of this office."

"I do have something in the meantime, if you're interested," Staton inquired.

"I'm listening."

"The agency is looking into cigarettes being smuggled in from China and Haiti. We need someone to head down to the Naval Base in Key West to check it out."

Who refuses a paid trip to Key West? I was in warm sunny Florida in under three days.

∞

Key West was beautiful. There were palm trees, sandy beaches, blue waters and random roosters running everywhere. I walked around the area, my feet in flip-flops, feeling relaxed. I drank tropical cocktails, feasted on pink shrimp and conch fritters, and took in the sights. I sat along the piers, an iced coffee in my hand, dangled my legs over the side and monitored the boats that came in and out. The first thing I noticed were the amount of overstuffed duffle bags that soldiers carried when they walked off the ship that weren't inspected upon arrival. The next thing I noticed were the ported shipping containers. I took my time, locating the crates with tickets from China and Haiti. I wasn't allowed to dig deeper, per Staton's instructions, and was only meant to gather facts that I found interesting. The first thing that came to mind were the lack of stickers some crates carried. If each sticker was to show documentation of their port location, it struck me as odd that some containers had loads of stickers, while others only had a few. I wrote down each ship's serial number, along with the serial number on the crates and containers it held.

After two days of gathering material, Staton wanted me to return home and deliver my findings. As much as I didn't want to leave the relaxed atmosphere of the Keys, I was positive I'd uncovered something that Staton would find usable and I'd be back.

❦

"We tracked your numbers," Staton replied, passing me a mound of paperwork from across his desk. "Turns out some of the ships and container logs were inconsistent, as you guessed. Shows they stopped at the Dominican Republic and few other locations, but they didn't document that in customs. You caught something here."

I beamed with happiness. Key West, here I come again!

"However," Staton interjected, interrupting my tropical cocktail fantasy. "The agency believes it's too extensive for us to take on at this time. They've handed the details over to the cigarette companies. The bosses thought they'd be interested in using their tools and materials to help pursue this further than we can right now."

"So I'm not going back down there," I said, disappointed.

"I'm afraid you're not," Staton said. "I have something else in mind for you."

I perked up, my eyes rising to meet his.

"Yonkers."

"Yonkers?" I repeated, confused. "You're sending me Downstate?"

"If you're interested," Staton said. "I've got a warehouse ready to go, a few hundred cases of cigarettes and some new cars. Pay looks pretty good too."

"Who's on board?" I inquired.

"Other than Tony, who we know is out, and DEA Dave, who will be healing for some time, looks like it'll be you and Jeff and a few guys of my own."

I raised my eyebrows with the mention of new guys.

"Billy, trust me. You'll like them. If you don't then we'll figure something out."

I sat quietly, absorbing the fact that my time in sunny Florida had transitioned to a warehouse in Yonkers.

"How soon do we get started?" I sighed, sitting back in my chair.

CHAPTER TWENTY-TWO

OPERATION KEYSTONE

Operation Keystone's new key players included El Bobo, a large, ethnic-looking undercover who was fluent in Russian, Polish and Bosnian, and was highly skilled in computers, and Nick at Night, a smaller undercover compared to Bob-O, who was a little under six feet, weighed around 190 pounds and had a thick mustache that made him look like Dirk Diggler from the '70s. Though his appearance threw me off, Nick spoke Arabic, feared nothing and was noted for the surveillance work he'd completed on a few high-profile cases. McNally oversaw our operation, while Rubino remained in charge of our tactical team and movements. Brihiem was back on the scene with surveillance, while Big Chaz, Russell the Muscle, Deerslayer and Jeff ran the warehouse's security.

We also had a Confidential Informant named Sayid, who Brihiem would become responsible for. As a transplant from Tunisia, Sayid had begun working with Staton after he was apprehended for smuggling items onto the black market two years before. He was to be our golden ticket in the operation, as Arabs only did business with fellow Arabs. I was happy he had that going for him, because he didn't fare well in the looks department. His nose was too large for his face, his eyebrows were too hairy, and he had excessive saliva that seemed to rest in the corner of his mouth as he spoke.

Operation Keystone was set in an empty warehouse enclosed with a barbwire fence and electronic gate. The scope of the warehouse and surrounding area was so congested that it took Staton's team two weeks to complete the audio and video surveillance. The only bad thing about the warehouse was the missing electronic gate opener, which Staton was working to locate.

"As you know, we're fighting hard to get these fucking terrorists out of our country, and that means cracking down on their cigarette sales. It's time to cut off their funds for good and lock these assholes up," Staton said as he prepared us for our new operation.

Staton's plan was simple. He placed an ad in the local Arabic newspaper advertising cheap cigarettes, and we waited for their call. Sayid oversaw the phone calls and scheduled times for the buyers. So, compared to everything else we'd just done, this sounded off-beat, but who was I to judge?

In order to keep our operation safe, and our buyers separate, Nick suggested we keep an hour between each sale.

"Are we going to get recliners for this job or what?" I asked him. "Seems like a lot of downtime."

"Trust me, you're going to be busier than you think."

Our first ad launched on a Wednesday, and by Thursday Sayid had secured three appointments.

"If you show up one minute early, we'll not sell to you," Sayid informed each caller.

The first day went smoothly. The three drivers arrived, purchased a few cases of cigarettes and left with a promise to return the following week.

"Tomorrow I'm definitely bringing a chair," Jeff said as we sat around, bored.

ভ

Just like with the bar owners, word began to catch on about our operation. By the end of the month we had 25 customers locked in place, as well as lounge chairs, which we had shipped to the warehouse.

By the second month some of our bad guys began creeping up on their schedules, so Sayid had to remind them about our time policy. They played along for a few weeks until they showed up early again, paranoid that someone was going to purchase all the cigarettes and leave them empty handed.

Jeff or I would come out, reaching for the gun in our holster, and the group would tear out of there faster than their tires could roll. Word got out that we were a crazy bunch of assholes yet, as much as I yelled and threatened to shoot people, they always returned, because they were greedy.

While our surplus of clientele continued to grow, our supplies quickly depleted. Tired of going to the state and filing paperwork for additional funds and then waiting for approval, Staton came up with a new approach. Ripped, as Staton called it, was formulated to repurpose our cigarettes. Basically, Staton made a deal with the Yonkers Police Department. After a big deal, we'd notify a specific unit of the vehicle make and model. In turn the YPD would flip the switch, locate the bad guys, arrest them, and confiscate the cigarettes, which they'd return to us. It may not sound like much, but reselling the cigarettes we'd already sold put us in another bracket and eliminated Staton's fight for additional funds. The extra money became so heavy that Staton hired a state accountant just to track those transactions. It was a win win for everyone. The Yonkers Police department was bringing in numbers, names and fingerprints, which they fed to the FBI, while we showed the need for a continued number of undercover stings within our unit. The guys and I were suddenly swimming in an operation that didn't require a lot of back and forth. Life seemed to be a bed of roses, even with our fair share of headaches.

One afternoon Jeff had dismissed a buyer when he noticed black smoke and tall flames shooting from the roof of the vacant building beside us. By the time we ran out to survey the scene, the building was fully engulfed. The four of us tore into our warehouse like mad men, loading ourselves with as much product as we could. We were certain the building was about to go down, possibly taking our warehouse with it, and we sure as shit didn't want to risk losing thousands of dollars' worth of product if we could help it.

As we finished our last load, Jeff noticed an elderly gentleman approach the scene. Carl, as we learned, owned an upholstery shop two warehouses down from us.

"I knew that empty building was gonna go," he said to us. "Been telling the landlord for years. It's a place for squatters and rats. Someone probably torched it."

The fire caused us to put the operation on hold for six days. But once we reopened it seemed like all hell broke loose. For the next three months we were busier than ever. New customers called every day and our loyal buyers began showing up in rented U-Hauls and trucks, anxiously hoping to fill them with product.

We closed our operation just shy of $50,000 a day. Add two to three sales days a week and we're talking about a monthly cash-in-hand revenue of $400,000 that the state was seeing.

Brihiem was in charge of transporting the money from our warehouse to Albany. An honest guy, who I often referred to as Dudley Do-Right, Brihiem was one of the most trusted guys on our unit, which might explain my solo transport with him.

During that drive, I'd made it to the New Jersey Turnpike before I turned and gave Brihiem a quick smile and nod to the sack of cash in the backseat.

"You got two options here," I said pointing to the road. "We could head north or south with this cash Which one will it be?"

"Don't start with me today, Billy," Brihiem stated. "I'm not in the mood for your philosophy bullshit."

"What philosophy? All I'm saying is I could easily make a call. I'll have a buddy show up. I'll take a gunshot to the shoulder, you take a hit on the head, and he runs away with the money. We meet up later and give him twenty percent. No one would be the wiser. What do you think?"

"I think we have tons of audio devices in this vehicle and you're trying to get us in trouble."

I watched Brihiem tug at the collar of his shirt, which only urged me to go on.

"Okay, so then we head down to Atlantic City and take a chance."

"Brilliant plan." Brihiem was growing red. "And when you lose all the money then what?"

"Then we go back to plan A. It's perfect."

I'd frustrated Brihiem so much that he never allowed me to transport anything with him again.

As far as he was concerned working one on one with me was too much of a liability. As for the rest of the unit, any questions about allotted funds were history. The only issue going forward became the number of bad guys that continued to turn up.

CHAPTER TWENTY-THREE

SUNSHINE

The warehouse fire had given our buyers a few days to think about their purchases, as well as ways to analyze our operation. And, when it came to bad guys and financial analysis, greed always overruled logic.

One of the miscalculations we didn't factor in was the empty lot that now sat beside us, which the Arabs began utilizing to spy on us from. They'd park their U-Hauls, pull out their binoculars and write down who we were doing business with, what car they drove, how much they purchased and if they seemed friendly with us. Obviously, this was very concerning to us when we uncovered the facts. But for weeks we were like sitting ducks, clueless as to what was happening. Until we discovered Sunshine.

Sunshine pulled onto the lot in a slick black mustang. The windows were as dark as the car and the silver, shiny rims seemed to sparkle as it inched forward. The guys and I stopped what we were doing, all straining our necks to see who was going to emerge from the ride. So when a black female stepped out, we almost lost our shit.

Here was this nicely dressed woman with a fluffy afro, tight body and red heels that matched her fingernails walking into a dusty warehouse, typically filled with sweaty Arabian men and old beat up trucks. A large black gentleman opened the passenger door and strode up beside her, breaking our gaze. This guy had muscles on top of his muscles, which made me concerned for the veins that seemed to push through his skin.

Sunshine was professional. She offered her hand to Sayid, and a smile and a friendly wave to the rest of us gawking at her.

"What do you boys have?" she asked as Sayid escorted her over.

Our rowdy crowd stood speechless as Jeff showed her our inventory. She placed an order for four cases, to which Muscle Man fronted the money and then stuffed in the back of the mustang.

"What are you going to do with those?" I inquired, managing to find my voice.

"Same things everyone else does. I'm going to sell them," she winked.

Sunshine exited the warehouse with an appointment scheduled for the following week. There was something about the way she carried herself, the way she did business that made my radar go up.

"Listen to your gut," Staton said at our weekly meeting. "If you think there's more there then by all means, dig deeper."

Sunshine became one of our Tuesday regulars. I made small talk with her and tried to hit a few jokes, but sanguinity was limited due to our time.

Upon our third arrival Sunshine brought the boys and me coffee.

"How'd you know what we needed?" I joked, happily taking the tray.

"Well, I'd say you're an easy giveaway," Sunshine said, gesturing to all the empty Dunkin Donut cups around the warehouse.

"So you not only drive a great car, you're observant too," I teased.

"Well, I am a woman."

"So we've noticed." I laughed. "Guys and I don't get to see too many of you here."

"How unfortunate for other women." Sunshine smiled. "It's a shame when men are collecting all the business prospects."

"You don't find this a little rough?" I asked.

"What? Older men in dirty t-shirts and a set of used recliners?"

"Ouch. I can't believe you'd say that about our t-shirts. I thought we were looking sharp."

Sunshine laughed, which I took as my key.

"Hey, next time why don't you let me take you for coffee while these guys load your supplies? There's a diner right up the road. Let me pay you back."

"Is that what you want to call it? A payback?" She smirked.

"Would you rather I call it something more official?"

"Payback is good," she said, turning towards her loaded car. "I'll see you next week."

The following week I escorted Sunshine to the diner one block away. The diner, famously known for their thick milkshakes, was busy. I grabbed a booth by the window, ordered us some coffee and a slice of apple pie to share.

"You're not sick are you?" I winked from across the table.

"Not any sicker than you are, I'm guessing," she replied, picking up a fork.

Sunshine was surprisingly open for our first meeting. After a few minutes of small talk, she told me that she ran a successful brothel three miles from our location. The cigarettes were an incentive to clients who frequented her establishment.

"Back up," I said, almost spitting out my coffee. "You're a madam?"

"Are you surprised?" she laughed.

"Yes, I am surprised! I figured you were going to tell me you're were the head of some crime family or worked for a big drug lord. But a madam. That I did not expect. I didn't even know that was still around."

"Well, if that's the truth that's very sad for you and your gentlemen crew."

"Especially if they all look as good as you."

Sunshine's cheeks flushed and she tucked part of her afro behind her ear.

"You know, if you've got all those ladies around, I know a vendor who's trying to get rid of a bunch of counterfeit purses and shit. I can see if he can strike a deal with you?"

"Are you all business all the time?" Sunshine questioned.

"Only 90% of the time. The other 10% I'm sleeping."

Sunshine smiled and agreed to look at what my friend had to offer.

"But if I'm going to continue doing business with you, then you have to do something for me," Sunshine stated.

"What's that? Continual coffee dates?"

"Not quite." She smiled. "You need to handle the men who are watching you. It's disturbing to be eyed when I pull up. Could be dangerous for you guys as well."

I immediately questioned what Sunshine knew and how long she'd known about them.

"Just this week," she shrugged. "When I pulled up they were there. I'd normally let my security handle it, but that looked a little too involved for me."

When we walked back to the lot, Sunshine discreetly pointed out the run-down truck, which appeared to be empty. Sunshine assured me it was not.

Surveillance was on the truck the moment the conversation came across the wire. El Bobo had the Yonkers Police waiting in the wings, ready to apprehend whoever was behind the wheel. The plan, he informed me, was for us to leave the area, as if we were going to lunch, so the police could swarm in.

I had to say it was a beautiful plan, because it went spectacularly. The Yonkers Police Department arrested the two men, stripped them of the information they'd gathered, and handed them over to proper authorities. The idiots were none the wiser, because within three weeks they were back on the scene.

"You idiots almost drew attention to us," Sayid yelled as they pulled up. "My guys in there knew you were watching them. They are very upset. They say you're going to get everyone arrested for your behavior. They don't want to do business with you anymore!"

The two men began to speak in rapid Arabic, which Sayid quickly translated for us: They were sorry. They didn't mean any harm. They just wanted to see who their competition was. Were we giving other people better deals and more cigarettes?

"Is this a joke?" Sayid said. "Better deals? We give how many cigarettes you order. This isn't an auction house. What do you want?"

The men wanted twice the number of cigarettes they'd previously obtained.

"Not today," Sayid said, knowing we couldn't afford to hand out that much. "You've made my men very angry. They want you to leave."

The men were shocked. They cried to Sayid about money and how badly they needed this sale.

"Come back next week," he said, directing them to head out. "Don't spy on them again. It's bad for customers. You're going to make a riot here. They don't want to draw any attention."

As the men carried on, I stepped out of the warehouse, my chest puffed, shoulders back, and hand on the gun that was strapped to my waist.

"Sayid!" I yelled in my best angry voice. "We got a problem?"

Before Sayid could answer, the two men put the truck in reverse and sped out of there, leaving us in peace for another week.

கூ

"You're in the clear," I told Sunshine as I handed her a box of counterfeit scarves, purses and Jimmy Choos I'd picked up from an undercover in Chinatown. "We got rid of those guys thanks to you. We're indebted to you, so these are on the house."

Sunshine stood on her tiptoes and gave me a hug, thanking me for the loot.

"You're one silvery fox, you know that," she said, messing up my hair.

"You taking a dig at my age again?" I joked. "A man's ego could really get hurt that way."

"Yeah, but you're not that type of man," Sunshine said, hitting me with her hip. "You're not sensitive and shit. You're strong and all business."

Sunshine walked away with her box of apparel, giddy as a teenage girl.

CHAPTER TWENTY-FOUR

NEIGHBOR CARL

As the operation continued to build momentum, Jeff grew irritated. We still hadn't acquired the automatic gate opener, so Jeff had to stand outside, pulling it open and closed as customers arrived. "It's like trying to manage a bunch of teenagers!" Jeff shouted, referring to the customers who arrived early or without an appointment. Dragging the gate open and closed between each client weighed on him. He'd complain about his abandoned recliner, nag Staton to harass the landlord, and whine about all the manual labor he had to do. One day, two Middle Eastern men began fighting over who arrived at the lot first. Jeff and Sayid were behind the closed gate, instructing the two idiots to back up. Paranoid they'd lose their spot, both men continued to inch their U-Hauls forward, attempting to block the other. Back inside the warehouse we heard Jeff yelling, "Back up! Back up!" Jeff hardly ever raised his voice, so his bark drove us out of our recliners and onto our feet within seconds. El Bobo and I exited the warehouse to find two men yipping, "I'm next! I'm next!"

"Back up!" Jeff shouted. "You're going to break the fence. Back up!"

Before we could get down to the gate, one of the men stepped on the gas, jolting his U-Haul straight into the fence. Jeff and

Sayid dove out of the way, just missing the gate as it went flying off its hinges.

"You stupid bastards!" I screamed, running toward them. "Look what you did! Are you crazy?"

The man whose truck broke the fence stepped out to survey the damage.

"Get the fuck out of here!" I screamed. "You're done. You hear me? You will never buy a fucking thing from this warehouse again, you understand, asshole?"

"Please, please, my family!" the man carried on.

"You should have thought about your family before you broke the fucking gate!" I hollered. "Get back in your truck and the hell out of here!"

I turned to the other U-Haul driver who was sitting behind the wheel, smiling at the show.

"You too!" I yelled. "Turn on your engine and get the fuck out of here. I'm not selling your ass any cigarettes either. You assholes are done here."

"No, No, please!" the man begged. "Please, my family."

"Fuck your family!" I hollered, looking at the fence. "Look what you did to our property! You want to pay for this too?"

The driver put his hands in the air.

"I did not do that. You cannot blame me."

"You're as much to blame as this idiot!" I said, pointing to the short, hairy man who was looking at the ground. "Both of you were too selfish to figure it out. Because of that you're both done. Now get the fuck out of here!"

I placed my hand on my holster, acting as if I was going to pull the gun out. El Bobo did the same. The man who did not hit the gate took one look at us and put his U-Haul in reverse.

"Please, I am so very sorry," the fence hitter exclaimed, still standing outside his U-Haul. "Please help me and my family. I cannot lose this sale. My family needs it for our business."

"Our family needs a secured gate!" El Bobo interjected, holding his pistol towards the ground. "You gonna take care of that?"

"I don't know how to fix a fence, but I have a friend."

"Get the fuck out of here!" I jumped in. "A friend. You think we're going to let you bring a friend down here? You trying to get us busted now too? Get in your truck and get the fuck out of here!"

Fence hitter walked back to his U-Haul, his head hung low, and slowly pulled away.

"Can I come back next week?" he asked Sayid as he drove past him.

"Get the fuck out of here!" I screamed, running up and kicking the back of the U-Haul. "GO!"

The driver sped off, leaving us to assess the damage he'd caused.

"You guys have a lot of stuff going on here," a voice said.

El Bobo and I jumped a mile. We whipped around, guns in hand, to see Carl standing there, arms raised in defense.

"Jesus!" I exclaimed. "We almost shot you! Don't you know better than to sneak up on people?"

"I wasn't sneaking. I've been behind you the whole time. I ran up as soon as I heard the commotion."

I eyed El Bobo. So far we were 0-2 when it came to knowing what the fuck was going on around us.

"Looks like a big repair job. Let me know if they need a duplicate gate key," Carl said, stepping forward to get a better look at the fence.

Jeff spun around.

"You have a gate key?"

"Yeah, I found it inside the warehouse months before you guys moved in." He shrugged. "Some idiot must have left it behind. I didn't want anyone to get it. I've got some important stuff in my area too. So I took it."

Jeff told Carl that we'd been missing the opener this whole time and went on to explain how he'd spent hours opening and closing the gate by hand every day.

"Well, shit, partner. This is all yours then," he said, tossing the opener over.

Jeff had a shit grin on his face for the rest of the day. I believe the first thing he said to the fence repair man was, "Please don't disable the remote."

It took two days for the repairman to fix the fence. Jeff was happier than shit to resume our operation now that he had his little button presser. He also became best buds with Carl, making his daily pop-ins a regular with the team.

Carl, the upholstery man, was a likeable guy. He seemed harmless enough, with his little furniture business and skinny son who sometimes came to help him out. He was also fascinated with what we were doing. He thought we were involved in the mob and running some secret operation for one of the head bosses in Long Island. We told him he'd watched too many Godfather movies, but we didn't deny his idea all together.

As weeks grew into summer, the warehouse became stifling. We'd often leave the garage door halfway open to let a little ventilation in between customers. One afternoon Carl happened to walk by. Catching sight of the opening, he decided to peek in. Our cameras caught him getting down on his hands and knees, attempting to look inside our permanently closed walls. However, our surveillance crew did not. Here were investigators with over twenty years of experience and a handful of security and a surveillance crew all sitting around and bitching about the heat, oblivious to the skinny white man who was crawling underneath our garage door.

I wish I had a Polaroid to capture the look on Carl's face when he stood up and saw us lounging in chairs, automatic rifles draped across our laps. Before Carl even caught the surprised look on our faces, he began talking.

"I knew you guys were mobbed up. This is amazing!" he exclaimed

"You think we'd have let you get this far if we weren't?" Jeff said. "We've had men on you since you started walking over here."

Jeff's beautiful response was automatic. That was the real shit of undercover that people didn't realize. It wasn't about just faking who you were. It was about being able to think of shit off the top of your head.

"Wow, this is great!" Carl squeezed out, looking around the warehouse. "I was on my way to pick up a pizza and came to see if you guys wanted some. But, wow!"

Carl's eyes bounced around the warehouse, fascinated with what was in front of him.

"You guys sell all these cigarettes?" he inquired.

Jeff explained our untaxed cigarette operation.

"I won't breathe a word of this to anyone," Carl said, raising his two fingers, in what I gathered meant Boy Scout honor. "Maybe I can help you. I can be a selling agent on the side. Help you move some of this product?"

We enjoyed the little amusement Carl was bringing us, so we went along and offered him a few cases as a standard beginner's test. This was prime real estate for Carl's ears. He sped off to pick up pizza, which we happily added our order to, with five cases in hand.

"How much do I make off each case I sell?" he asked before he left.

"For you," I said, still sitting in my lounge chair. "We'll give 10 percent."

Carl hardly seemed like the criminal type, so if he was able to sell a few cartons, why not let him make a little profit? After all, the government was already seeing their fair share.

While our unit had brought in over $3 million for New York State, helped them obtain several arrests and positive identifications for the Terrorist Task Force, the grandeur of it all was causing other complications for Staton.

"The Yonkers Police Department needs us to relocate," Staton informed us. "They're concerned with all the traffic coming in and out of the area. If they need to take someone down, or if something goes awry, they feel other people could be put at risk. They're not wrong. We need to have a clear area. I'm looking for a larger location now, but I need you guys to be prepared for a quick move."

However, before anything would be put into play, a giant fish would fall right into our lap.

CHAPTER TWENTY-FIVE

WE BOUGHT A BOMB

A week after Carl's warehouse discovery, he approached us, forlorn.

"I can't move the cases you gave me," he said, disappointed. "I thought it would be easy, but I can't get my people to bite. They're too much money. I can sell a shit load of cartons, though."

"We don't deal in cartons, Carl. We only deal in cases," I said.

Carl went on about how badly he felt, but it was another hot day so I wasn't interested in hearing anyone else complain. I nodded for Jeff to jump into the conversation to appease Carl. Yet, just as I was about to walk away, I overheard him ask for help purchasing a silencer.

"Who the fuck do you think you're dealing with?" Jeff smirked. "Of course we can get you one. But why the fuck would we sell you one? You can't even sell the cigarettes we gave you."

"What if I can exchange something for it?" he inquired nonchalantly. "Something you'd be really interested in."

Jeff and I tried not to laugh.

"You got better lounge chairs in your shop?"

"No, but I have a bomb."

Jeff and I froze. What were the freaking odds that skinny Carl had a bomb, I thought to myself, wondering if it was all bullshit.

"Okay, please tell us how the fuck you got a bomb," Jeff asked, hiding his smirk.

"I built it," Carl said as smoothly as if he'd just told us he had eggs for breakfast.

Jeff and I tried to gauge if Carl was being serious or if he was a little touched. Carl saw the hesitation on our face.

"I've been building bombs since I was 11," Carl explained. "That's what my shop is really for. I'm a guy just like you, conducting business in secret down here."

My stomach had begun to seize. I was certain the surveillance team was calling this in as we spoke.

"You're telling us your furniture business is a setup?'" I asked.

"I do sell some pieces, but mostly I'm making money for my expertise."

"Wait, you're an expert bomb maker?" Jeff inquired.

"I consider myself one, yes," Carl exclaimed, straightening himself proudly. "I started toying with devices in my parent's basement when I was little. My father had a collection. I had pipe bombs mastered by the time I was 15 and was selling them by 16. Best money I ever made. Bought myself my first ride with that check."

Nick and Bob-O had to be salivating over this story.

"Building bombs pays more than furniture ever will."

I was struck with the realization that Carl hadn't had any customer traffic the whole time we'd been here. I'd just supposed he didn't make things people liked.

"I've been a leader for the White Supremacist Organization for over ten years," he continued. "I've helped them with some beautiful shit. My work is well known, so they'd be happy to vouch for me if you need."

"I think we're good," Jeff said, his voice a bit shaky.

"I've been bringing my son to groups with me. I'm trying to get him to lead a new group we're establishing here. It's hard going in these parts."

"I bet."

"Never been caught by the police, either," Carl boasted ironically. "I'm very thorough. I can make you a bomb designed to look like an accident when it goes off, or something larger if your boss needs. I'm very diverse in my makings. And not a fingerprint or part can be traced. I make sure to use pieces from leftover machines. I'm at the junkyard a lot."

"That must be interesting work," Jeff responded, since I'd become temporarily speechless.

"You guys want to come over and take a look?"

Carl looked like a little kid eager for a playdate. Despite how badly I wanted to run away from the monotonous cigarette operation and straight to the bomb site, I stayed put. I'd learned my lesson about leaving the scene during the last crack house visit.

"We can't leave the warehouse unattended. We've got a few more sales coming through," Jeff replied.

"How could I be so stupid?" Carl said, slapping himself on the forehead. "Of course you can't come. You're busy."

"How about you show us tomorrow?" I asked. "I'm pretty interested to see what you've got."

Carl's original excitement re-emerged.

"And you'll get me a silencer, right?"

"If what you have is legit, we'll get you more than that."

Carl practically skipped back to his warehouse, leaving Jeff and I there to absorb the reality of what had just happened.

∽

Just as I'd imagined, Nick and Bob-O had been on the phone with the higher ups the moment the word bomb slipped from Carl's lips.

"We've got a meeting at 7 p.m. tonight, down at the lodge. All personnel needs to be present," Nick stated as we walked inside.

By 7 p.m. that evening, our team was sitting inside a cold, air-conditioned lodge beside members of the Bomb Squad, the Yonkers Police Department, their SWAT Team, ATF, the State Police and Staton.

There was more gold and ribbons on the shoulders in that room than I'd seen in my entire life. Yet, despite the apparel and stiff nature of the men around the table, the meeting was somewhat relaxed. The ATF had run a background check on Carl with little to see. He was a high school graduate, wife was a teacher, son was a delinquent and, other than a DWI, he had no prior arrests.

The Bomb Squad laid out the details. They wanted us to purchase the bomb in a safe location, which the SWAT Team identified as a nearby park. However, the one thing the Bomb Squad and all agencies enforced was their need to be present. If I, or anyone from my team, were to collect the bomb under non-surveillance conditions we would be stripped of our badges and arrested for criminal negligence and interference. None of us had an issue with the agency's stipulations, mainly because we didn't want to fuck with a bomb.

The next day we carried on with business as usual while we waited for Carl to arrive. I was so distracted and anxious that I happened to clip myself in the eye while pulling a case of cigarettes off the truck. My eye immediately began to swell and turned black. When Carl arrived, he took one look at me and asked if a nigger had gotten to me.

"Yeah, fucking blacks. I hate them all," I said, testing his reaction.

For the next thirty minutes Carl spoke passionately about White Supremacy, the leadership qualities they instill and why I should join. Small balls of spit formed in the corner of his mouth as he worked himself up.

"You should really come meet them," he exclaimed. "They would love you." He seemed a bit wired as he went on. His anger and passion over his group made him overly excited.

After five minutes I cut him off, pretending to be annoyed and dismissive.

"How about you show me this so-called bomb you've got before we talk groups?" I said. "I've got enough bullshit to do at the moment."

Carl's eyes lit up.

"I want to bring it to you tomorrow. You'll really like it."

"You can't bring your shit here, Carl," I said. "You know that, right? If you're going to show us something it must be done off premises. We're already worried about cops and people watching us. Who knows what shit you could cause if you really have a bomb."

"You guys don't believe me?" he questioned.

"Carl, all I believe right now is that we're fucking busy and you're over here shooting shit about a bomb and all kinds of crazy stories. If you really have something, we're interested in seeing it. But not on our fucking lot. Got it?"

Carl apologized.

"Stop with the fucking apologies too. There's a park up the street. Meet us there tomorrow around 10 a.m."

☙

We obtained final clearance from the Bomb Squad, who would be on site at 4 a.m. alongside the NYPD, FDNY, ATF, since he requested a silencer, and the FBI. The SWAT Team, who would be with us, inquired about our time of arrival.

"Around 9:30," I responded.

The SWAT Team almost choked on their own saliva.

"You can't get there thirty minutes before!" they hyperventilated. "We need you there two hours before."

"I'm not sitting in the woods for hours to wait for a guy who's right around the corner from me," I replied.

It took an hour for all the final details to be set in place, and for us to narrow our time down to 9 a.m. Jeff and I were to be in position on the hillside, a quarter mile from where the team was set up. Within minutes of the bomb's reveal, the SWAT Team and Bomb Squad would storm from the woods directly behind us, and overhead, via helicopter, to apprehend Carl.

The plan sounded smooth. However, the next morning, with everyone in position, Carl never showed. A million scenarios floated around. Did he see someone? Did he figure us out? Was he bluffing the whole time?

Raid discussions were rampant. The SWAT Team wanted to seize the warehouse, but the Bomb Squad and Government agents wanted something bigger. If we could obtain a bomb with intent to sell, we had a stronger case. If we didn't, this asshole could plead a lesser charge for tinkering with explosives in the privacy of his business. In the end, it was agreed that we would wait for a possible sale, and headed back to the warehouse to see if Carl would show. Sure as shit Carl walked straight up to our warehouse two hours after we'd returned.

"Where the fuck were you!?" Jeff shouted as Carl walked towards the truck we were loading. We were all irritated at this point.

"I'm so sorry guys. I overslept."

"You overslept!" I yelled, stepping off the loading dock towards him. I couldn't believe my fucking ears. Today of all days, this asshole slept in!

"Carl, you made a date to show us your shit and you choose to sleep in? I'm calling bull. I don't believe you have any bombs or any of the shit you say you do. I want you to stay over in your little furniture-making warehouse and stop harassing my guys with your fucking stories from now on, you got that? I can't have someone in here wasting their time."

Carl stood there, his mouth open, waiting to say something.

"What the fuck are you standing here for? I said go! This is a real business over here, Carl. Real businesses need real money. You just spent our morning pay. So go find someone else to feed your tales to."

Carl walked away without a word.

"You think you were too tough?" Jeff asked when he was out of sight.

"No. If he really has something, he'll show it to us now. Let's just wait and see what he does."

Thirty minutes later our surveillance crew went on high alert as Carl returned to the scene.

"Can you see anything?" I radioed Nick.

"He has something in his hand. I can't tell what it is."

"Okay, everybody be ready," I said. "Jeff, try and talk him down."

"You think he really has a bomb?" Jeff asked, his eyes wide with fear.

"We're about to find out." I smiled. "Play it cool. Nick, make sure the crew's contacted the Bomb Squad to notify them."

Jeff walked out to greet Carl, placing his hand on his shoulder and engaging him in small talk. I could tell by Jeff's face that he was concerned. Carl's lips were tightly pressed together, his cheeks flushed and he was walking at a rapid pace, with a large can of Campbell's tomato soup in his hand.

I stood up, ready for whatever was about to go down, as he stormed into the warehouse.

"What the fuck is that? You bring us lunch?" I asked, pointing to the can.

"It's your bomb," Carl sneered, looking directly into my eyes. An uncomfortable feeling immediately rose up my spine.

"This can of soup is the bomb? What the fuck kind of damage will this shit do?" I said, the feeling rising to the back of my neck.

Carl pointed to our 26-foot rental truck.

"It will blow the back end clear off that truck," he grinned before raising his arm and slamming the bomb on the table beside me.

My heart leapt into my throat and the warning in my spine shot throughout my body. Carl was trying to reclaim power with his slam. But his attempt that was designed to scare me only pissed me off.

"You just slammed that shit on my desk!" I spat, springing up from my seat. "You trying to fucking play me? Because right now I see a shit ass bomb maker whose bomb did nothing!"

Jeff's face tightened, while Carl's grin widened.

"Why don't you step out of the warehouse and I'll show you what my lunch can do?"

"Jeff, your buddy here is trying to get us all busted. He wants to fuck around with his little toys here and send us all to jail. This is the type of person you bring to our warehouse?"

Jeff was as white as a ghost.

"Billy, I didn't know he was going to pull this shit," Jeff played along, his voice strained. "Please don't tell the boss."

Carl stood there, watching our exchange go down.

"I don't have to tell the boss. This asshole just cost you the operation."

"What?" Jeff interceded. "I didn't know he was unstable. I had no clue he was going to be dumb enough to bring a bomb into the warehouse."

"It's your job to know," I exclaimed, pointing to the door. "Leave on your own terms or feel free to take a ride with me."

Carl butted in.

"NO, Billy. This is my fault," he said.

"You're still here?" I said, glancing at him. "Carl, as far as I'm concerned, you're no longer a part of this business or this crew. You promised something you couldn't deliver, you backed out on a deal, went against our wishes, and brought a can of soup into our warehouse claiming it's a bomb."

"It is a fucking bomb!" Carl shrieked.

"THEN WHAT THE FUCK IS IT STILL DOING IN MY WAREHOUSE?" I roared, all my anger spewing out like a lion.

Carl stepped back. I'd scared him. Hell, I think I scared myself. After a minute of silence, Carl broke.

"I'd be happy to give you this as a peace offering," he stuttered. "I don't want any problems and I don't want Jeff to lose his job because of me. This is all my fault."

I stood there, still breathing heavily, and looked into Carl's eyes. A little more life had come into them since he'd arrived.

"We don't take handouts. If it's the real deal, we'll buy it from you. You think you can wake up on time and meet us at the park tomorrow morning, like planned?"

"The train doesn't go in that direction, and I don't want to carry this over there in case I get robbed. I'd really like you to just come to the warehouse. I have everything for you right now."

"Carl," I said, talking a calming breath. "We are not going to leave our site to visit your warehouse. Nor are we going to dislodge a bomb here. I for one don't plan on going to jail any time soon, and I think you feel the same, correct?"

"Correct," he meekly replied.

"Okay. So then you meet us here at 8 a.m. tomorrow and we'll escort you to the park. If your shit is real, like you say, and it blows up that dirty park, we'll offer you a deal to purchase a dozen right then and there. How does that sound?"

Carl's eyes brightened.

"A dozen?" he questioned.

"For now. We can discuss larger sales if the product is good."

Carl was happier than a pig in shit. He agreed to the morning meet-up, and promised to set his and his wife's alarms so he didn't sleep in.

"I'll call my son now to prep the orders. You're going to be so impressed!"

Carl was so excited that he began to walk away with his bomb still on our table.

"Carl," I called out. "How many times do I have to explain about your shit in our warehouse?"

Carl placed the can under his arm and walked back to his warehouse with a goofy grin on his face. He talked to himself the whole way back.

❧

Jeff was pissed that I'd agreed to transport Carl and the bomb, the surveillance crew was annoyed, since they had to include an additional onsite and van interior set up, and the Bomb Squad was quick to ask if we were certain our guy would show up.

Just as I was rallying everyone, pumping them up about closing another case, gunfire broke out around us.

"Hit the floor!" our surveillance team yelled.

Our crew scrambled to the floor, crawling to the side of the warehouse, guns drawn and ready. Millions of thoughts flew through my mind as the bullets pinged off the sides of the warehouse. Had I pushed Carl too far and he'd returned on an angry rampage? Was this part of his White Supremacy group? Were we being robbed by one of our Arabic groups?

"What's going on out there?" I called out to our surveillance team.

"Stay where you're at," they radioed. "We've got gang activity happening just outside your door. Stay down. Police are on their way."

We'd learned about the heavy gang problem that surrounded the neighborhood within days of moving in, but we'd never experienced any problems as we were said to be in neutral territory.

Sweat rolled down my face and dripped onto the floor as I waited, my pistol aimed at the door. My heartbeat consumed my ears, making me wonder if it had blocked out all sound. I no longer heard the pops and pings against the wall. After a few minutes, distant sirens filled the clouded silence. It wasn't my ears. The gunfire had stopped. I sat there, unable to move from the adrenaline that was surging through my veins.

Language, unsuitable for children, sprang from Bob-O's mouth. He was pissed, and with good reason, for in this moment we were all growing tired of the tense situations that seemed to be engulfing us.

∾

Back at the warehouse the next morning, everyone was quiet. Unlike the usual back and forth bullshit we'd throw at one another after an exciting night, this silence was consuming. Everyone sat around, sipping coffee from the corner deli, until it was time to go over the details of the exchange. The silence became so uncomfortable that a large sense of relief filled my body when Carl walked onto the scene.

Carl hopped into our van excitedly. He happily fed our audio devices the precise details of the bomb he'd created for us.

"My son and I finished two last night. You're going to love them!"

"Your son sounds like a hard worker," I said, trying to ignore the bomb that was resting on the floor behind my seat.

Jeff pulled onto the intersection, which was already jammed with traffic.

"Look at this shit!" Carl exclaimed. "This is why I would never drive in this god-forsaken city."

Carl went on, complaining about the traffic, while Jeff inched his way through the cars and I tried to hide the rising panic that was filling my chest. We'd weaved through three cars in twenty minutes before Nick rung in. I leaned towards the window, so Carl wouldn't overhear the conversation, thinking it was going to be an accusation over our timing.

"You can't go to the park with the bomb! Turn around! Do you copy?" he screamed.

"Says who?" I asked, in case Carl heard him screaming.

"You can't transport a fucking bomb through the middle of Yonkers you idiot! Do you hear me? Turn the fuck around!"

During all the hype of the bomb purchase, some idiot missed the fact that President Obama was in town. Not only was transporting a bomb a breach in every contract we'd ever made with police, but if something happened while Secret Service was there all hell would have broken loose.

"Go back to the warehouse now! Obama is in town. Do you copy?" Nick shouted. "President Obama is here."

President Obama was literally three blocks away from us. Hence the early traffic jam.

"Tell him you can test the bomb at our site! Things are set in play. Just turn the fuck around!"

I calmly turned to Jeff, who was looking at the closed road straight ahead.

"God damn it, turn around Jeff! Fucking Obama is here and Secret Service has closed the fucking roads!" I said, tossing my phone on the dashboard. "Let's just test this fucker at our site. We can't put Carl's life in jeopardy. We can do some real fucking time if we're caught with this shit."

"Are you fucking kidding me?" Jeff responded, his eyes wide with irritation.

Worry spread across Carl's face as well.

"Obama is here?" he questioned.

"Yes, you two crazy assholes!" I yelled. "So turn this goddamn car around before I turn that wheel myself. I ain't going back to jail for you two idiots."

The closed roads led to major traffic clusters, so we sat in the car for another 25 minutes making small talk to keep each other calm. Once we made our way through our gate, bright lights streamed through our rear window.

"What the fuck?" I yelled, turning to see the cars quickly approaching us. "You better pray they're not for us Jeff!"

Jeff quickly played the part, pulling the van over and telling us to remain calm.

"They don't know shit. It's probably a simple blinker I missed or some shit. Everybody stays calm. Don't blow this."

I wondered if he meant that sentence on purpose. Within seconds our car was surrounded by multiple law enforcement agents, their guns drawn and ready. The surprise caught Carl off-guard. He kicked the bomb under my seat and raised his hands. The police lunged in and dragged him out before he had a chance to think.

Jeff and I were pulled out and arrested for Carl to see as well. The agency couldn't afford to jeopardize their cash cow operation with our possible exposure. After all, people talk in jail.

Carl looked at me from the back of the police car, scared. I shook my head and put on a fearful face from the car I was detained in. As Carl's officer drove off, I swear he mouthed the words, "I'm sorry."

Once out of sight, the Bomb Squad came rushing in, securing the bomb, while the SWAT Team tore into Carl's warehouse, retrieving three bombs, two rifles and a box of explosives.

Other positioned units stormed into Carl's home, retrieving eight homemade bombs, 14 rifles, thousands of rounds of ammunition, and $500 worth of fireworks. They seized his home computer, arrested his elderly father, who was living with them, as well as his son—who was in the basement building a bomb when they arrived. Another team arrived at the local elementary school, where Carl's wife worked, and arrested her as well.

The arrests lead to national headlines and, for the betterment of the operation, a relocation. Yet, the greatest satisfaction I received was in a message from my family.

"So I just saw on the news that a man making bombs was caught and arrested after he'd been schmoozed by an undercover. I'm guessing that had to be you. We're all proud of you."

Some may not grasp the deeper meaning of that message, but for me it was huge. My family knew me. Without even telling them, they knew what I'd done. There was a great satisfaction in that.

CHAPTER TWENTY-SIX

THE PARTY GETS BIGGER

After the hype of the bomb, everyone wanted in. The FBI became a permanent fixture in our unit, as well as the Terrorism Task Force. Our new location, which was set in an air-conditioned warehouse in Marshalls Creek, Pennsylvania, required us to bring Pennsylvania State Police and the PA BCI unit on, as well.

If the relocation was an issue, we didn't see it. Here we were, an hour and a half away from our original location, yet every customer followed us. They'd formed a sense of trust with us, knew our products and built their own businesses off them. It was fair to say they would have followed us to Alaska if we'd asked. We had them in our back pocket. However, what we also had was a larger warehouse and a shitload of other agencies looking to work with us.

Our weekly advertisement in the Arabic paper had brought in a surreal amount of additional clientele, which made enough work for everybody. Staton had sat down with the Terrorism Task Force and the FBI and came up with an additional delivery scam that would allow the FBI and Task Force to see where people lived and worked. Using our new distant location as an excuse, we offered to drive products to people, and the bad guys bought right in.

While the FBI pursued their weekly leads, and the ATF explored the weapons that most of our criminals were arriving with, I dipped into Sunshine's returned visits.

Sunshine had promised to follow us the moment I told her about the bomb takedown that had happened at our warehouse. Within the first week, she arrived, her security intact, and checked out our new place.

"This is much nicer than your last place," she said, walking around the lot. "You boys must be doing better than I thought."

"Knock on wood," I said, tapping on the steel warehouse. Sunshine laughed.

"You're still as crazy as ever, though."

"I don't think a location can change that." I smiled.

"I hope you boys have a good plan set up here. It's a bit far from your original location."

"Doesn't seem to be a problem so far," I said. "We're booked for our first week. And we're starting to deliver, since we'll be in and out of New York. You let me know if you want me to swing by."

"You and your boys should come by." She smiled, leaning up against her car. "I've got a lot of pretty girls down there for you."

"Well, there seems to be only one pretty girl I'm interested in right now."

Sunshine beamed.

"Hey," I said, leaning in closer, "you think you can help me out with something?"

"I think I can manage to help you out in several ways, if you're asking."

Blood rushed to my cheeks.

"I'm looking for a little coke," I whispered. "You think you can help me?"

Sunshine stood back and looked at me.

"You do coke?"

"Occasionally," I replied. "The stress here has me all wired. I can't keep up and I don't want the guys to see me slowing down."

Sunshine leaned in and fixed the collar of my shirt, letting her fingernails trace the skin on my neck.

"Let me see what I can do," she said, standing so close that I could feel her breath on my neck.

"Billy!" Jeff yelled, sensing my situation. "Help me grab some of these boxes."

Grateful for the distraction, I thanked Sunshine for the help and busied myself with Jeff. Sunshine wasn't even out of the driveway before surveillance had the Drug Task Force lined up and ready to go. One more agency in the loop.

CHAPTER TWENTY-SEVEN

CHIN LU

As with all our prior operations, this one began running operations within operations as well. While Sunshine had become the host of our prospective drug buy, a new guy on the scene would lead us in another new direction.

Chin Lu was our first and only Chinese buyer. Unlike our Arabs or the new African group we'd acquired, Lu, as we called him, arrived at the detail in tailor-made suits, polished shoes and dress shirts, which were always crisp. It was so out of character compared to our other customers that we automatically took an interest in him.

Lu had an energetic personality. He arrived happy, with jet set speed, ready to pay for his merchandise and go. There was no dawdling or idle chit chat. This guy was all business.

Lu didn't assist in carrying any of the product, either. Instead he slipped our guys money to load everything into the trunk of his white BMW. While he waited, I noticed his inability to sit still. He'd readjust himself in his seat, drum the steering wheel or wiggle his fingers, making me wonder if he was strung out on coke. And, if so, did he have more to offer us than cigarette transactions?

During his visits I harassed him a little, to gauge where he stood.

"Chin, you're always dressed so nice when you come to see us," I said, leaning into his open car window. "I'm beginning to feel like you like us."

"Nah, I only love the casino. I have a date with her later. I show her my style, she shows me the winnings."

After a few weeks, Lu began scheduling double deals. He'd arrive early in the morning, load his car and then drive down to Chinatown and then return, which often pissed us off because he was our last, and often late, customer to load up again.

During these deals I always attempted to further the conversation.

"You're always running," I'd say. "When do you relax?"

"When I'm at the table," he'd say, referring to his love of blackjack. "I'm late now."

"Where are you going anyway?" I inquired.

"Atlantic City," he replied in horror, as if I were stupid to ask. "No other place in the world compares. I'm there every night."

I wondered if Lu's cigarette hustle was the result of a gambling debt. *Maybe he was in trouble*, I thought. If he was in trouble, that could be my way in. So, the following week, I decided to feel it out.

"Lu, you in trouble?" I asked.

Lu looked at me as if a skunk had just crossed his path.

"In trouble?"

"In trouble with gambling or something? I'm just asking because I have some people who might be able to help you out."

Lu looked around, as if he were on hidden camera.

"You crazy, Billy?" he said. "You see my car. My clothes? I have no trouble. Trouble comes to me for help."

"If you're sure," I said aloofly. "My help is here if you need it. No pride at stake."

Lu laughed.

"You should come to me for help, not me to you. You're really funny."

"As long as you're okay, guy," I said, tapping his car. "We watch out for our customers, that's all."

Lu must have thought about my offer, because the following week he arrived with a business proposal.

"I have something for you," he said during his evening pickup. "It's a business deal."

The words 'business deal' are like flies to shit for undercovers.

"I sell tax stamps." Lu smiled. "You want in?"

"Tax stamps?" I said, puzzled.

"Yeah, you know tax stamps. For the cigarettes. To make it look more real."

I stared at him, scrambling for my move.

"You fucking idiots don't know tax stamps? They're on the side of the cigarettes you sell!"

Lu pulled a pack of Marlboro lights from his pocket and pointed to a tiny marking on the side.

"You see this? This is the tax stamp," he said, directing his finger to the gray marking. "You get caught with cigarettes without this stamp and you can go to jail. It's illegal."

I walked over to our supply and pick up a carton. Lo and behold, the little tax stamp was sealed on the side.

"We already have tax stamps," I showed Lu. "What the fuck would we need yours for?"

"You don't have to have them," he said. "I make them for you."

"Lu, you're going to have to enlighten me here," I sighed, honestly confused. "Why would I need you to make me a tax stamp when I have tax stamps?"

"For counterfeit," he replied, waving his hands in excitement. "You sell people fake cigarettes and I sell you the tax stamps. Nobody knows any different."

"Where the hell do I get fake cigarettes from?"

"Oh, I have plenty of places I can take you to. They come from all over. We have them in our warehouse."

"Lu," I interrupted him. "If you have fake cigarettes in your warehouse, why the hell are you coming here every week?"

"Fake cigarettes taste like shit. My guys want real smokes. But your other customers—you can trick them."

I wrestled with the opportunity in front of me while the guys shut Lu's trunk, finished with his order.

"I've got to admit you've got my interest," I said, rubbing my hands across the side of my face. "Why don't you let me talk to my partners and get back to you next Thursday?"

"Don't think too long," Lu replied as he stepped into his car. "You waste money that way."

❦

Staton was all over Lu's proposal. Within two days he had our crew shutting down our operation early Saturday afternoon for a scheduled debriefing at the Philip Morris plant in Richmond, Virginia Sunday morning. It was another weekend on the job and away from my family. Needless to say, my wife and kids weren't happy, but the drive to go deeper helped me ignore their disappointment. After all, we were talking about meeting some of the pioneers of the tobacco industry!

Any exhaustion I may have felt melted into the private driveway that held a sea of gentlemen waiting to greet us. I felt like royalty as they opened the car doors for us, excitedly shaking our hands and escorting us into their facility.

After a few minutes of introductions and travel talk, the gentlemen offered us cool glasses of iced tea topped with a splash of bourbon, and gave us a brief tour of their property, explaining their history as we went along. It was amazing to hear the stories of some of the founders, see where the factory had expanded, and learn about all the things, both good and bad, that had made them who they are today.

The tour ended in the CEO's large conference room, which was filled with prestigious leather chairs, a 12-foot-long hand-carved wooden table and a feast of deli meats, breads, fresh fruit, salads and tobacco-smoked meats.

We loaded our plates and tore into delicacies too profound for a bunch of sweaty warehouse workers, while their Director of Tax Fraud passed out bound packets of information. Smoked prosciutto wrapped around sweet slices of cantaloupe unfolded to the fight that large companies, such as Marlboro, had been up against for years. The fact that we happened to stumble upon it was a blessing in their eyes, and one they were proud to join forces to help us beat it.

As much money as these companies were making, they struggled to keep up with the billion-dollar loss they'd been facing the last five years. All because of pirated cigarettes.

They'd established their own private team, who they hired to find and shut down the operations that were responsible for smuggling, housing and selling these products. That team had located the production facilities, which were housed in China and South America, and determined the ports that allowed them into the United States. The problem was that the pirate organizations had become so good that it was nearly impossible for customs to tell the difference from the real products and the counterfeit.

A tall, skinny gentleman in a black suit and navy tie placed the two products in front of us and asked us to choose the fake pack from the original. I was amazed at how identical they looked and, as hard as I tried, I couldn't spot the difference.

The first thing Navy Tie showed us were the jagged points throughout the M in Marlboro. It was a signature the founders had made a point of noting when they labeled the brand. The counterfeit packs had straight lines in the M, which you needed special glasses to detect. Another way to determine the cigarette's authenticity was to open the pack and check the cellophane wrapping. Authentic brands held a cellophane that came off in one piece, whereas the counterfeit cellophane would break or fall apart when peeled. Again, for the untrained eye, you'd probably never notice or think twice.

Of course, the third option was taste, which I took their word for since I'd never been a smoker. Marlboro cigarettes were made with high quality nicotine plants. The imposters were made with crap. Therefore, the moment a smoker held the cigarette up to his lips and took a drag they'd experience a horrendous mouthful of smoke. And, if that smoker had unknowingly purchased a pack of these cigarettes, the loyal buyer now became dismayed with Marlboro's product and began sampling other varieties.

When it came to the tax stamps there were various ways to detect their authenticity as well. The first involved a portable blue light, which Navy Tie shined on the stamps. True tax stamps were created on thick, matted paper that prevented light from shining through it. So if we could see the package behind the stamp, then the stamp was counterfeit. It was a great concept. However, border patrol didn't have the time or the manpower to stop trucks loaded with Marlboro cigarettes and shine a light across each stamp.

Marlboro tried to create stamps with different intricacies every year to help weed out the fraudulent suppliers, but it was always just a matter of time before the forgers would adjust their stamps to resemble the new ones and the process would begin again.

"This shouldn't be our job, Billy," Navy Tie said, looking across the table at me, "but the ring is larger than any agency can seem to get a hold on. The bureau has failed us for years and we've spent millions of dollars on our own accord to try to combat this situation."

The rest of Navy Tie's team chimed in, sharing stories of past losses and unsuccessful undercover smuggling stings. You could tell they were frustrated and a bit apprehensive, which was understandable, but I assured them our agency would do everything possible to take down the guy we were working with.

Dalton, the Director of Marlboro's Accounting Department, had more bound booklets, which broke down the cost and loss of revenue that stamps caused for the states and tobacco companies.

New York State had the highest tax stamp, and New York City, which held an additional tax stamp on top of the preexisting state stamp, was through the roof. This put a prime target on the Metropolitan area—exactly where Lu was located.

Whether it was a mom or pop shop, a large corporation, like Wal-Mart, or a wholesaler, every place of business had to apply for a retail license and document each pack of cigarettes sold. It was then the State Inspector's job to verify their records to help detect any loss in revenue. However, it didn't do anything for the thousands of bodegas and small shops, which were selling pirated cigarettes. That's where the company needed us. They were hoping to add additional funds to bulk up on manpower so we could begin breaking down each and every one.

As we departed late that afternoon with an understanding of what we needed to do, I was eager to jump into business with Lu and see where this new niche could take us. And, when I turned to check in on the crew, I could see that every one of them was ready too.

CHAPTER TWENTY-EIGHT

GIFT FOR SILVER FOX

While the cases and operations were different than Operation Spirits, I stuck to the same mentality: Don't rush. Don't show eagerness. And don't break routine. Therefore, we had to wait four days until Lu's Thursday appointment.

Sunshine and her anticipated cocaine arrival got us through Tuesday.

"Hope this helps you, Silver Fox," she said, slipping an eight ball into my hand while standing on her toes to kiss me on the cheek.

"Who's better than you?" I said, studying what she brought me. "This is definitely going to help."

"I've got something else I need to talk to you about," Sunshine said. "It's serious so I need you to focus."

I turned to Sunshine and gave her my full attention.

"You've been doing business with a group of Africans, correct?"

"How do you know about…"

"Just listen," she hushed me, placing her fingers on my lips. "Those Africans are bad news. I caught them down the road getting a drink. Word is they're going to rob you."

We'd been dealing with the Africans for only two weeks, and in that time they'd already landed themselves their own internal investigation as they'd used counterfeit money to purchase their cigarettes.

"They're coming in long trench coats with shotguns underneath. They're looking for cash."

I called Sayid over and checked on the day's itinerary. We were two hours away from their slotted time.

"Okay, I need you to get out of here," I said, pushing her towards her car. "I can't work unless I know you're far away from any danger."

Sunshine smiled at me. But as we approached her car door her expression changed to concern.

"I'm nervous for you," she said. "Do you have a gun? Anything to protect yourself with?"

"I'm not carrying right now," I shrugged. "But I'll make do."

Sunshine reached into her glove compartment and pulled out a 9mm semi-automatic revolver with a silver barrel and black handle.

"For your protection." She winked, handing the gun to me. "Take it and be safe."

"Are you sure?" I asked. "I don't want to take your protection away."

"I have more. Don't worry about me. You need to focus on your guys and getting them properly equipped. Those little pistols they have aren't going to compare to what the Africans are coming with."

"I'll take the gun," I said. "Now get out of here. I've got to get the guys prepared."

I kissed Sunshine on her forehead and stood in place as she drove off, thinking about the can of worms she'd just opened for herself. The moment she was out of sight I scrambled towards the guys. We had some big shit to get ready in a little amount of time.

Rather than shooting the Africans on sight, the guys agreed that the best course of action was to catch them off guard, to confuse them.

As the Africans pulled up to the warehouse, Sayid went into action, just like planned, as Jeff, El Bobo and I stood in the dark, waiting.

"My boss wants to see you," we heard Sayid tell the Africans. "You need to follow me to the office."

"They bought it. They're following Sayid in now," Bob-O radioed. "They're wearing trench coats. Watch their hands."

Sunlight streamed under the door as Sayid escorted the Africans into the warehouse. The door opened to the office we were silently standing in, and we watched as Sayid took a seat behind my desk. The Africans glanced at each other, unsure of what to do. One of them reached into his pocket and pulled out a wad of money, which he placed on the table. Sayid grabbed the money and ripped it up.

"You think we're fucking stupid?" he shouted, tossing the torn bills at them. "You think we don't know this is counterfeit? You try to steal from us?"

On cue, Jeff, El Bobo and I stepped forward and jammed our guns into the back of their heads.

"Nothing better than to kill a brother right before Martin Luther King Day," I shouted. "So go ahead and do what you came here to do."

The Africans put their arms in the air and began blubbering.

"We don't want no problems," mine said. "He's got money in his back pocket."

"No more of your shit money," Sayid said, stepping around the desk. "You're trying to get us all busted."

"We want your weapons," I said, pulling on my guy's trench coat. "Reach down and place them on the table."

The Africans tried to face each other, but we pushed the guns harder into the back of their heads, making their effort in vain.

"You think we can't tell you're carrying? You guys really are some stupid bastards. Now unload before we do!" I yelled.

I think the trio kept hoping someone was going to come up with a quick idea. But neither swayed from the course. After a moment of hesitation, the Africans pulled their sawed-off shotguns from their coats, along with a pistol and two knives. This shit was real. Sunshine had just saved our lives.

"You fucking so much as show your face around here again and I will blow it off. Are we clear?"

"Clear! Clear," Jeff's guy yelled.

We held the guys for a minute, letting them whimper and beg for their release, before we let them go.

"One wrong move and we shoot," I said, nudging my guy to walk forward. "You come back to this spot, or even attempt to do business with our fellow partners, and we'll blow your heads off in your sleep, understand?"

"Yes, yes. We will never be back. We're sorry," El Bobo's guy cried as he shook nervously.

The Africans scrambled to their car, our guns still aimed at their heads, and peeled out of the lot. The three of us stood there, grounded in position, until surveillance radioed that they were officially off the lot and on the main road.

Pennsylvania State Police apprehended their vehicle five miles from our warehouse, just as planned. The Africans were charged with attempted armed robbery, passing counterfeit money, and purchase of untaxed goods. It was fair to say we wouldn't be seeing those guys for a long time.

CHAPTER TWENTY-NINE

HE'S A FUCKING COP

On Wednesday we pulled into our tactical meeting, which was held in the back parking lot of an abandoned grocery store, to find it full of cars from agencies across the board.

With so many cases at stake, we had different units arriving every week. There was the FBI, who had uncovered several possible terrorist affiliates throughout our dealings, eight of which were on the terrorist watch list. Others had ties linked to Al-Qaeda and Hezbollah, which brought the U.S. Army on board. Then there was the ATF who were tracking our customers, since they were all carrying, as well as the State Police who helped with arrests, the Narcotics Unit, who were hopeful for a successful turnout with Sunshine, more PATB agents, here to learn and study our case with Chin Lu, and the U.S. Attorney. And here we were, the quarterbacks of the case, and we couldn't even get to our own meeting. There were so many cars in the lot that we had to park 1/4 mile down the street and walk up. Talk about a way to make someone stay humble.

After the encounter with the Africans, Staton wasn't taking any chances.

"If you are all here to benefit, then you will need to help the operation," he told each agency that came on board.

The small loft inside our warehouse became an alcove for extra surveillance equipment, agents and Army personnel, complete with scope rifles for our protection.

෩

By the time Chin arrived on Thursday, everything had been arranged, unbeknownst to him, and put into place. All morning, when customers arrived, the agents above our head would be as quiet as mice. The moment they would depart, the warehouse would spring alive with chatter, radio broadcasts, phones, faxes and the pounding of computer keys. By the time Chin pulled onto the scene, I was ready for some peace and quiet. The week between had seemed so long, especially after all that had happened, and having him here signified the beginning of the end of something.

"Long time no see, boys," Chin said as he stepped out of his car. He was dressed in white slacks, a blue dress shirt and brown dress shoes.

"I thought you weren't allowed to wear white before Labor Day?" I asked, referencing his slacks.

"I say if you look good, you fuck the rules and wear what you like," Chin said, walking up to me and shaking my hand. "How've you been?"

"I've been thinking about our deal, actually. I'm hoping you brought me a sample. My guys aren't so sure your stamps are legit."

"You're not sure of my stamps?" Chin laughed. "You idiots didn't even know about the stamps you were selling."

"True," I shrugged off. "But we'd still like a look. If they're good, we want to buy in."

"Not good." Lu smiled. "The best in the country. Everybody in the business knows who I am."

Lu pulled a small Ziploc bag of stamps from his pocket.

"You tell me how good," he said, handing me the bag.

Inside were three different stamps. One from New York state, another from Pennsylvania and the other from New York City. I pulled out the Pennsylvania stamp and held it against an authentic stamp on a pack of Newports. I stared at the stamp for five minutes, unable to spot the difference. I called Nick over, trying to see if he could tell the difference, but as hard as he tried, he couldn't spot it either.

"Okay," I said, looking at Nick. "I think you've got yourself a deal, Mr. Lu. What do we have to do to get started?"

"How much you think you want?"

"I guess our question for you would be how much is too much?"

Lu smiled, shaking my hand.

"You boys might be smart business leaders after all. I'll give you numbers next week."

Lu drove off, fully stocked with cigarettes, while we sent the stamps to the lab. In seven days, Lu would be back and we had to execute a plan.

❧

While Chin was in the works, Staton approached me about another side sale the ATF wanted me to explore.

"Sunshine," he said. "They want to test out any gun connections she might have."

"What about the Drug Task Force?"

"They're aware and on board with it, too."

"Let's go for it then," I said, automatically regretting the protective nature Sunshine had displayed to me.

❧

The ATF set me up with one of their guys. George, as he was called, was dressed in khaki pants, a cream dress shirt, a brown belt, matching shoes and a military haircut to boot. I was unimpressed from the start.

"He looks like a fucking cop," I said during our meeting. "No fucking way."

"I know how to look casual," the cop look-alike said. "Trust me, I'll be much more relaxed than I am now."

I didn't trust him. There are somethings you just can't cover up and run from, and everything told me that George disguised as a regular delinquent was one of those somethings.

"Billy, I am a fan. I have wanted to work with you for some time. I promise I won't disappoint."

"I'm not scared of being disappointed," I said. "I'm scared of being there when you get made for a cop."

The ATF agents went back and forth and, eventually, I reluctantly caved. There wasn't much I could do to change their minds. They wanted George on the case with me and no matter how hard I fought they were going to get what they wanted.

Upon Sunshine's arrival, I let her know how scary the African situation was and how grateful our guys were for her help.

"And you're right. My guys needed extra cover. You think you can help us?"

"You know I can, baby. Let me see how much product I can get for you."

❧

Sunshine called me that afternoon with a meetup location in the Bronx.

"I have a new guy," I informed her. "He's looking at purchasing some merchandise. I'm going to bring him, if that's alright with you."

"If he's okay with you then he's okay with me," Sunshine said. "No later than 10 a.m., though, Silver. The girls have a busy day tomorrow. It's Fleet Week."

The next morning, George showed up wearing a yellow button-down shirt, crisp blue jeans and black boots.

"What the fuck are you wearing?" I yelled as he approached our van. "You look like a fucking cop!"

"I do not!" he exclaimed. "I'm casual."

"Listen dude, I am not comfortable with what you're wearing. You're going to have to change."

"You know, I've been on the job for fifteen years and I've never had anyone around me so anal as you. We have a job to get done. So let's stop focusing on what I'm wearing and go buy some weapons, shall we?"

"I'm not getting in the fucking car with you like that. No way."

"Well, you're technically not allowed to purchase guns on your own. And we have a team of backup and surveillance already out there waiting for us to get the show on the road."

I glared at George. Inside I wanted to grab him by the throat, rip off every fucking button on his ugly yellow fucking shirt and shove it down his throat. Instead, I paced the lot until I opted to get in the car and get the day over with. If he got made that would be on his agency. There was no way I would vouch for him and risk my operation.

We pulled into the back of a sketchy convenience store, located in a high-crime area, and parked closest to the exit so surveillance had a clean shot from the street.

Sunshine pulled into the lot twenty minutes later, her security guard seated in the passenger seat as usual. As she approached the van, she took one look at George and furrowed her eyebrows at me.

"This is your guy?" she questioned.

"Yep," I said, playing it cool. "George meet Sunshine. Sunshine, this is George."

George shook her hand.

"Nice to meet you," he said.

Sunshine pulled her hand back in disgust.

"He's a fucking cop, Silver!"

"No," I said, shrugging her off. "He's just an idiot. Thinks he can hustle guns down in Maryland."

"Maryland?" Sunshine said, appalled. "You trying to take guns to Maryland?"

"Yes, I am," George said flatly.

Sunshine looked back at me, cocking her neck. She was pissed.

"Silver Fox!"

"Sunshine, what can I say? He's a fucking idiot, but he pays well. Get in the van so we can talk."

Sunshine nodded to her security guard who produced a black bag from the backseat.

"I'm not getting in," Sunshine stated. "Not with him in the car."

"Come on," I said. "He's not that bad."

"Silver, how many deals have you done with this guy?"

"I've sold him some stuff and he's sold me some stuff."

"I'm telling you he's a fucking cop," she said as her security guard tossed the black bag through my open window.

I glimpsed into the bag to find three 9mm automatics and two hand pistols.

"These are beautiful, Sunshine," I told her. "You really are an asset for our team."

George moved his body closer to mine and peeked in the bag. Then, like a moron, his mouth gave it all away.

"Can you get us some machine guns?"

Sunshine pulled back from the car, outraged.

"I fucking told you he was a cop, Silver," she shouted as she walked back to her car, the white envelope of cash I'd handed her sticking out of her back pocket. "He's a fucking cop!"

Sunshine tore out of the parking lot before I could react.

"You think she can get machine guns?" George asked, pulling the bag from my lap.

"NO, I don't think she can get machine guns, asshole! You just blew my whole fucking cover. She knew you were a cop! You been on the field for fifteen fucking years and you don't know enough not to ask a criminal for something in less than five fucking minutes of being introduced? You're an embarrassment to your whole fucking unit!"

George ignored me and radioed for Sunshine's takedown.

"Are you fucking serious?" I yelled. "That wasn't the fucking deal we signed. We're not done with Sunshine! She's the key in our drug operation right now."

George ignored me and continued calling in her location.

I grabbed my radio and yelled for everyone to stand down.

"You do not have approval to pull her over!" I screamed. "We have a direct order from the Governor on this case. Everyone stand down!"

At the same time that I yelled into the radio, I pulled my phone out and dialed Staton. He immediately contacted the head of ATF and within minutes Sunshine was removed from a possible takedown and George was out of my van.

"Somebody pick up the yellow-shirted motherfucker. I left him on the corner," I radioed in, satisfaction rolling over me.

෬

The ATF lambasted me, claiming I'd ruined the case. But Staton, the Drug Task Force and every other agency in our lap backed me up. Staton refused to go any deeper with the ATF, leaving them to launch their own investigation on Sunshine if they desired. But, try as they might, they were never able to get her back on board.

As for Sunshine, I had no choice but to give her a little space. In the midst of the meeting, Lu had called requesting our presence at his warehouse in the morning. He wanted to show us his operation so all buy-in questions we might have would be put to rest. Staton, the FBI, the Governor and the U.S. Attorney weren't willing to let this opportunity pass us by. So, despite my exhaustion and mental drainage from the day, I had to prepare myself for the new task at hand. Therefore, Sunshine's dealing had to wait.

CHAPTER THIRTY

SEX SLAVE TRADING

Despite five solid hours of sleep, Jeff and I arrived in Chinatown at 6 a.m., raring to go. Fitted with cameras and surveillance equipment, we pulled up, miraculously finding a spot in front of the warehouse on Catherine Street.

The smell of fish immediately permeated my nose as we stepped out of the van.

"Ah, my boys. Breathe that in. It's the smell of fresh morning success for our fisherman," Chin said, walking out of a side alleyway to greet us.

I looked at Jeff who was holding his nose.

"Seriously?" I said.

"What? I hate the smell of fish."

"You white boys are crazy. You never been to an open market before?" Chin smiled. He was dressed in a nice pair of slacks and a crisp light blue dress shirt. "Come inside with me. It smells better."

Jeff and I followed Chin through a narrow alleyway to a side door, painted black. Chin escorted us up a stairwell that was crammed with boxes.

"Morning delivery," he said.

Once we reached the second floor Chin stopped in front of an old steel door, which rolled open via tracks above our heads.

It made a loud noise that echoed throughout the warehouse. I counted seven girls, all of whom had stopped what they were doing to watch us.

"These girls are my stockers," Chin said, clapping his hands. "Back to work, girls."

All seven quickly diverted their eyes from our presence and continued loading the empty boxes with cartons of cigarettes, which the back end of the warehouse was piled with.

"They arrive weekly from the port," Chin said, catching my stare. "They come in with the fish. Nobody wants to check stinky boxes of fish, so they come through without a problem."

"Sounds like a job for you, Jeff," I teased.

Chin led us through the stockroom and into the production end, which was separated by another large steel door on wheels. Again, the noise from the wheels made the five girls in this room stop what they were doing to look at us.

I was surprised to discover that the women were working on rolling machines, identical with what Marlboro had in their factory. I made a point of walking around and analyzing the machines so my button camera could get a full profile, while stopping in front of the serial number on the side.

"You like these?" Chin smiled. "Someone stole them last month from Phillip Morris trucks. I have guys who watch them. The guys who delivered their machines work for us. We pay them guys to keep us informed of what they're getting into so we can do the same."

It was fucking genius. Here were underground criminals working for the exact company who was spending millions of dollars to outsmart them.

"My operation is different than yours." Chin smiled as he led us out of the manufacturing point and through a garment area. "We focus on the poor. So no one notices."

"You mind explaining that a little?" I said as we passed through the heavily employed garment area and into a large kitchen where two elderly women were gutting fish. Jeff immediately plugged his nose again.

"Poor people don't complain about taste if it's cheap," Lu said. "They just want the smokes. So, we sell to owners in corner markets and on the street. The owner pays us for the cigarettes and then charges his customers the regular price. So he makes money from the tax and cigarette price in one. The people don't know any better, or have anywhere else to go, so they continue to buy. Everyone's happy."

Chin pointed to one of the elderly ladies.

"This is my mom."

Chin's mom scrunched her nose in distaste and looked us up and down.

"That one is fat," she said, pointing to me. "Shows he's greedy, doesn't know when to stop. That's no good, son."

His mother's bluntness struck me.

"Mom," Chin interjected. "These two have lots of money, very successful. They're going to be our new partners."

"You can't trust him," she said, continuing to point her finger at me. "Fat people never trustworthy. They take more than they should. Not good for business."

Chin shook his head, said something to his mother in Chinese and directed us out of the room.

Off the kitchen, Chin led us through another hallway, which was poorly lit. I tried to watch my steps and cover all angles of the hall, but I kept thinking about how Chin's mother had just called me fat.

The dim hallway led to Chin's office, which was set in the corner of a room, surrounded by tables and several workers busy adhering fraudulent stamps onto cartons of cigarettes.

"I like to keep them in my eyesight at all times," Chin said, gesturing for us to take a seat in front of his desk. "I don't like any tricky business here."

I turned in my chair to get a closer look at the girls' process.

"You have a lot to learn, big man." Chin laughed. "I teach you when you invest."

"Tell me what you need," I said, ready to make a deal.

"$5,000 for five cases."

"Lu, that's a $1,000 a case." I laughed.

"You'll make double that when you sell them."

Chin pulled a roll of tax stamps from his desk drawer and tossed them to Jeff.

"The state only gives these to banks for cigarette companies," he stated. "Today, I am that bank."

Jeff and I examined the roll of stamps. No question, they were good. I ran my thumbnail against a stamp and attempted to peel or scratch it, but it didn't budge.

"Told you my shit was precise." Chin smiled. "We got a prime factory here."

I managed to get Chin down to $4500 for five cases, which wasn't as significant as Staton would have liked, but it was something.

"I'll have delivery set for you on Thursday," Chin assured us.

That was just enough time to wrap up his case—something the State, Staton and I couldn't wait for. We hadn't had a day off in weeks or a big arrest to give us that high we needed. A closed case would do us good.

❧

By the time Chin arrived, in pressed steel gray pants, a crisp white shirt and tan shoes, every agency on board was in place, salivating over what this takedown was going to mean for their unit. Yet, just as we got close enough to taste the end, Chin dropped one more bombshell onto our lap.

"Billy," he said, gesturing for the guys to remove the product from his trunk. "Long time no see. Come look at the beautiful items I brought you."

I walked towards the trunk and inspected the cases. Again, I couldn't spot a difference.

"Did I tell you or what?" Chin smiled, happy with his delivery.

"You told us. These look great, Chin. Jeff has your payment all set."

I gestured for him to follow Jeff, where our takedown would begin, but Chin remained in place.

"I have something else for you."

"What's that? Did you come into some new stamps?"

"No. This better. I have a proposal for you and the guys."

Even though every ounce of my body screamed to leave it be, my curious nature couldn't let it rest. So, I let him talk.

"I know you have connections with mafia," he said, putting his hands up to protest any argument from my side. "It's okay, I work with Chinese mafia. I never tell."

His line seemed ironic since that's what he had just done.

"I need a boat," Chin stated seriously. "I have an order of girls coming from China to America. I need help getting them here. My driver already has too many."

"What kind of girls? Family?"

"No, not family. Girls to work."

"How many girls are we talking?"

"For your boat, 16. They'll take care of your guys during the ride to entice them. They like girls, right?"

"Chin," I said, lowering my voice. "Are you asking me to bring sex slaves into the country?"

"No, not all are sex slaves. Some are clean," he stated matter-of-factly.

"But some ARE sex slaves?"

"The dirty ones, yes. The clean ones we show off until we get a good price."

I couldn't believe I was having this conversation.

"Chin, even if I could help you get these girls into the country, I'm not sure I want to. Human trafficking is a whole different level. We run cigarette scams for fuck sakes. I wouldn't know the first thing about getting people into the United States."

"I take care of all that, you just provide the boat."

I stared at Chin in disbelief.

"Billy, it's a lot of money for you and your guys. Buy you a better warehouse," Chin said, looking around our coveted spot in dismay.

"Let me talk to the guys and see what I can do," I said. "I'll have an answer next time you come."

"Don't wait too long. Chinese girls get horny."

"Chin! You said they weren't all sex slaves," I yelled as he walked over to Jeff for payment.

"Only the ugly ones." He laughed as Jeff handed him the money. Clearly, he'd been told that a takedown would no longer be happening that day.

కో

The entire unit stood down, per Staton's request. Groans and several choice words flooded the warehouse. But it didn't matter. Staton needed to dig into what Chin had just offered. The sex trade industry was huge, and the government was working overtime to try to crack down on it.

Staton reached out to the trafficking agency and had two agents on board the next morning. I handed over Chin's details, his warehouse location, his gambling habits and his current proposal. However, there was a political catch. The Attorney General and the Governor were itching for a positive outcome on the counterfeit stamps, especially since it was taking thousands of dollars away from the state. So Chin's new turn was off limits—for us. However, we agreed to help them with specific instructions, like the routes Chin used, how he bypassed border patrol, and any insight we could get on the hundreds of boats and transportation routes other slave trade owners were using. And, as for Chin's arrest, the trafficking agency couldn't touch him until after we'd closed our case.

When Chin arrived at the warehouse the following week, three additional trafficking agents were positioned with our surveillance crew. The space had become so crowded that I began to feel as if I were crawling out of my skin. The background noise annoyed me, the people talked to me too much and the causal laughter that would spring from the loft grated my spine. I found myself needing to escape the confines of my once comfy lounge chair vicinity for the fresh, crowd-free space outside its walls.

"You're waiting for me?" Chin said as he drove up to the warehouse. He was dressed leisurely, compared to his usual getup. So I used that to my bullshitting advantage.

"Actually, I came out to see why you're dressed like such a slob. Khaki pants and a polo are a bit casual for you, no?"

"I have busy day today. You understand, sometimes you have to get your hands dirty."

"I hear that. Anything I can assist with?" I inquired.

"Not this one," he sighed. "You find the boat?"

"I believe I did."

Chin's eyes widen.

"You have a boat? You are in?"

"I'm not in until you let me know everything this involves. If I don't like the details I'm out."

"Of course I give that to you," Chin said, a bit overly excited. "But I only know about the boat. We pick up and drop off for a price. I'll be with you."

"You on the boat with me might break the deal," I joked.

"You don't speak Chinese, asshole. How you going to speak to girls? They're not going on a boat with hairy, white man in dirty pants."

"Ah, you got me there." I smiled. "How long are we talking I'm on this boat with you then?"

"Two days," he said. "They pay us $3,000 per girl."

"That seems a little low. You say you have 16 girls. You have to pay for the boat, gas and food to feed them. We'll need more money."

"Billy, these are not good guys," Chin stated. "We are only the transportation. You don't want problems with them. They will kill you."

"You leave those problems to me," I said. "My guys and I can handle them. Now, what's the route like?"

Chin explained that our job was to pick the women up in the Bahamas and transport them to the Florida Keys.

"How do the girls get to the Bahamas in the first place?" I inquired.

"Through Cuba. I have another guy who sets that up. He calls me when he has the girls and then calls me when the girls are secure and ready for pick up."

"Wait a minute!" I interjected. "Do we have to share our money with these guys too?"

"No," Chin stated. "He's already taken care of."

"I don't know, Chin. This seems like an awful lot of work."

"It's a side job, Billy," Chin said. "It's a little extra in your pocket."

"My interest is going down, Chin."

"Billy, it's easy job. Pick up in Bahamas and drop off in the Keys. It's like a vacation. You do good and I'll bring you on the Mexico job. That one is good money."

"You're transporting girls from Mexico too?" I asked.

"Just Chinese girls. We have a lot of them."

I played aloof, and turned to talk to Jeff and the guys about warehouse issues, allowing Chin to try to pull me back in.

"This is unbelievable opportunity, Billy. Lots of money for you."

"I'm not too worried about money right now, Chin. I thought our side business was doing pretty well."

"No, no, Billy," Chin said, putting his hands up. "Our business is doing great. This is just another side business to work together."

"Kidnapping women and dragging them to America? I can't say that's a business my partners and I want to be a part of."

"No kidnapping," Chin exclaimed. "They come on their own. They want to come to America for a better life. Their parents give them to us for money. They come willingly."

"That I believe we're in disagreement on, Chin."

"Okay, Billy. What would you want to make this happen?"

"I would need detailed maps of where my boat would be loading and dropping off, port names and locations and the name of the guy we're picking the girls up from."

"I can't do that. He's very secretive."

"Then I can't help you," I said, shrugging my shoulders. "I'm not driving across waters to be surprised by a man I don't know. I want to do my own research first. Make sure this guy isn't a cop or doesn't pull any surprises."

Chin thought about it for a minute and reluctantly agreed.

"How soon can you get your crew together?" he asked.

"As soon as you can provide me with the things I need."

"Okay, I come back in two days. What kind of boat you got anyway?"

The funny thing was, in all our planning and arranging, we'd never discussed boat details. I didn't have the slightest boat knowledge. So I flew by the seat of my pants, per usual.

"A 16-footer."

"16! What do you mean 16?" Chin screamed. "You can't transport people in a 16-foot boat! We'll all die! The boat will sink!"

"Chin, I'm just teasing you." I laughed. "I've got a 23-footer."

Chin yelled in Chinese and threw his arms and hands all over. By the looks of his red face a 23-foot boat wasn't exactly cutting it either.

"Chin, relax. I have a good boat. You bring me what I asked for and I'll show you the boat."

Chin stood in place, his chest still heaving.

"What? It was a joke." I laughed. "It was almost as funny as your money offer."

"You're a funny man," Chin said flatly. "Almost gave me the heart attack."

"Heart attack or not, I'm not picking your skinny ass up off my warehouse floor," I teased. "Now get the fuck out of here before our next appointment comes in."

"Okay, I'll have the shit in two days. In return, you show me boat!"

"Chin, if that shit isn't highlighted with everything I asked for don't bother bringing it. I ain't stepping foot on any boat with you unless I know all the details up front. Any funny shit on the boat and I'll turn around. So make sure you cover all your bases."

"I can do that for you, Billy. You'll see. No funny shit. Just more money."

Chin slid into his car with a wide grin on his face as I stepped away with a big sigh of relief. Who the fuck knew there were so many boat sizes?

༄

The Immigration office was ecstatic over my work. They praised me on my diligence and coyness, and had guys lining up to work the case. However, while those details were being sorted out between outside agencies, our agency was busy trying to close our case. You see, even though we'd made a deal that Chin was off limits, there's a sticky line that allows greed to slip in. Each agency begins to see the numbers and press that would come from an operation of this sort, and they begin to quietly justify why their case is more important than the others. So the chance of someone stepping in and jeopardizing your operation suddenly becomes very real. Therefore, our team made a secret plan to take Chin down the moment he handed over the paperwork. It would be another weekend that I wouldn't be returning home.

CHAPTER THIRTY-ONE

CHIN TAKE DOWN

Chin's arrest happened early Saturday morning. Summer had begun to wrap up, and the chill in the air seemed to foreshadow what was to come.

Jeff and I arrived at the warehouse at 7a.m. with a picture of the boat in hand, and handcuffs strapped under our shirts in the back. Staton's only request was for us to be thorough and discreet.

"There's no room for errors here," he said over the radio. "Take your time and stay off any other stations. Word does not get out until after we have everyone secured."

Once our crew gave us the go ahead, Jeff and I approached the black door in the alleyway. Chin arrived at the second knock, welcoming us to his office. Jeff dropped a wedge under the door, preventing the door from locking as I engaged Chin in bullshit chatter to distract him.

As we made our way up the dim hallway, I showed Chin the picture of the boat.

"That is beautiful," he said. "Where is it docked?"

"Off my friend's pier in Long Beach. If you have the information I need it's ready to go."

"I love you guys," Chin said, opening his office door. "You're all business, no bullshit."

I made a point of looking around before I took a seat beside Jeff, so surveillance could count the five women in the room.

"Okay," Chin said, handing me a sealed yellow envelope. "This should be everything you need."

I opened the envelope to find the port listings, maps, boat styles and names. He'd done it. Chin had handed us everything we needed. It was over. My adrenaline kicked in.

"Alright Chin, looks like our work here is done," I said, my code for surveillance to begin the takedown.

Within seconds screams filled the warehouse. Chin jumped up from his desk as alarms sprang through the rooms and the steel doors echoed.

"We're being raided," Chin said, reaching for his drawer.

"Not so fast," Jeff yelled, pointing his gun at Chin. "Keep your hands where we can see them!"

Chin looked at us in horror.

"You are police," he said, the reality of who we were coming together.

"Yes, sir," I said as agents flooded the room.

Chin lowered his head in defeat and slumped in his chair.

"No time for sitting, buddy," an agent said, pulling him up from his seat. "You'll have plenty of time to rest in prison."

Chin didn't look at us as they escorted him into the hall. I felt bad for him actually. This would be the end of his casino trips and fancy tailored ensembles. From now on he would spend his days in orange jumpsuits, possibly washing dishes once he made good behavior. However, as for his mom, that was another story. I made a point to walk by her, cuffed and seated in the hall among several other women, and smiled.

"You know what this fat guy is going to do tonight?" I said, squatting down so she could hear me. "I'm going to go home to my nice couch and big TV and order a shitload of Chinese food. Hope your night is just as good."

Chin's mother just sneered at me and turned her head.

It was 8 a.m. by the time Jeff and I got back into the van to head back, our work with Chin officially over. By 2p.m. all units had dismantled everything within the warehouse, arrested 25 workers along with Chin, and collected enough information to keep them pulling overnights for weeks. Agents from Phillip Morris were permitted to come down and claim their machines, and the trafficking unit was open to a plea deal. Everyone seemed to be happy, including Jeff and me, who were allotted a day of rest. But come Monday, the hype of the closed case pushed the remaining agencies into overtime. They were like dogs who'd tasted blood. Every single one of them wanted more.

CHAPTER THIRTY-TWO

SUNSHINE WARNS AGAIN

Drug trafficking agents urged me to phone Sunshine so they could close their case.

"I thought you were smarter than that," she said into the line. "He was a cop, Silver."

"Sunshine, no one was more shocked than me when he asked you for machine guns," I said. "Maybe he got turned. I don't know, but I'm done with him. I kicked him out of the van and left him in the Bronx. He might still be there if you look around."

"Well, no one's knocked on my door. So maybe we are in the clear."

"He's out, Sunshine. We don't have to worry about him anymore. If he was a cop we would have been arrested on the spot, I promise."

The agents began to do a little happy dance around the warehouse as Sunshine set up a time to see me the following week.

"I'll take you for ice cream," I said. "It'll be like old times."

"It's a date, Silver Fox."

While the Drug Task Force was eager to see how far we could go with Sunshine, fate decided to throw us yet another curve ball.

"You have Albanians you're dealing with, correct?" Sunshine phoned a few days later.

"You know I can't disclose customers. What makes you ask?"

"I met them a few weeks ago after a sale. They've been visiting my girls and one of them heard something."

"Where the heck did you meet these guys after a sale?" I inquired, curious.

"At the Dairy Queen down the road. That's where all your businessmen meet before they come up there. Don't you know anything about your surroundings?"

I could see Nick scrambling to get a crew down to the Dairy Queen while I continued the conversation.

"Anyway, they're setting out to rob you. A stupid one told my girl their plan. They're coming disguised as cops. They going to pretend to be undercovers and seize your products right under your nose. They're going to have guys in the woods too. They're armed. They are planning to take everything."

I couldn't make this crap up if I tried. Criminals working with undercovers had planned to show up acting as undercovers to rob them. This was some Ocean's 11 shit.

"See if you can find out anything else," I told Sunshine.

"Will do, Silver," she said. "And about that date?"

"I've got something nice planned, just you and I," I said, trying not to sound too dismissive. "A nice dinner where we can talk about white picket fences, a little house, and maybe a ring and some little ones."

"You really are the real deal, aren't you, Silver?"

"I don't know about that," I replied. "I'm only who I can pretend to be."

Sunshine laughed, mistaking my truth for comedy.

∞

Our security detail went into overdrive for the next two days concocting ways the Albanians could break in. When the time came, the entire event went down just as Sunshine said it would.

The Albanians showed up, as scheduled. The two men we'd dealt with walked into the warehouse, making idle chitchat. They looked Russian. Short, with broad bodies, chiseled faces and a worn exterior. They questioned our inventory.

"How many cigarettes you go through a week?" the one with a rotten front tooth asked.

"What the fuck is that your business?" I responded, stepping towards him.

"No business," he said, smiling. "I'm just making the talk. You know, being friendly."

"We don't do friendly here," I said.

Jeff's phone rang.

"They're coming through the woods. Dismiss the Armenians now!" Bob-O yelled into the line.

Jeff turned towards the two men.

"You two get the fuck out!" Jeff hollered. "We've got people roaming around in the backwoods."

The men's faces dropped.

"How do you know that?" they asked.

"You think we don't have security on this place?" Jeff said, as if the men had asked the dumbest thing he'd ever heard. "Now, get the fuck out!"

Jeff whipped his pistol from the back of his pants and aimed it at the Armenians.

"NOW!" he yelled.

The Armenians scrambled to the door, blubbering about their lack of cigarettes. I bolted the door behind them as Jeff sealed all other entrance points.

"We've got six guys spread through the woods," surveillance radioed. "They're slowly approaching. Get ready."

Having an army at your back was a welcome treat in times such as this. We climbed up to the loft, got into position and aimed our puny guns at the door. Meanwhile, our team of soldiers were spread out on the warehouse level, their scope rifles shining on various parts of the door.

The warehouse was quiet. Sweat trickled down the back of my neck as I contemplated everything that could go wrong. My biggest fear was that one of the Albanians would notice the agents with scopes pointed at them and react before we had a chance to.

"Two men are approaching the door," surveillance stated.

Red dots from their rifles covered the door.

The door handle jiggled and twisted. But to no avail for the guys on the other end.

BAM!

"They're attempting to kick the door in."

BAM!

I knew they weren't going to have much luck with a steel door, but I was still ready.

BAM!

BAM!

After the fourth attempt the warehouse went silent again. I waited, listening, but nothing happened.

"They have a crowbar," surveillance said after five minutes of empty air.

Body-chilling scrapes, like nails on a chalkboard, echoed through the vast space. Over and over again, the scrapes, pounding, twisting and manipulating of the handle continued. As the pounding sped up, I knew the guys were getting impatient.

One of the agents began murmuring, "please break, please break." Keyed up to shoot someone, the agent's red dot was framed in the center of the door in hopes of a direct head shot.

BAM!

"They're using their bodies now. Two at a time. These guys are persistent."

BAM!

Between the slams the Albanians began to argue. I couldn't make out what they were saying, but based on the tone and quick nature, I knew it was tense.

The crowbar began to smash down on the handle as the men slammed into the door. Again and again and again. Until it suddenly stopped.

Silence filled the warehouse.

No one moved. We sat there, waiting for what felt like an eternity.

After ten minutes surveillance radioed back in.

"The site is clear. You're free to move about."

No one jumped up from their position. Everyone seemed to linger, contemplating how close we'd just come, once again, to another shootout.

"Goddamnit," the trigger-happy agent said as he removed his dot. "I wanted to take on those fuckers firsthand."

The rest of the guys joined in, each talking about who would have shot first and who had a better position. But I knew the truth. Besides Trigger Man, everyone was just as nervous as I was. The sweat that soaked through their dirty shirts said as much.

I stretched my legs over the loft and made my way down the ladder, listening to these fools argue. Trigger Man wanted to explore the woods and had two agents ready to go with him.

"Guys," I said, stepping into the warehouse. "The surveillance crew is on them. We need to stay put until they confirm they've apprehended them."

The rest of the crew moaned and carried on some more. Even those who I knew would never follow Trigger Man chimed in with a few "chicken shit" comments. I wasn't bothered, though. I knew it was just a bunch of idiotic guys pent up on testosterone.

Thirty minutes later, surveillance radioed back in. Once the Albanians realized they couldn't get into the warehouse they drove to the local Dairy Queen, where four other groups were waiting to purchase cigarettes, and robbed them. Dairy Queen had it all on tape, along with three different bystanders who called 911.

The police followed them across state lines back into New York, where they arrested them on multiple charges. Our name and operation had been saved once again.

CHAPTER THIRTY-THREE

HIRED AS A HITMAN

We continued to find multiple criminal angles within our clientele. Some of those angles, like a bomb deal, turned out to be legit, while others faded away. One of our largest Middle Eastern customers happened to be a prime example.

This particular group showed up, religiously purchasing $100,000 worth of cigarettes in cash each week. Needless to say, this was a big deal for our operation, as well as for the Terrorism Task Force, who was tracking them to the full extent.

While the large transactions were done exclusively with them, this group often sent transporters to pick up smaller orders if they ran short. During one of these visits their count came up short. Angry, the group drove back up to our warehouse for an unscheduled visit, and accused us of robbing them.

"Why would we steal cigarettes from your guy?" I questioned, stepping into the angry group of men who were yelling at Jeff. "Look around. Do you see a need for more fucking cigarettes, you idiots? I think you need to turn around and head back home to check your guy before things get a little colorful here."

The men stood their ground, attempting to taunt us with their ugly sneers.

"Did you hear me?" I asked, taking a step closer to their circle. "Get the fuck out of here! Go home and see what you have going on with your guy. And when you find out it was your guy I want you to bring your ugly asses groveling back here. You owe my guys and myself a big fucking apology."

The men reluctantly dispersed, only to return three days later with an apology in hand, just as I'd told them.

"Don't ever accuse us of such a stupid thing again, understand? We don't operate like that."

The men apologized profusely. But when their sorrys were over they hand-delivered a new line of criminal intent.

"We want you take care of the guy," the tall-skinny one spoke up.

"Take care of how?" I questioned.

"We are just businessmen. We want our money back from the guy who stole from us. We need to send a message to other people in our community."

"So, we're talking what? You want me to rob him?"

"In our country we deal with things of this nature differently. We don't want you to just rob."

Obviously I knew what they were implying, but if I were to push them or say the words myself their attorney could claim I trapped them or misunderstood what they'd implied. Therefore, having these guys state exactly what they wanted me to do was of the utmost importance.

"Do I look like I'm from your country, guy? Stop playing around and tell me what you're looking for. I'm busy."

"We would like you to kill him," the tall one said, watching my face for a reaction.

I gave myself a few seconds, hoping to appear as if I was considering their deal. The two fat gentlemen behind the tall skinny one began giving each other the eye, while the tall one slowly rocked back and forth on his toes. Their discomfort gave me a sense of enjoyment.

"Well, something of that extent is going to cost you around $100,000," I said, settling my hands in my pockets. "You boys got that type of money?"

The three Middle Eastern amigos huddled together to discuss.

"Okay, what if you were able to get the money back for us? If we get our money we just want him shot, but no murder."

"So you just want to show him harm if he has the money," I repeated. "You don't want him dead, correct?"

"No, only wounded if he has the money. If he no has the money we want him dead," the fat one interjected.

"Sounds fair enough. Would you give me a week to think about this?"

The men were excited and happy to grant me whatever time I needed.

Once again, the surveillance crew was going nuts upstairs. After all that had been tossed our way, we didn't think it couldn't get any bigger. Yet the cases kept coming. If we played our cards right we now had an attempted murder case to add to our resume. It was thrilling to say the least.

When the men arrived the following week we had FBI and ATF agents waiting in the wings.

"I'll need a gun," I told them.

"You have gun already," the skinny one said, pointing to the small pistol attached to my side. "Use that one."

"Are you out of your fucking mind?!" I yelled. "Why would I use my gun, which could be traced back to me? The deal is you show up with a gun, free of any of your grimy fingerprints, and the guy's address. I'll take care of the rest. Got it?"

I don't know if they were getting cold feet or whether the money was an issue, but their plan had changed as well.

"We decided we no want him dead, just shot one time," the former murder-hungry fat one said.

"I don't work like that, gentlemen. If I am going to shoot someone I can't have them come back to identify me. It's bad for business."

The men began discussing the terms, while I wondered if they'd come through or not. The answer was not.

"We cannot do murder," the skinny one said. "We're already in trouble. We can't afford the risk. We want out."

"What if I lowered the price? You tell me what you boys can afford."

"No more shooting," the skinny one stated flatly. "We no want to shoot any of our people. Too much problems."

The deal was null and void and, again, if I attempted to push the issue I could cost the DA the case in the end. But if I couldn't get these guys for conspiracy to commit murder, then I was definitely going to make sure they spent several years behind bars for their cigarette operation. So for now I had to take the loss and play it cool.

"You do what you need to do. You change your mind I'll be here with the same conditions."

While the hire-to-kill crew continued to frequent our business they sadly never spoke about murder possibilities or injury enforcement or anything that didn't pertain to our day to day transactions again.

CHAPTER THIRTY-FOUR

I CHOOSE YOU

With Chin arrested and the Albanians nailed, it was time to wrap up Sunshine.

I went home that weekend for the first time in months. But my energy was too depleted to engage with anyone. I spent two solid days mostly asleep. When I did wake up, I'd move to the couch, put on a show and fall asleep again. I'm not sure if it was the safety of my home, the softness of my bed, or the lack of fuel that I'd been running on, but try as I might, I just couldn't stay awake.

"I don't know why you even bother to come home if you're just going to sleep while you're here," my wife said.

She had grown restless and irritated with my caseloads and schedule.

"They're working you too hard! You should have had a break after your last operation, but they didn't give you one because they don't care what happens to you! They only care about what cases you can close for them. You're going to burn yourself out quickly. You need to pull back."

Instead of taking my wife's knowledgeable advice, I mistook it for nagging. My mind was so caught up in my work and all the great I was doing that I couldn't see all the damage it had caused my family. I was so adamant about being right about my agency, and her being so wrong, that I cut my weekend at home short. I left after dinner on Sunday evening to get a head start on the next's morning's work.

I called Sunshine to speed up our last case. "I need more. You think you can bring me a kilo of coke tomorrow?"

"Billy," she said, "what are you going to do with a kilo?"

"You'll see," I snickered. "Can you bring it?"

"I'll see what I can do," Sunshine said. "Billy, should I be nervous about you?"

"That's the last thing I want," I sighed. "I've got enough people nervous for me. I need someone confident in me."

"Then that you shall have," she said as she clicked off the line.

Sunshine rolled into the warehouse Tuesday morning with two girls tucked in her backseat. The girls were beautiful. They stepped out of the car alongside Sunshine, their long brunette hair reaching the middle of their backs, highlighting their tight dresses and sleek heels.

"Are you interested?" Sunshine asked, sliding up beside me where my mouth was hanging open.

I quickly pushed my eyes back into my head.

"Of course not," I said, putting my arm around her waist. "I'm not into brunettes."

"Well, you have to pick one if you want this kilo," Sunshine said, her security guard displaying the bag from his window.

"Pick one? What do you mean?" I questioned, praying this wasn't going to turn into another Chin Lu situation.

"To get that bag you have to fuck one of my girls."

I laughed, assuming Sunshine was playing with me.

"I'm serious, Silver. I need to make sure you are who you say you are. If you're not a cop you'll fuck one of my girls."

"I'm a cop if I don't have sex with these girls?" I said, raising my eyebrows at her. "That seems a bit twisted."

"You have your way of doing business and I have mine. A kilo is a big jump all of the sudden. So I need a little security."

"I'll give you all the security you want," I said, stepping closer to her. "I want a ring on that finger, a family, a house in the country. I want it with you. That's security enough. Is it not?"

"All of that doesn't matter. My dealer gave me instructions. You're to fuck one of these broads before I leave."

"Then I choose you."

Sunshine looked at me in surprise. My heart raced. I didn't know how the hell I was going to get out of this shit. But I did what I always did. I winged it. I grabbed her hand and pulled her into the warehouse bathroom, praying my mind would pull something out.

"I'm going to tell you something right now," I said, leaning her up against the sink. "There is no way I am going to have sex with you in a dirty warehouse bathroom. That is not going to happen. You deserve more than that and I'm going to give it to you. But it sure as hell ain't going to be when I'm stinky and smelly and working with a bunch of animals."

"You've got to give me something better than that. Those are just words." Sunshine smiled up at me.

"I'll tell you what," I said, turning her around to face the sink. "I've always had a fantasy of doing a line of coke off your beautiful ass. How about you let me blow a line?"

"You're one kinky bastard, aren't you?"

"Give me a line and you'll see."

In one swift motion I pulled Sunshine's pants down to her ankles, spread the coke she handed me on her ass and pretended to snort a line. I have to say, the sight of her ass outside of her jeans gave me nightmares for days. Who knew a pair of blue jeans could make something so dimpled and saggy look regal? I whipped Sunshine back towards me, her pants still down, and looked her in the eye.

"You ain't seen half of what is going to happen between you and I."

"Silver Fox, I can't wait," she said, kissing me on the lips.

"Fix yourself up and meet me outside," I said, pretending to wipe my nose.

Nick, El Bobo and Jeff were frozen in horror as I walked out of the bathroom. I gave them a broad smile as Sunshine walked out behind me. I took her hand, still playing into the boyfriend role, and escorted her to her car, where she picked up the kilo from her security guard.

"I hope all you say is true, Silver. I want to build a life with you," Sunshine said.

"Dinner in New York next week?"

"Best dinner you've ever had."

I smiled and grabbed her ass.

Sunshine giggled and trotted back to her car. As soon as she sped out, the guys were all over me.

"You're in huge trouble. You know that, right?" El Bobo stated.

"I got the coke," I said. "Nobody is going to care about shit, other than the fact that this case is about to come to a close now too."

Within minutes I could hear the screams coming off Jeff's phone from Brandy, and Rosso's coming over El Bobo's line. In that moment I was actually more scared of facing those two than I was facing bad guys.

CHAPTER THIRTY-FIVE

SEXUAL RELATIONS

I was summoned back to New York City within hours of the warehouse deal. Rosso went down one side of me and up the other before Staton could close the door.

"I know you are crazy. You've been a crazy bastard since day one. But this is too much. You're having sex with girls in the bathroom. Have you lost your mind?"

"I didn't have sex with her!"

"Don't try to give me that bullshit! Respect me enough to tell me the truth. I know you had sex with that girl. We all do! You've possibly just put this whole operation in jeopardy by your selfish move!"

"Staton, you know me better than that," I pleaded. "I did not have sexual relations of any kind in that bathroom. Even I'm not crazy enough to do that."

"Then why pull her into the bathroom, off camera?" Staton questioned.

That was the first time Staton didn't have my back, and it hurt. I felt like a wounded dog reprimanded by its owner.

"You've broken every rule we've given you. You've defied orders and went about cases on your own. And now you've finally gone too far. It's always something with you. We're always cleaning up your mess to insure the case for the state, yet you keep giving us more spills to handle. Spills that you like to pour in our faces and smile about."

"Guys, I'm sorry. I know it seems like a lot of chaos at times, but I bring you the end result that you need. Don't I?"

"At what cost?" Rosso sneered. "How the hell do we explain how our prime undercover walked off the tape with the perpetrator who he stated he was going to have sex with? Are you going to take the heat and explain to the world how you managed to take a woman, who arrived requesting you have sex with her two hookers, into the bathroom, without having sex with her, yet still managed to obtain the coke she wasn't willing to give you?"

"Give me the forms and I will sign right now. This was my fault and I will take the responsibility," I said, suddenly aware of what my actions might have caused me.

Rosso sat there, glaring at me.

"Staton, you have to believe me," I said. "I would never have sex with that woman and put our whole case in jeopardy. I acted out of instinct. Taking her in the bathroom was all I could think to do in the moment, and it worked. I got the coke and further deals in line. I sacrificed myself and took a risk for the team and it worked out."

"If you feel that's what you did, then I agree you should take the heat on this one. You'll have a lot of questions that are going to come from this. But if you feel this was your best options as an undercover then I will back you."

Rosso pulled a piece of paper from his drawer and slid it across the desk.

"Better get to writing then. Staton and I have a lot more to discuss."

I exited the room and wrote up exactly what had happened, leaving no detail unturned.

When I walked back into the office Rosso took one look at my statement and ripped it up.

"You really are a fucking moron," he said. "You're going to make every single one of us lose our jobs."

Rosso pulled another sheet of paper from his drawer and began writing. I sat there beside Staton, and watched his angry scribbles fill the white sheet.

"Now sign it," Rosso said as he passed the paper to me.

It read: Due to the integrity of the operation and safety of officers involved, I made the perpetrator bend over a sink and, with her face turned away from me, gave her the impression that I did a line of coke off her buttocks. While the act was conducted off camera, there was no other way to get out of the situation. As the prime undercover, I made the choice to protect the safety of the officers involved by taking matters into my own hands. From my actions we were able to secure a sale of cocaine and regain our undercover to continue with the operation.

The statement was distinct, intelligent and to the point. I picked up a pen and signed it.

"Now that's that out of the way," Rosso stated, "we need to discuss the end of this operation."

The words caught me off guard. My head shot up in Rosso's direction.

"It's gotten out of hand. It needs to end. Staton and I have agreed that we want all arrests to come over state lines into Yonkers. We'll establish a new home base, give the Terrorism Task Force time to set up, and take down each unit as they arrive."

"How soon are we talking?"

"This will be your last week," Rosso said coldly. "You'll begin informing all customers of your move, providing them with the new address, and begin gathering your goods. Two weeks from now Operation Keystone will no longer exist."

It was hard to believe that all of this was going to come to an end. Yet, at the same time, a wave of relief washed over me. We were about to leave, unscathed, unharmed, undetected, with a positive closed case in hand once again. This time I didn't feel like a punishment had just been handed down. Instead, I felt like a vacation had been awarded.

"Billy, you're one crazy bastard," Rosso said as I rose from my seat. "But you have balls of steel and a big heart. When you finally get killed, we'll make sure we put that on your gravestone."

Most people would have been offended by his statement. I was too far gone to recognize any ill will. Instead I found myself walking out of the office thinking about how cool my gravestone would look to those walking past.

CHAPTER THIRTY-SIX

MY GUARDIAN ANGEL

We relocated to a new warehouse in Yonkers two weeks later. It was smaller than our Pennsylvania location, but it was in a fenced off salvage yard, away from residential housing. The garage, which acted as a tire rotation service, was owned by a former CI who owed Staton a favor. He was paid for a little vacation while we spent the next week bringing customers in the front and arresting them in the back.

The takedowns were easy on our end and proved prosperous for the Terrorism Task Force as one of the individuals held an entrance ticket to the Twin Towers in his wallet. The ticket was dated September 10th, the day before the towers were hit. By the end of the day, the Task Force had sealed and contained every member of this guy's family and working relations, as well as all the individuals and their family members that he did business with at his corner shop in Brooklyn.

By 5 o'clock we had successfully gone through a dozen procedures. However, the next one would be our doozy.

During our cigarette operations the bad guys often pulled up with someone new, someone they wanted to show the business off to. On any other day we welcomed newbies. It was another case for us and another lead. But today was a day of closing. We had everything marked to the wire. So I told Hussein, our customer for the past three months, that we couldn't allow any new clients. Huessin looked at me, confused.

"He's a good guy," he said.

"I don't care what he is, he can't be here today," I repeated, leaning onto the driver's side window.

The passenger looked at me with pure hatred.

"Who the fuck are you?" he said, his words drawn out and heightened with anger.

"I'm your buddy's fucking supplier," I said, standing upright. "And now your buddy needs to turn the fuck around and let himself out."

Before my mind could process what happened, the passenger reached around and grabbed a 9mm from his seat, stretched his hand out and pulled the trigger. BOOM! It was that quick. My ears buzzed from the shot and my body went numb.

I watched the Arab jump out of the truck and run towards the front gate. As I watched him, a surge jolted through my body. No way was this motherfucker getting away from me! No way was I spending my life in fear of someone who'd seen my face, tried to shoot me and gotten away. As I scrambled to my feet, suddenly aware that I hadn't been hit, I saw El Bobo take off after him. Stunned, I walked to the gate and watched as he chased the bastard for two blocks—right until another police unit rolled on to the scene and threw him to the ground.

I stood there listening as the Arab yelled things I couldn't understand. Nick later explained he was wishing us death. As the officers peeled away, with the Arab stewing inside the car, the sky opened and it started to rain. The drops felt cool on my skin, which was burning from adrenaline.

Jeff met up with us on the street, making sure El Bobo and I were okay. I needed a moment. I was shaken, but I didn't want the guys to see. I wandered around the dilapidated area, looking for a place to piss as an excuse to get away.

At the end of an alleyway was an old Ford truck, its hood lifted and its parts stripped. I leaned on the side of the truck and a voice shouted.

"You're peeing on my house!"

I was already rattled, so the shout startled me even further. Without thinking I grabbed my gun and whipped around to see a thin, black man peering at me from the truck bed.

"What you gonna shoot me for?" he said. He had very few teeth. "You the one peeing on my house."

Through my shock it dawned on me that this man was living in the truck.

"I'm sorry," I said as I lowered my gun. "I didn't realize anyone was here. You frightened me."

"That's okay, man." He smiled. "Ain't no one want to be arrested for indecent exposure around here anyway. You want to come in and get out of the rain?"

For a moment the thought of escaping into his truck sounded enticing. But as I looked to the main street, I could see Jeff pacing back and forth waiting for me. I politely thanked him for the offer and excused myself. We had three more takedowns to go and our day would be officially done. I couldn't stall any longer. At this point, everyone needed the day to be over. The Arab had been the final kicker for a life that had been filled with too much excitement.

The rest of the takedowns went on without incident, though I was on edge with each car that pulled in. We kept it smooth, quick and to the point. We didn't have any more runners, any problems, or anyone not willing to talk. Even the Arab who'd been so quick to shoot me dead was the first to rat on his boss in hopes of avoiding an "American jail," as he'd put it. Apparently, the American jail was worth my life, because had the gun not backfired, I would have been dead.

We couldn't leave the warehouse until 10 p.m. that evening, when we'd finally detailed the last sting.

"You okay to go back to the hotel yourself?" Staton questioned as we locked down the warehouse.

"I'm fine," I assured Staton, and everyone else who seemed to have watched me with a close eye. "I just need a nice swim and a good sleep."

As it turned out, sleep was the last thing my body wanted to give me. Even after a hard swim in the hotel pool and a hot shower, I laid in bed until 3 a.m., watching the clock. I didn't know if I finally drifted off or not, but when I reopened my eyes, I saw my great nephew Joey hovering above me. There he was in his little white burial suit and hat, with these little wings. My body calmed at the sight of him and I finally fell asleep.

It wasn't until I woke up that afternoon that I processed his image. Joey, who was only three months old when he passed away, had been gone for a mere five months. My head flooded with the knowledge that he had been watching over me that day. He was what had caused the gun to misfire. I wouldn't tell anyone that story for months, as I was afraid it made me sound crazy. But in that moment, I curled over in the hotel sheets and cried uncontrollably.

The shock of what had happened sat with me for a while. Here I was a cop with 32 years under my belt and 10 years undercover, and I couldn't shake the fear I had. Couldn't shake the adrenaline or the memory of looking straight into the barrel of the gun.

CHAPTER THIRTY-SEVEN

COWARD ON THE BQE

While the cases wrapped up, there was one last matter at hand: Sunshine. The Drug Task Force had arrived at her brothel at 9 a.m., the same time we'd begun our takedowns at the warehouse, and arrested her, her girls and a few men who happened to be inside.

"She says she won't talk unless you come down to the station and admit you were an undercover the whole time you were with her," the detective said over the phone.

There was no way I wanted to face this, but Staton and the guys wouldn't have it any other way.

"You worked too hard. Clear your name and get her a good deal. She saved us too many times, Billy."

It took every bit of courage I had to walk into that station and face the woman who sat waiting for me—her wrists handcuffed and attached to the table. I had to give the woman in front of me a double take as she no longer resembled the woman I'd spent the past year doing business with. This woman looked worn. Her afro, which turned out to be a wig, was gone, revealing the little stumps of regrowth on her shaved head. Along with her bald head was her missing eyelashes, which were apparently fake as well. Who knew fake eyelashes could make such a difference? Her eyes looked miniscule and drawn out, which made her somewhat easier to talk too. It was as if the woman I'd spent time doing business with and the strange, bald woman in front of me were two different people. Any emotion or trepidation I'd felt walking in fell to the wayside with one glance.

"You lied to me. This whole time!" she cried as I took a seat across from her.

"I know. And I'm sorry," I said, trying to find Sunshine in the woman across from me... "I really did like you as a person. I think you're a beautiful female who's bright and great at business. It just wasn't the business that you should have been doing."

Tears rolled down her cheeks.

"I thought you were the real deal. You promised me a white picket fence, a house, a family."

"In another time, another life that could have been," I said.

Sunshine's shoulders shook as she cried harder. Snot began to gather at the tip of her nose.

"They've got a deal for you," I said. "Have you considered it?"

Sunshine nodded her head up and down, causing the snot to run down her mouth and chin.

"I want you to take it, Sunshine. You're someone very special to us. You helped save our case. Hell, you helped save our lives. Twice. It's our turn to take care of you."

"What about my business and everything else? It's all gone. You've taken that from me."

"We're giving you the chance to start something better. I know you can do that. You're too smart not to. Take the deal, Sunshine. You'll be out in under two years. That's plenty of time to plan your next steps. Figure out what you can do when you get out."

"Is that all you got to say, Silver?" Sunshine asked. White salty streaks smeared her face.

"I came to make sure you talked. Give them what they want. You're not who they're looking for. You're only small potatoes."

"If that's all you have to say then you can go. I've heard what I needed."

I sat for a minute, waiting to see if there was anything left to debate.

"Stay safe in there, Sunshine," I said as I stood up from my seat. "If you need anything, or if you decide you want to talk, you have our number."

Sunshine refused to look at me as I exited the room. By the second day I learned that she'd taken the deal and given up everyone—along with a statement that showed my innocence in the bathroom with her. Her case was closed. She was out in 16 months, based on good behavior. I never heard much about her whereabouts once she finished her time. I only hoped the college classes she'd reportedly taken while in prison had served a purpose and granted her a degree once she escaped the confines of the cement walls.

ɕ⌀

During my dealings with Sunshine, Staton had dealings of his own. The PATB began putting pressure on him to create a new sting in Virginia. The FBI and Terrorism Task Force wanted exclusive use of Sayid, who'd been spending his days working counter-surveillance with us, for their current investigations, and requests from hundreds of other officers who wanted to be included in further undercover stings began piling in. Yet, while everyone wanted some sort of in now that our takedowns were all over the news, the Ivory Tower became lackadaisical.

When Staton succumbed to the request and agreed to take our unit to Virginia, the Ivory Tower showed its so-called support with a signed refusal for new undercover vehicles. For them it was a waste of money. All our bad guys had been arrested, so there wasn't a need to revamp everything because there wasn't anyone to hide from. For Staton, it was a matter of protection. What if someone from our past did remember us by the vehicles we drove? What if the bad guys were giving up intel in jail? Seeking out our whereabouts? No matter how Staton fought for our protection, the Ivory Tower could not be swayed.

Never one to wait or play by the rules, Staton went ahead and set up warehouses in Dalgreen, Virginia, purchased cigarettes with the state's allowance and took out an ad in the local Arabic newspaper. Once that was all was set, he reached out to the local police department and set up the same Ripped principles we'd used with the Yonkers Police Department. The only change we had this time, besides the lack of support from the Ivory Tower, was Sayid's absence.

The recent attention from the FBI and other agencies had made Sayid feel at risk. He had been speaking to Staton at odd times throughout the days leading to our new sting. Calls would come through at 2 a.m., his voice wiry and shaky on the other end. He'd been woken to strange noises outside his home. He'd sworn people were outside, ready to bash down his door and take him and his family into government custody. When that didn't happen he'd call, concerned about the random phone calls that were coming into his home or the strange cars that were parked across the street, watching his children play on the front stoop. But the final frantic call came through one day before our departure to Virginia, when two agents cornered him on the street, demanding his help and threatening his family's U.S. residency. According to a friend, Sayid hung up with Staton, packed his family up and fled to Africa in the middle of the night. Staton had no knowledge of where he had gone or how to get in contact with him. Yet Staton would spend the next two years facing criminal accusations and an open investigation with the state for aiding Sayid in his escape from the U.S. The case would eventually be pulled out of the system due to lack of evidence. It was a rightful win for Staton, but a festering loss for the state and one woman in particular.

Without Sayid, Staton had to bring in another CI. This one had helped undercovers imprison a terrorist set to conduct a mass shooting at a local high school. He was professional enough, but could never really take the place of Sayid. However, with a new CI on our side, it left me room to negotiate bringing Chaz and Briheim, my former coworkers, onto the detail too.

Within the first week we acquired a dozen customers, just as we'd expected, along with two successful Ripped cases with the local police. But instead of purchasing more cigarettes with the extra income, Staton used the money to purchase new vehicles for our unit. It was a huge middle finger to the state and one they didn't take to kindly.

Over the first two months our caseloads had become so standard that I took furniture from my house and brought it to our warehouse so everyone could be comfortable on the job.

While our comfort continued, Staton's discomfort with the state began to grow.

The newly appointed Inspector General began to ask questions—thanks to Staton's middle finger. The inspector had been notorious for investigating and shutting down operations that had embezzled money. Her name and wide-eyed stare spread across New York headlines like a California wildfire. She was boasting her success. And now Staton, and our unit, were on her radar.

The inspector began looking into our numbers, riding Staton about how much or how little we had in our account. She rechecked what the state and the accountants received and attempted to find a missing balance. The money infringement and questions made Staton's blood pressure rise. His temperament caught a few people off guard every now and again. But when it came to our detail, he was as focused as ever. So, when a sister agency outside of New York City requested assistance with a case per the state's recommendation, Staton proudly sent me to clear the way.

The state allotted me two days off the Virginia detail to help the agency track a supplier. When I arrived the unit informed me of their lead—a rusty, white van. With trackers set up and a rotating surveillance crew, the team had monitored the van as it crossed the New York, Connecticut, New Jersey and Pennsylvania state lines several times a week. They had video surveillance of the van entering verified warehouses responsible for the sale of untaxed cigarettes, both in and out of the area, as well as footage of cigarettes being loaded into the van. I almost felt bad telling the guys that their surveillance didn't show a kingpin of an operation, as they believed. They'd merely discovered a driver.

Disappointment showed on every face in the room. A few guys questioned my conclusion, and one pompous investigator challenged every detail I explained to the team. The room quickly heated up. The pompous investigator challenged the other investigators for listening to me, another investigator announced he wanted to quit and others began arguing with everyone as emotions and exhaustion from a case they thought they were about to crack came bearing down. I sat quietly, examining their footage, until I noticed something of significance. They'd followed the driver to his home.

"What do you know about where he lives?" I interjected over the shouting.

The room began to quiet as the heated investigators walked over to check out what I'd pulled up.

"As far as we can tell there seems to be six children in the house, along with a wife and grandmother," the lead officer explained, leaning into the screen.

"Do the wife or grandmother leave during the day?" I questioned. "Do they work?"

"No. The women stay cramped inside the apartment," the pompous investigator sneered. "They only come out to shop at the corner market and get the kids from the school bus."

"He'll talk then," I informed the team. "Your work wasn't all in vain. You have something big here."

They all looked up at me warily.

"If there are six children in that house and two women who don't leave, then he's the only one bringing in a salary," I explained. "A family of nine reliant on one income can't afford to lose it. You put that threat on the table and he'll tell you everything you need to know. He's your bait for the bad guy."

The look of gloom across the team's face began to melt. Smiles spread as they grabbed pens and began jotting down notes.

"We wait for the van to cross state lines tomorrow, with product in hand, and take him down," I announced. "Your case should have a name by afternoon and be closed within 24 hours, if all goes right."

The team was eager to get started. We mapped a plan. The pompous investigator and I would wait for the van to cross the

Long Island Expressway after his first pickup, and follow him to his next destination in Brooklyn, where we'd take him down. Everyone nodded in approval, except for Pompous—who made it obvious that he wasn't thrilled to be riding with me. He wasn't exactly the guy I wanted to be beside when catching a criminal lead, either, but part of me wanted to break his balls. Having to sit with me in a car for a number of hours when I knew he disliked me seemed like the best way to do that. After all, if I was there to help their unit get a pat on the back, I should be able to have a little enjoyment too, I thought.

The next morning I pulled myself into the passenger seat, pushed my seat back and slurped my morning coffee. I commented on Pompous's driving, offered him lane directions and changed the radio stations. For three hours we sat along the LIE waiting for the van to approach. Pompous wasn't shy of letting out a giant sigh of relief and a loud "Thank God" when word of the van's movement came across the wire. I smiled, knowing I'd gotten under his skin as much as I'd intended, as we waited for the van to get closer.

In time with the surveillance crew, we pulled onto the LIE and kept our speed to a medium crawl until the white van caught up with us. It was 11 p.m. and traffic was heavy with stop and go madness. Pompous remained two cars behind the van, just like he'd been instructed at driving school, while we followed the van from the LIE to the BQE. It took everything I had to not jump into the driver's seat and take control.

As we passed the Van Wyck exit, the van began to swerve. I quickly noted the back rear tire had gone flat.

"Careful," I warned Pompous.

The van's warning lights went on as he attempted to push into the right lane. The location couldn't have been worse. Traffic from the airport was thick, drivers were impatient and backup was miles away. But my instincts told me it was now or never.

"Pull off behind him," I instructed Pompous.

"Are you fucking kidding me?" he shouted. "I'm not pulling over here! We'll get fucking killed!"

"Pull over or you're going to lose your case," I advised as I picked up the radio.

"Be advised, I'm going to assist the target," I said.

The radio buzzed back with excitement.

"No. It's too dangerous! Stand down and wait for him to get back on the road."

This team was stupid, to put it kindly. They wanted our unmarked car to pull over and watch the van we were following, which would be less than 10 feet in front of us, until it was back on the road. It was idiotic! It was now or never.

"Guys, we're going in," I reported, turning down the radio to ignore the chatter that came across.

"Pull off behind him," I said, gesturing to the van.

"This is a horrible location!" Pompous whined. "We're going to get killed sitting here."

"If you say the word killed or die one more time, I'm going to kill you myself, you understand?" I said through clenched teeth. "Pull the fuck over!"

Pompous reluctantly did as he was told, flinging the car in park and leaning back, cRossong his arms across his chest in defiance.

I ignored his childish antics and watched as a Middle Eastern man, approximately 5'4" and 180 pounds, stepped out of his van and surveyed his wheel. Our car jerked with each car that flew past. I knew there was no chance pussy boy was going to get out of the car, so I opened my door and stepped out, just as the man looked up.

"Hey, buddy," I yelled over the traffic. "Need some help?"

"This fucking tire," he yelled, gesturing to his wheel. "Piece of shit."

"You got a spare in there?" I asked, nodding to the back of his van.

"Yeah, I don't know," he said, running his fingers through his hair.

"Open it up and I'll help you take a look," I said.

The man naively walked to the back hatch and pulled it open. There, in the midst of all the dangerous traffic, sat a full inventory of untaxed cigarettes—all piled above the spare tire.

There I was, standing on the side of the BQE with the perp this unit had been following for over a week, helping him unload cases of cigarettes. It was comical. I'd fill my arms with the untaxed cases and turn to the side, flashing a smile at the lame investigator who was snapping pictures.

Make me look good, asshole, I thought as I proudly displayed the merchandise this guy was handing me.

"Hey, hey, not like that!" the man said, turning my body to the right of the vehicle. "Somebody see you with all these cigarettes and we're going to get robbed! You going to make the police come."

"Oh sorry," I said, giving one last smile to the camera. "We definitely don't want the police here."

"No," the man said, pulling out his tire.

I stood beside the man, holding the van's lug nuts as he bent down and replaced his tire, while Pompous flung his hands up, frustrated with what I was doing. Vehicles far too close to my liking continued to fly past us.

After what felt like twenty minutes, the tire was in place and the man was happily walking to the back of the vehicle beside me, slapping me on the back and shaking my hand.

"Thank you. Thank you." he repeated.

"No, thank you," I said, holding his hand tightly. "You just saved me a full day of work."

"I'm sorry?" the man questioned, trying to pull his hand back.

"We were supposed to follow you up to your usual exit on the Outerbanks Bridge. But, now that you showed me your product, we get the pleasure of arresting you here."

The man turned white and his eyes darted a second, which I quickly interrupted.

"Ah, don't run," I said, still gripping his hand. "It will only make it worse. We have this whole area waiting for you."

The man's eyes darted around again before settling on my partner, who was still sitting behind the wheel.

"Let's go, guy," I said, weighting my other hand hard on his shoulder. "Quietly step inside the vehicle and I might be able to help you out for being so cooperative. I think your wife and kids would like that."

The man jerked his head towards me, everything suddenly sinking in.

"By the way, is the elderly woman in your house your mother or your wife's mother? We couldn't tell."

The man's eyes filled with tears and he lowered his head in defeat.

"They don't know about this. Please leave them. They know nothing."

"Let's walk to the car and we'll talk," I said, pushing the man forward.

"Fucking tire," he mumbled, tears rolling down his face.

"Ah, don't be too hard on your tire, buddy," I said, opening the rear car door for him. "We would have gotten you either way."

I closed the door and turned my radio back on.

"We're going to need vehicle assistance," I radioed in. "We have your guy in custody and are just waiting for permission to move forward."

"Did you just ask for permission?" an angry voice responded. "Your investigator has called police to the scene. They'll pick up the suspect. You will get the truck back to the station without so much as a scratch. And that is a direct order, in case you need further explanation!"

"Loud and clear," I replied, a bit too perky.

It was obvious I'd overstepped my bounds. However, I felt that was justified given the state of the idiot investigator they'd sent me with. If he'd gotten out of the car he could have helped remove the cartons of cigarettes or been the one to arrest the perpetrator.

I leaned into the passenger window and told Pompous I'd bring the van back while he waited for the squad car. But once I tried to get into the van I realized I couldn't fit. The driver's seat was busted. No matter how much I tried to jam the seat back, it wouldn't budge.

Reluctantly I headed back to the car.

"We're going to have to switch," I said, opening the investigator's car door. "My ass can't fit inside."

"That van's a piece of shit. I'm not driving that thing!" he said, trying to close his door.

My face must have looked like the man in the back of the vehicle's two minutes before.

"Guy, the bosses want the truck back to their location," I said. "What don't you understand? I can't drive it there. That means you need to get behind the wheel and do at least part of your job."

"Fuck you! I heard them over the radio. They ordered you to deliver the vehicle, not me. You think I'm stupid enough to let you sit here and take credit for this asshole as well? Fuck off."

It took everything I had not to reach inside the vehicle and drag him out by his neck. Luckily for his sake the flashing lights of the squad car loomed behind us at that exact moment.

The investigator, who'd failed to remove his scared ass from the vehicle, suddenly jumped out and began walking over to the officer. I leaned against the car and watched as he eagerly shook his hand and explained the situation. This idiot was grinning ear to ear as he escorted the Middle Eastern man out of his car and into the squad car.

"Officer," I called out after he'd secured our guy. "I'm going to need you to follow me back to our site."

The officer walked over, looking apprehensive.

I showed him the van and explained the situation.

"I'll call a unit in to transport it," he replied.

"No can do. Unfortunately they need all eyes on this vehicle and are requesting one of us to drive it back. Since coward boy over here is too scared, it's going to have to be me," I said, stuffing myself into the van. My knees were up to my chest.

"I'm not sure this is safe," the officer responded.

"Neither am I, but if you can just turn your lights on and get me safely through the traffic, I'd be greatly appreciative."

The officer was more than happy to comply. He walked past the investigator, whose original proud tone was now a bit more annoyed, and slid back into his car, flicking his lights on.

I followed the squad car through the BQE, my knees and chest beginning to pulse, and off the highway for another 40 minutes until we reached our destination.

Once the vehicle was secure and the team members were safe, I addressed the gutless investigator. I told him he was done, that he would never work with me or anyone in my unit again, and then I marched into his superior's office and had the event documented minute to minute.

"You might question how I handle situations or how I conduct my operations," I stated. "But that's precisely why you called me out here. Sitting behind a vehicle cowering isn't going to get you the numbers or success rates you desire. Nor is it going to get the job done. Idiots like that are what damage an investigation and put a team at risk. I can't imagine the state would approve of the actions your pompous investigator just displayed."

I left my signed form on his desk and walked out of the unit, confident that I'd done my job well.

The unit did get pretty far with the Middle Eastern man and were able to shut down the operation he worked for six months later. They received recognition from the Governor's Office and the press. However, the coward on the BQE wouldn't be there for that. He'd been moved to a smaller office Downstate, where he sat behind a safe, cushioned desk. Unfortunately, that was just the fuel he needed when the Inspector threw out her most wild accusation: our unit was missing one million dollars.

CHAPTER THIRTY-EIGHT

A MILLION SHORT

"We're being audited by the state," Staton said during our weekly meeting.

"Audited for what?" I asked.

"They believe we're short one million dollars. They're looking at everyone on the unit."

Jeff and I looked at each other in disbelief.

"But we have accountants that can verify everything."

"That was true until word got out by your BQE boy. He's claiming you bragged about allotting your team extra overtime when it wasn't needed and cash that wasn't accounted for."

"That sleazy motherfucker!" I exclaimed. "Where the hell did he come from?"

"He's an enemy. You put him in a bad spot."

"He put himself in a bad spot!"

"True, but most people who put themselves in those spots don't see it that way, now do they?"

"So, from this idiot's claim, they're going to open up an investigation?"

"Seems like it," Staton said.

And that was just what they did. For two months, while we brought in case after case, the state dipped into our financial records, checked our personal accounts and rechecked every second of overtime that we'd accrued. Overnight, we'd transformed from a unit that was breaking cases and pulling in high crime individuals to the cast of Goodfellas.

The claims tainted our names. People who once looked at us as high profile investigators began wondering if we were what they believed us to be. Meanwhile, here we were building a large case in Virginia that left us securing access to a military base, which was five miles away, and forging more ties within the Terrorism Task Force. Things on the business and investigative side were pretty good, yet just while our time in our Virginia investigation grew bigger, Rosso came in with orders from the state to begin closing it down.

"She's heated right now," Rosso said. "She's calling for all operations to be closed so she can dig further."

"Further into what? The criminals we've brought in?" I yelled, the blood rising to my face.

"The Inspector is claiming that terrorism is slowing down," Rosso smoothly stated. "She's convinced the state that someone can claim that the state is trying to entrap and target the Arabic community."

"Entrapment!" I spit, the words barely making it out of my mouth. "She's worried that the terrorists that we HAVE caught, the terrorists that HAVE been validated by the state's task force, that HAVE purchased illegal, untaxed cigarettes and sold them to profit from their criminal maneuvers, might make the state look bad? Are you fucking kidding me?"

I wanted to explode. The rage that began to build inside me left me feeling as if I could reach inside my stomach and rip my intestines out whole. I wanted to hurt someone. To make every fucking suit wearing asshole hang from the Ivory Tower, showing the criminal negligence and bullshit that they were in fact responsible for.

"Billy, I'm going to need you to calm down," Rosso stated. "This is just temporary. Nobody is thinking clearly at the moment. Once everyone takes a step back and assesses what is happening around us, and the false accusations that are being made, I think the situation can be re-approached."

"Re-approached nothing!" I exclaimed. "If they want to fuck this operation and put our names in the mud, then they can take this job and shove it up their ass."

"No, Billy! Don't go there. That's what they want."

"That's one thing we agree on then," I said.

"You cave and give in to them, and you cave and give in to all the operations you stood for."

I sat there, stewing in my anger.

"Think of who you are. Bust their balls and stick around, just out of spite if nothing else."

I let the conversation with Rosso linger in my mind that night. I tossed and turned, thinking of all the things I wanted to say to the Inspector, how I could show everyone how wrong she was, how off she was. But all that got me was an evening without sleep and nerves that were as frazzled and frayed as if I'd spent the evening tangled in electric fences.

No matter how angry the team or I were, we couldn't prevent our shutdown, which was announced two days after Rosso'd delivered the bad news.

"We'll be back," Staton declared. "The operation is not over. It's just on hold."

Our unit was solemn over the next two days. The friendly, fun conversations died with the news of our closure, filling the space with anger, sarcasm and loathing. Luckily for our egos, the one thing we had on our side was the wounded egos of everyone on the Terrorism Task Force. To shut one of our operations down was one thing, but to suggest an entire agency's purpose and day to day affairs may be invalid was an entirely different offense. We shut down our operation with 13 arrests, 10 of which all had valid ties to terrorism involvement.

As the FBI stepped in, quick to lap up the rewards and present these "entrapped" individuals to the state and press, we taped up our boxes and headed home, leaving the Terrorism Task Force to battle the state and the inspector who'd done a good job blindsiding them all.

Staton encouraged our team to take a little respite.

"We'll be back," he assured us. "The cases are not over. We have a world of criminal activity to tap into. Go, take a moment. Clear your mind and get some rest. I have a new operation already underway. I'll reach out to you with the details, but not before I know all of you have taken a step back from this. I don't want anyone returning to the next operation with a grudge or chip on their shoulder about the government's policies. It is what it is. Let's keep our heads up, remember what we've accomplished and go back to being normal guys for a day or two."

While respite meant a family vacation and trips to Disney World for some of my coworkers, my respite was sitting poolside in Florida, tanned with information.

Ronnie was known as a drug educator for special police units. He was always on the cusp of drug prices, knew what was hot, what was bad news and, most importantly, what the criminal world was lapping up. Despite the headlines and never-ending news coverage of our "scandalous" undertakings from the state, I arrived in Florida ready to relax and begin what would possibly be the next phase of my career.

Ronnie was all smiles when I arrived. He was quick with the jokes, and even quicker asking for a little side money.

"We'll talk money when you talk insider information," I joked.

Unfortunately for Ronnie, his drug knowledge had put him a little too close to the spotlight a few years back. He'd spent three years in prison as a result.

Ronnie and I spent two days catching up, checking out Florida's coast and exchanging information. However, as most stories go, the relaxed, tourist feeling that was just setting in lasted right up until my phone rang.

"They need you to come home for questioning, Billy," Staton replied.

"You can let them know that I'm on vacation, and unless those assholes are willing to pay for my flight back and forth they can shove their questions up their ass."

Ronnie shot a look at me.

"When are you set to come back?"

"I have two more days. I'm not budging, Staton. This is the respite you encouraged."

"Enjoy it, like I said. But when you come back you need to set up a meeting. They're working fast on this one."

By the time I arrived at the Ivory Towers, the inspector had already met and interviewed everyone from my team, the police departments we'd worked with, the Governor's office and the Attorney General, who thankfully still had our backs.

"Your operation was responsible for bringing in millions of dollars into the state, Mr. William," the inspector stated. "You were the first operation to offset your own costs and negotiate your own needs, with minimal state security. Would you find that statement to be correct?"

The inspector's conference room seemed sterile and cold. I couldn't tell if it was the room itself, the eight other boring suits quietly watching as the inspector attempted to interrogate me, or the inspector's absent personality that seemed to drain the room of any emotions or feelings.

"That's correct," I replied, my wind pants making a squishy noise as I rested one leg on top of the other.

"Was there ever a time, with all this money floating in and out of the warehouse, that you or someone you worked with was tempted to dip into the pot?"

I couldn't help but laugh at the question.

"Is this really your approach? You're questioning to see if I'll admit that I was tempted to take money? I hope your other interrogations didn't come off that easy."

"I'm glad you find the humor in wasting your time and ours today," the inspector sneered. "We're not here for your jokes, nor do I appreciate being asked about my tactics."

"I apologize," I said, trying to quiet my smile. "I'm sure you know what you're doing. Please proceed."

The next few questions went the same as the first. Had I witnessed anyone take money? Had other people, besides Jeff and me, been allowed to touch the money? What did we do once we had the money? All the answers were met with the same response.

"We had a unit and an accountant to handle that part of the job," I said. "Once the money was in our hands it went straight into the safe. The only one to see it after that was the accountant."

"But, surely, having access to that money every day, all day, made it hard for anyone to stay clean. Even your outstanding unit."

I could feel the dig as the last words weaseled their way through her teeth.

"Well, as I'm sure you can see from my rich mansion on the hill, luxury cars, and private camps on the foothills of the Adirondacks, we were tempted every day."

"Mr. William, again may I remind you that time is of the essence. Let's move fast and stay away from the jokes, shall we?"

"If you're implying that we don't have houses on the hill or luxury cars or camps, then I assume you looked into all of our household finances. I also assume that means you turned up nothing. Because there is nothing. Not one of our hard-working members ever dipped their hands in the pot, as you say. You know why? Because all of us were hungry to nail the bad guys that came our way every day. We didn't see money. We saw arrests. We saw power. We were high on takedowns and adrenaline and hoped to nail the next big guy that came our way. Not one man on this unit considered the financial aid papers they had to fill out for their child's college or the second mortgage they had to take out on their house because your employers would rather pay you top dollar and leave us men on the field with just enough money to take our family to Disneyland. Maybe we should have. Maybe thinking like that would have served our families. But I guess a unit as outstanding as ours wasn't that bright."

The inspector sat back in her chair with a heavy sigh. She wasn't going to get anywhere and she was disgusted. Here we were, a unit filled with degenerates that had been able to do something so profound, and yet she couldn't find the loophole.

"Because there isn't one to find," I said, hoping to end the conversation. "There was nothing wicked or vindictive in anything we did, other than nail down the criminals and terrorists that you say no longer exist. What you're searching for isn't money, it's how we made the system work for the agents, and not the state who tries to make everything black and white."

"What we're searching for is $1.3 million. Mark my words, Mr. William, we will find it."

☙

The days after the inspector's interrogation were dry. We all spent our time sitting in the Syracuse office, waiting to hear anything. Yet day after day no news arrived.

"The agency has a soft operation for you," Staton muttered two weeks into our downtime. "It's nothing big, but it's work."

Staton sounded as worn down as we felt. All this fighting, moving from warehouse to warehouse, operation after operation, to sitting stagnant behind a desk, waiting had settled into his bones. He was angry. And, as I later learned, anger always makes you speak out of turn and make decisions you may have otherwise thought unfit.

"It's a tax evasion case. Nothing major, but a lot is riding on it. Be thorough, precise and get it done in a timely manner."

Jeff couldn't be more excited about the task at hand. And to be frank, they could have offered me a job sorting through dog crap for a dime bag and I would have taken it. I was desperate to get out of the office and back on the field.

Yet, one day before our assignment was to begin, Staton made a decision. Tired and overwhelmed with the inspector's "hold," Staton took our criminal arrests, money brought to the state and pages of facts to a journalist at the New York Post. His timing was spot on, as the day of his sit down the investigator launched a new development.

Our unit sat there the next day, reading the headlines of the paper, with our hearts in our throats. We were being replaced by a machine. The inspector hadn't even had the courtesy to tell us that we were being broken apart. But I suppose my lack of compliance had given her reason not to. I imagined the smile that had spread across her face as she decided to announce our fate through the press. I imagined it was just as similar to Staton's smile the day he decided to do the same.

With her head held high, and the state police and Governor behind her, the inspector proudly introduced a new coding software system that was designed to manage and improve the illegal sales of untaxed cigarettes and fraudulent tax stamps in New York State. The system was arbitrary, to say the least. Yet, when the headlines came in, the outsiders bought it.

The inspector proposed to offset the cost of the highly expensive software by disbanding our unit. The software, she promised, would help to eliminate the sale of untaxed cigarettes for good. But Staton and the rest of our disbanded unit knew better. No matter what technology they'd try to develop, the bad guys would always catch up. There'd always be someone smarter and quicker, someone who'd take the inspector's "a common goal" and unravel it.

eↄ

With his loss of power, Staton found a way to fight through the straitjacket that the inspector had put around us, and went straight back to the journalist with another statement. Staton spoke to the people about our $13 million revenue. He listed our closed cases, number of arrests and asked the public to consider why a woman of this stature would want the state to disband something so profitable.

Staton used his anger to unleash powerful accusations, referring to the inspector as a sore loser, since she'd fought to show criminal intent within our unit and had come up empty-handed.

Staton's facts and structured argument sent the inspector reeling the next morning. But his fight wouldn't stop there. *The Albany Times Union* and other surrounding newspapers and press outlets both small and wide would print glowing articles, courtesy of Staton, for the next three weeks. The powers-that-be couldn't do a thing about it, either. For when they stormed into his office the morning of the first release, they found his letter of resignation, gun and badge neatly placed on his cleared desk.

Over the next few months Staton continued to expose our unit's skills and operations over the air and to any paper that would give him a slot. The inspector would go after him, slandering our team's name and the actions we took, but she could never clear Staton's accusations. Not even when Staton announced her candid statement about the downsizing of terrorism in the United States—two days after a terrorist drove his car into a crowd of people in Times Square.

Staton, the founder of the PATB's largest arrest in history, continued his fight to clear our name, while the guys and I headed down to Fort Plain, ready to prove our unit's importance for the last time.

CHAPTER THIRTY-NINE

BOUGHT A BAR

Our unit was set to crack down on a group known for tax evasion, loan sharking and drug trafficking. The director in charge of this operation knew of our undercover operations, specifically with Billy the Liquor Guy, and had reached out for help.

Rubino, who was our temporary supervisor, happily signed us onto the case with one condition.

"I know you guys are antsy to get back on the field, but everyone here will have to be on their best professional behavior," he instructed our team. "I want this case pushed with a quick, positive outcome, meaning felony tax evasion and felony drug charges."

Rubino turned to face me.

"I would appreciate it greatly if none of your antics come out, Billy," he stated. "Please try to be professional at all times. This investigator is serious and runs a smart town. Your unit is being tossed in the press like gunfire, so let's try to regain our reputation and put it back in a positive light."

While I wasn't sure how confident Rubino felt with my answer, I agreed wholeheartedly to his request. Like a child, there was that small glimmer of hope in my mind. If we could prove ourselves worthy and the inspector could find nothing on Staton, maybe he'd come back and we could be one happy unit once again.

We arrived in Fort Plain with our Syracuse Supervisor, Timmy, one week after our meeting with Rubino, and held our first meeting under an old pavilion next to the Erie Canal, since the town's police station couldn't hold all of us.

The investigator and his team of one happily welcomed us. The chip on my shoulder expected the investigator to be like Barney Fife. Instead, I was greeted with a tall, intelligent man who was extremely proud of his town.

Chief, as I called him, worked as a part-time investigator for the town and a full-time firefighter in a larger city not too far from the area. He was surprisingly street smart, well-educated, and ready to shake up the small town he grew up in. I immediately understood why Rubino wanted our team, and me in particular, to act professional. This guy believed in what we were doing, and he'd come to us with confidence that we could get the job done.

The Chief passed out a set of profiles on the targets and the barmaid, which was standard. However, his notes went beyond the black and white. His team had gone on to list the type of liquor the patrons liked, who was into drugs and who might raise concerns about a new guy walking into a small hometown bar. They also linked each patron with a description and picture. I found myself eating any words I'd ever mumbled about small town investigators.

After looking through the material, I picked out the motorheads, who I steered Jeff to interact with, and the gamblers and merchandisers looking to make a buck, who I'd go after.

I also chose to go after the barmaid who they'd listed as the drug distributor.

Chief listed the owner as an arrogant, unfriendly bastard who thought he was better than everyone else.

"That's great. Assholes are my favorite type of target to take down," I said.

Our first meeting was scheduled for the following Monday at 7 p.m. The plan was for Jeff to try to forge a discussion with the remaining happy hour customers about bikes and whatnot, while I sat at the bar loudly complaining about how badly I'd taken a beating on the last two Monday night games.

All our audio devices had been tested and secreted on our bodies, just like on our previous ops, but for some reason I felt more relaxed than I had in a long time. I didn't know if my calm demeanor was a result of the proximity of my family, or if it was because I was back in my natural environment, selling wares as a degenerate gambler. It wasn't very complimentary, but it wasn't a biker or Jamaican bar filled with criminals that I had to try to infiltrate, or a terrorist who I had to cozy up to while they attempted to stockpile cigarettes.

Even with these thoughts, I had to remind myself not to get too comfortable.

As Jeff and I walked into the dimly lit bar I immediately recognized several of the targets on Chief's list. Dan, the owner, was standing behind the wooden bar, writing something on a piece of paper; and Lisa, the barmaid, was tending bar as expected.

The joint itself was an average dive bar. It had the standard dart and shuffleboard station, a few wooden tables and an old, L-shaped bar with wooden stools. Even the lack of light couldn't make this place look good.

Jeff headed towards the dartboard, hoping to engage in a game, as I casually walked up to the bar and ordered a Jack and Coke.

"Hey, can we switch the game on?" I asked Dan. "I gotta lot of money riding on this one."

Just as Chief told me, he was an arrogant asshole.

He mumbled something about being a stranger and about respect before ignoring me and walking away. However, to his dismay, his move invited a conversation with Lisa.

Lisa was polite and all smiles as she strutted over to the television and switched on the game.

"There you go, Silver Fox," she winked.

My stomach dropped with her last two words. Silver Fox. It was like a flash in time. Sunshine sprang to my mind, which was funny, because for as bad as I'd felt when she was arrested, I'd stopped thinking about her a long time ago.

I sat at the bar for the next hour with an order of chicken wings and the nightly game, while Jeff played darts with an older gentleman who swayed every time he threw a dart. I made a little small talk with a few locals as they came in to watch the game, and by halftime I'd managed to rally a discussion around the side liquor business I dabbled in.

"You know, Dan over there might be interested in some of that liquor if you really have a supply," Lisa chimed in as she leaned across the bar towards me.

Bingo!

I played aloof and focused on the game.

"I'll have to let him know," I mumbled, pretending not to notice her lean.

The blind-eye worked. Lisa wanted my attention, but the game had it. So she did what girls who need attention do. She walked over to her boss and told him all about my side gig. Within minutes he was by my side, along with Lisa, who was proudly smiling.

"Lisa says you're over here bragging about some half-ass liquor business you have," he grunted.

"I wouldn't necessarily call it half-assed," I said, feasting on a chicken wing. "But I'd be happy to show you some stuff after this game."

Lisa smiled and nudged Dan.

"You should see," she exclaimed. "He might have some really good stuff."

"I've got a few cases of Jack Daniel's and half a dozen bar racks left," I stated.

I could see Dan trying to take me in as I yelled and carried on about the most recent play. It was a tactical move I used to distract him from overthinking my position and it worked. Dan agreed to see what I had and I agreed to head out back, despite my current involvement in the game.

Within ten minutes I was back in the bar, finishing my wings and carrying on about the game, while Dan carried in the last two cases of untaxed Jack Daniel's I'd sold him.

It was a great first night, and one the Chief and Rubino were proud of. Arrogant Dan had bought into my sale hook, line and sinker.

❧

I returned the next night in time for the evening game. Lisa already had it on for me.

"I was hoping you'd come tonight, Silver Fox," she said, sliding a glass of Jack and Coke to me. "That's on the house. Dan was really pleased to see your stuff was the real deal. I think he wants to do more business with you."

"That's good," I said, nonchalantly. "How have you been?"

Lisa took my invitation for conversation and ran with it. She told me about her job, bar patrons, who she liked, who she didn't like, how long she worked, how often she took a break (hint), and how curious she was about me.

"Don't get too curious," I said. "There's not much more than this."

I looked back up at the television, which made Lisa desperate to talk more. She'd been waiting for me, it seemed. She wasn't an awful looking girl, just a bit sloppy.

"So what other types of liquor do you sell in that van? I'm sure I could get Dan to buy more! And I know a lot of other bar owners I could introduce you to. I can help you get big in this town if you'd like."

"Ah, sorry Lisa," I shrugged. "But I don't have that type of supply."

Lisa tended to another customer while I turned to check on Jeff who was shooting the shit about car engines with two patrons.

"How much do you have?" Lisa said, interrupting my Jeff observation.

"You know what you might be interested in?" I said, turning to face her. "Handbags."

"Handbags?"

"Yeah, Gucci handbags, Gucci scarves. I can get them for you and you can sell them if you're interested."

It didn't take much for her to sign on the dotted line. I chatted with her between commercials and sold her boss another case of Jack Daniel's before halftime.

We waited a few days before we reentered the bar, full of counterfeit items for Lisa. She gushed over the large box of purses and promised to sell them all by the end of the week.

"I slipped my number in the box," I winked as I took a seat. "Call me if you need anything."

Lisa gave me a seductive wink back and slipped me a drink on the house. She called two hours after the bar closed that evening. She was drunk and lonely. She spilled about her boss and her job, told me she hated it there and how awfully Dan treated her.

"Lisa, you're a smart woman," I told her. "You can do better than that bar."

"I can't," she sighed. "I have my reasons why I can't. I mean, it's close to my home and close to the people I trust."

"Do you trust Dan?"

"Yeah, I do. I grew up with these people, Silver," she said. "We all know each other like the back of our hand."

"So, can I ask you something personal then?" I said. "I don't want you to be disappointed in me."

"How could I ever be disappointed in you?"

I ran my coke speech. I told her my source in the city had dried up and I didn't know people here.

"Let me see what I can do, Silver Fox," she said. "I can't promise anything."

"Lisa, you really are a great girl, ya know."

And with that I opened the drug outlet Chief was waiting for. Lisa called me the next night. She had stuff.

"Meet me for lunch tomorrow," I said. "I want to thank you for looking out for me."

Lisa arrived 15 minutes late and was higher than a kite. She had on skintight jeans, a yellow tube top that her breasts spilled out of and spiked high heels that she couldn't walk in. She stumbled over to my table and sat across from me with a big smile.

"Guess what I brought for you, Silver," she teased, struggling to pull a Ziploc bag full of cocaine from her tight pocket.

"Ah, Lisa. I knew you were my girl." I smiled. "How about we get you some coffee?"

"I'm gonna get a sandwich," she slurred. "I'm dying for the homemade chips they make here."

Lisa and I talked for a while about her life, which had been hard up to this point. She didn't know her dad, grew up with an alcoholic mother who died when she was 21, and had never married. Lisa's demeanor was sloppy, which made it hard to feel bad for her. She was so high she kept missing the straw and poking herself in the cheek or eye, or her elbow would slip off the table, making her head jerk since she was leaning on it for weight, and her words rolled into one another. Worse yet, she didn't touch her sandwich or eat one chip!

"Can you come in and see me tonight?" Lisa asked as we wrapped up the afternoon.

"Not tonight, kid," I told her. "I've got a lot of deliveries to make."

Lisa was disappointed but perked up when I asked her if I could drive her to work.

"I drove here, Silver Fox."

"That's okay. You can get your car later. I like talking to you."

Inside I was dying to get out of the diner and away from Lisa, but I couldn't let her drive in her condition. I had to help her down the stairs and drove her to the bar.

"You think you can have another supply for me?" I inquired as she stepped out of the car.

Lisa smiled and said she'd make sure it was waiting for me.

∞

My next visit went as planned. Jeff and I arrived during the game, Dan bought alcohol and Lisa had another bag of coke in her pocket for me. However, this time Dan seemed a bit more comfortable with me. I'm not sure if it was because he knew I was buying drugs from Lisa and she hadn't been busted, or if it was because he felt confident with his liquor sales which, again, occurred without his bar being raided. Either way, Dan started bitching to me about the bar business.

"Really?" I shrugged, popping a pretzel in my mouth. "I was actually thinking about getting back into the business. I have a few investors lined up right now. I just need to find the right place."

Dan's eyes lit up.

"What's wrong with this one?" he asked.

"You want to sell it?" I questioned.

"I'm done, Silver." (Yes, even Dan referred to me as Silver now.) "It can be all yours if you want it."

I took a hard look around the dingy bar before responding.

"This would be perfect for me, actually," I said. "It's far enough away from my business in NYC, and close enough to Syracuse. It would be a great front for my liquor business."

Dan's excitement built.

"Tell you what, get your books together and show me what you really make here and we'll discuss a price," I told him.

The surveillance team was practically jumping up and down when I turned in for the day.

"Shit, Billy. You are no joke," Chief said, patting me on the back.

"Well, no jokes are free. I'm going to need some front money to show him I'm serious if we want this to work."

That night I fell asleep and dreamed of Dan pulling a gun from underneath the bar and pointing it at my head. I could see down the barrel and feel the cold steel pressed against my forehead. Dan pulled the trigger back just as I shot out of bed screaming for my life. It was 4 o'clock in the morning, but try as I might, I couldn't get myself back in that bed.

❧

Chief arrived with $20,000 in cash.

"This is all I can allow, Billy," he said, handing me over a classic brown briefcase with hidden markings. "It's my savings. Make it work."

Dan was all smiles when I showed him the front money.

"You got the books?" I said as he counted through the stacks of bills.

"Yeah, it's in the back."

"Dan," I said, leaning forward. "You know I need to see your second set of books before I agree to buy this place, right? Not the books you show the tax guys."

Dan smirked at my bar knowledge. For those unfamiliar with this term, a second book is the money a bar makes. The books auditors and tax collectors see are filled with the least amount of money a bar makes. We needed credible evidence of how much Dan was evading from the state.

"Yeah, I've got those books too." He laughed.

Dan bragged about the amount of money he'd hidden from the State for the last five years. His arrogance and stupidity made it easy to take this asshole down. He spilled everything. He led me through the back of the bar and into the basement, where he showed me where he stored all his untaxed liquor and beer.

"The trick is to underpay your employees, skimp on all the documents you provide to the State, and deal in cash whenever you can," Dan told me before he reached the back of the basement where his second set of books were waiting. To my surprise there were five books, one for every year he'd been in business.

"You mind if I take them back to my investors?" I questioned. "You've got quite an operation going on. I think they'd be interested to learn what you know."

"Not at all." He smiled. "I'm glad to be of help if I can. I can sit down and meet with them as well if they'd like to know more."

"I think that will definitely be a possibility. I guarantee they're going to want to meet you after they learn about all of this."

Dan was confident as hell. His chest stuck out and he had a little stride to his walk as we exited the basement.

"Thanks again, Billy," he said, shaking my hand.

"You got it, Dan. I'll be in touch soon."

I jumped back in the van with Jeff and pulled off as Dan stood outside, happily waving to me.

∽

While the Chief and his team dissected the books, I tried to find a way to get connected to Lisa's dealer.

I arranged another meeting with Lisa the next afternoon, back at the diner. When she arrived, she was higher than she'd been on our previous occasion. Her white tank top revealed track marks that ran down her arms.

"Lisa, the stuff you've been giving me is good, but I need a larger quantity," I said once we were settled.

"Wow, you're worse than me," she slurred.

"It's not all for me," I said, shooting her a smile. "I think I have a side business that you and I can get into together."

Lisa perked up with the mention of "you and I."

"I'd like to meet your seller to discuss my plan. He can be a crucial part of it."

"He's not going to go for that," she immediately stated, shaking her head.

"You let me handle that," I said, putting my hand on top of hers. "I might be able to sway him once he hears my deal."

After a bit more convincing and proper "you and I" word usage, Lisa agreed to arrange a meeting between the two of us. Two days later, Lisa advised me to meet her by the Thruway exit, where I'd follow her to his location. When I arrived, Lisa was out of her mind.

"You can't drive like this," I said. "Why don't you just come with me?"

"No," she said as she stepped away from me. "He won't come out if he sees that I came on your terms. If you want to meet him you have to let me arrive first."

"Alright," I said. My mind spun on how to get around this scenario. "Give me a minute to use the restroom and we'll head out."

Once inside the bathroom I radioed the team.

"You can't let her get on the road like that, Bill!" they yelled. "We have eyes on her now. She can't even stand up."

"Guys, we've got state police ready for this takedown, correct? Can we call ahead and have them stop traffic? We can bring two more undercovers out to box her in while she drives?"

A few choice words and "are you out of your mind" spat across the line. But just as I thought it was a lost situation, the Chief radioed in and gave us the go ahead.

"Just hold her off for twenty minutes so we can notify everyone."

Shocked by the Chief's decision, I bought time inside the gas station with Lisa, who tripped over herself.

"We've got to get going, Silver. He's waiting," Lisa said as she caught herself on the chip rack.

"He'll be fine," I said. "Let's grab a soda to celebrate our new future."

Lisa tucked her arm in mine and walked over to the soda machine, where I took my time pouring a drink and searching for money to pay.

"We've gotta go, Silver," Lisa tugged on my sleeve, which caused her to fall on the floor. I pulled her up while the gas attendant stared at me, and walked her back out to her car. I prayed everyone was ready to go.

"Go slow," I told her. "I can't get pulled over in this van."

Lisa saluted me and waited for me to get in, which I lingered doing. By the time we pulled onto the road, there wasn't a car in sight. I followed Lisa as she swerved through the toll booth and off the ramp, where two undercover vehicles waited, as planned. It took less than a minute before Lisa pulled off the ramp and drove straight into the grassy median between the highway lanes. The undercover cars and I acted fast. We pulled up alongside her and helped guide her car back onto the proper lane of traffic. But she jolted her car left and headed for the other side of the road.

"She's on the other side of the road!" Chief screamed over the radio. "End this now. Get this spaz off the road!"

The three of us blocked Lisa's car in and brought it down to a crawl. Her head darted around, trying to figure out what was going on. But she didn't need to. Within two seconds the state police swarmed the scene and pulled her over.

I immediately told the officers to arrest me so that she could see me handcuffed.

"Lisa!" I yelled, heartbroken, as the officers laid me in front of her vehicle and handcuffed me. "You promised you wouldn't drive fast."

"Oh Silver Fox," she cried as they faced her to me. "I didn't mean it. I'm sorry. I didn't mean it."

They placed Lisa and me in cars across from one another. As Lisa looked over at me I looked down in an act of heartache.

"Don't wait to go back to the office," I told the investigator behind the wheel. "Get her to spill now, while she can see me. Let her know you're going to send me away for five years unless she tells you where her dealer is located right now."

"Ten four, sir," the investigator said as he stepped out of the car.

I watched Lisa as she cried and carried on with the investigators. Within five minutes the case was closed. Lisa gave up her dealer's location, contacts and the number of weapons in his house. Police raided his house an hour later with triumphant success.

Lisa was charged with DWI and placed in a cell for the evening so she couldn't run back to the bar. Dan, who was behind the bar due to Lisa's absence, was rattled. Of all the things I liked about this sting, Dan's chicken wings were the best I'd had in some time. Since I knew this would be the last opportunity I had, I ordered a dozen "to go." Dan returned with my order ready to talk business.

"So, what did the investors say?" he asked.

"They're on their way to meet you." I smiled.

Dan stuttered.

"They're coming now? Shit. Lisa didn't even show up for her shift. She's probably high somewhere again."

"You've got time. I've got to drop an order off in 45 minutes and then I'll bring them back. Just wanted to give you a heads up."

Dan poured himself a shot.

"You know what, Dan? How many wings you got back there, anyway? Think you can whip up an order of 150 for when they come?"

I walked out of the bar, chicken wings in hand, and headed down to the local firehouse where the Chief and his team waited.

"You're all set," I said as I closed the door behind me. "He's ready for you."

Rubino glanced at my to-go container.

"Seriously, Billy. You ordered wings?"

I plopped myself in a chair by the window with the container on my lap.

"My work here is done, fellas," I teased. "There should be an order of wings ready for you guys too."

Rubino shook his head, suited up and walked out the door with the rest of the unit.

I propped my feet on the sill and enjoyed my wings as 25 police cars flooded the street.

The takedown went smoothly. Dan was arrested and charged on tax evasion without a fight.

I felt satisfied as I sat there and it all went down. My team and I had successfully closed another operation. Despite how unstoppable I felt in the moment, the truth was that was exactly what we were. Three weeks from the day, the powers-that-be would finally disband out unit and close our office. Overnight, our unit that sought terrorists, dealt with hard criminals, and brought in hundreds of millions of dollars for the state had dissolved into nothing. We were meant to be erased, blamed for missing funds that we never touched and left to ponder in a quiet office that saw limited activity. It was a slap in the face for our unit, all the men who worked these cases, and for the American people in general. But, like most things, people outside of our unit would never know that. They came to believe the lies they were told. To this day, they've never allowed the PATB to run a case or smuggling operation again.

CHAPTER FORTY

PTSD

There was no question that I had toed the line over the course of my career. I'd dabbled in drugs, engaged too closely with criminals and consistently pushed the envelope. I told myself that I did things, like utilize drugs, for the safety of my cover. But, if I were being truthful, all those things were bold warning signs that I had lost who I was. Unfortunately, I didn't recognize those moments for what they were until I was too far gone.

As my dangerous operations closed, the large takedowns, warehouse closure, and Staton's absence left a void. I became antsy, irritated and unsure of myself. Overnight I went from a fun, happy guy to one that couldn't handle the smallest situations. Minor incidents at home, like a broken dish or a kid that wouldn't stop running around the house, would send me into a frenzy. But that was only when I was engaged. Most of my time at home turned into a hibernation retreat. I'd head to my room within minutes of arriving home, throw myself in bed, and either sleep or watch TV for hours at a time.

At first, I chucked my new behavior off as exhaustion. I told myself the years spent on the field had caught up with me. The only problem with that theory were the restless nights I experienced. I'd wake up every night with my mind racing. Cases, situations, Nash, Double J, Steel, Staton, and the warehouse seemed to play with me and trying to untangle one thought from the next seemed impossible.

My wife frequently woke up to find me staring out the window at 3 a.m. As a social worker, she'd pull up a seat beside me and express her concerns about my stressful patterns, but I'd shut her down.

"This is why I don't like coming home," I'd snap. "I can't get any peace. I can't just be left here to think. Do you have any idea about all of the shit I have done? I've spent years in dangerous situations and no one in this family wants to take time to acknowledge that. I've done some pretty big things and nobody has any regard for that."

My words came out in anger. While everyone loved me and had spent most of their days and nights worrying about me in the field, my clouded vision couldn't see that. In my mind I was someone they laughed at, ridiculed and made light of. If I happened to catch a police show with my wife or son and I commented on the reality or fundamentals of the situation and they didn't seem interested, I took it personally. I built this overwhelming case in my mind that emulated their disinterest in my comments as a lack of respect for the work I'd done.

My irritation and fear left me afraid of crowded spaces, like arenas, festivals or anything where there would be hundreds of people around. My mind would go to dark places. I imagined a bad guy spotting me in the overpopulated crowd before I saw him. I thought of the violent altercations that might occur, like being shot in front of my wife and kids or, worst of all, I pictured the bad guy following my family and waiting for a time when I wasn't around.

One time my wife asked me to join her and my sister-in-law for a concert at the New York State Fair. I hemmed and hawed until my wife got so pissed that I caved and went.

"You think everyone is going to recognize you," she said. "You have to get that out of your head."

"In fairness, I'm over 6 feet tall, have white hair and large shoulders. I stand out in most places. And for a bad guy I arrested I most definitely stand out."

The State Fair was hot and crowded, just as I'd imagined. There were people everywhere so even choosing a direction to focus on was impossible. My palms were hot and a cold clammy sensation spread throughout my body. I walked next to my wife, making our way through the crowd to see the animals, visit the butter sculpture and, of course, the food court. While we waited in line to try a fried Twinkie I saw a man I recognized.

I told myself not to panic. Told myself to breathe. Told myself I was imagining him. That it was all in my head.

Yet, as I looked again, the man I recognized, who was standing beside a group of bikers, immediately had a face and a name. He wasn't anyone I'd arrested, but he'd been involved in Nash's group. I had a clear image of him taking his shirt off across from me in Nash's basement. My mind shot into work mode.

"Turn towards your left and keep walking," I whispered to my wife.

My wife began to protest since she hadn't ordered yet.

"Turn to your left and walk away now. We have to leave this spot immediately."

I remained three people deep as I followed her back to the horse stable. Despite my dark thoughts, I'd seen the bad guy before he saw me. Too engrossed in his beer and group of comrades he never looked my way.

"Are you sure it was who you think it was?" my wife asked once we'd stopped.

"Honey, the reason I'm still alive is because I can recognize these people."

Annoyed at my wife, but mostly at the situation, I departed the fair and waited in the car where I listened to music and napped until the concert was over.

The next time an event like this occurred my wife was ready.

We'd been driving along the thruway on our way to Buffalo, NY when we decided to stop at one of the exits to grab a coffee. We weren't in line for two minutes when I heard a familiar voice across the station.

"Oh my God, it's Billy the Liquor Guy!" a man yelled. "How the hell are ya?"

I told my wife to stay in line before I was greeted by Steve, a chubby bar owner who had more of an attachment to gambling than anything else.

The coffee line moved up and my wife moved forward while I stepped out.

"Man long time no see," Steve said as he approached me "Where the hell ya been?"

"Jail." I laughed. "I got busted with the guys in Elmira a while back. I just got out last month."

"No shit?" Steve said. "Well, where you headed now? You want to go get some lunch or something? Catch up? I haven't had anyone coming to the bar with liquor since you left. You starting that up now that you're out?"

"I might be. But right now I'm on my way to a funeral in Rochester," I said. "It was good seeing you though. I'll make sure to pop in some time."

"That'd be great. I'd love to tell the guys you're back."

"Me too. It'd be good to shoot the shit with everyone and see how they're holding up."

"Well once you come in I'll arrange it. Billy the Liquor Guy. Wow. So cool to see you here."

"You too, brother. I'll be in touch next week."

I headed to the bathroom and waited for my wife to call me once the coast was clear.

When we got back into the car I looked over at my wife.

"You see," I said, "I'm not crazy. These people are out there. You never know."

Incidents such as these only fueled the anxiety I believed I wasn't having. Within months my fear began to mount, which in turn fueled my anger. I became increasingly pissed at myself for being afraid. What the fuck could I be afraid of? Hadn't I stood shoulder to shoulder with some badass criminals? Wasn't I Billy the Liquor Guy? The one everyone in fellow agencies admired. Yet, there I was afraid to leave my house and my safe zones. It was ridiculous!

I dreaded waking up every morning because the vicious cycle would start the moment I opened my eyes. My fear, anger and lack of sleep left me feeling off. I became convinced something was wrong with me and that I was harboring an underlying health issue that was sure to be discovered any day.

A fear of driving, which I'd suppressed for years, emerged. Traditionally my safe space, the only time where I could kick back, open my windows and blast Willie without criminals, family members or bosses around, had become my hell. Random flashbacks of incidents that had happened on the road flooded my mind. I'd be lost in my thoughts when George, my former partner, would slam into my mind, on the hood and into my windshield. The image appeared out of nowhere and it was as real as the day we'd actually hit and killed a woman during a snowstorm ten years prior.

"What the fuck was that?" I could hear my old partner George yell, his voice on the edge of hysteria, as we rolled the car to a stop. "Billy, WHAT THE FUCK WAS THAT?"

I'd noticed our blood-scattered windshield and what looked like strands of long, dark hair before I'd discover the body of a woman in a nurse's uniform, lying feet away from the car in the snow. The snow was so heavy, the flakes made it impossible to see past her body.

I'd held her in my arms while George radioed in for backup. The nurse, who'd stepped out of her vehicle and attempted to cross over the snow-covered highway to help another car that had slid into a guardrail, would die before the ambulance arrived. And, George, who'd never saw her coming, spent the rest of his life rehashing the night.

"Billy," George said years later, his scrawny body sunk into his hospital bed. "You think I have cancer because I killed that lady?"

The comment had caught me off guard.

"I killed her, Billy," he said for the first time, tears running down his face. "I hit that lady and killed her. I think this is my punishment."

"Will you be fucking serious?" I'd said, leaning forward to look at him. "If people were given out illnesses every time they made a mistake or did something wrong in life the whole world would be dead."

George looked down, his eyes consumed with tears yet to fall.

"Look at me, for crying out loud!" I continued. "If that's how you think then I should have leprosy for all the shit I've done in my life."

ↄ⌀

I happened to be riding with a new coworker when one of these flashbacks occurred. I slammed on the brakes and swerved the car into the other lane, certain we'd just hit someone.

"What the fuck is wrong with you?" my coworker screamed as I pulled to the shoulder of the highway, sweat running down my forehead and my hands gripping the steering wheel tightly.

"I don't know," I replied in a moment of weakness. "I think I'm beginning to lose my mind."

I told him everything I had seen and confessed this was the third time it had happened. He listened and, after pulling over so he could drive, suggested I talk to someone about what I'd seen.

"Hitting someone is a pretty fucked up thing," he said. "You gotta get that shit right in your head or it will haunt you for the rest of your life."

I'd worked hard to build a name for myself. I was frequently approached by fellow undercovers, detectives and police officers for advice, tips and help on cases. "Billy" was a name everyone knew, no matter what agency. I couldn't lose that.

"It would mean a lot if what happened didn't leave this car," I told him.

My coworker agreed if I promised to speak to someone about it. Like hell was I going to speak to anyone about what was going on! I'd already done that. I'd seen Father Joe when we hit the woman. I wasn't going back. After all, what if the counselor realized how fucked up I was and took me off the job? So I lied and promised my coworker I'd schedule an appointment as soon as we returned to the office. After that, I buckled down and focused on beating my mind.

During my time with Double J and Nash, I'd experienced periods where I found myself short of breath and my heart would race. I was convinced these were warning signs of an approaching heart attack. On one occasion I'd had Chaz drive me to the emergency room, certain this was the big one. I sat on the cold hospital bed, miles away from home, scared that my family wouldn't reach me in time. But, after an hour of EKGs and every other heart attack/stroke test you could think of, the physician walked into my sheet-enclosed room and told me he believed I'd had a panic attack. I didn't know what the hell a panic attack was, but after he explained it I knew one thing: he was dead wrong!

There I was, the lead in an undercover operation, interacting with bad guys like they were my next of kin, and a doctor was telling me I had anxiety. I gave the small-town doc a few choice words.

"Get your stress under control or one day I will be seeing you for a heart attack," he said before walking out.

❧

Of course, trying to beat my mind was an ill-regarded mission. My mind was stronger than I could be. I returned home from work delighted to spend the evening hours sealed in my room. I told myself as soon as I got over this hump I'd have the energy to battle the demons I was facing. Those lies only led me to become a shell of myself.

I didn't want my kids or family to see what I had become, so I stayed in my room. I wouldn't eat, I couldn't sleep and I dropped weight. I went to my doctor, ready for them to diagnose me with cancer or a blood disorder. But every test they ran came back normal. My doctor told me she believed I was suffering from anxiety and panic attacks. And, again, I left angry and unconvinced.

Eventually, I began missing work. I had no active undercover roles to tend to, so there wasn't anyone to dispute my office absences. Without work or a medical diagnosis to explain why I was feeling this way I couldn't find a sense of peace within myself. I was living in constant fear of nothing. I'd be immersed in a show and suddenly I'd remember sitting in Nash's bar getting drunk with the bad guys or smoking hooch with Double J. I never considered the danger I had been putting myself into. I'd allowed myself to lose my judgment, told myself that I knew enough to get out if things got bad. The reality and fear of those moments now rose faster than I could suppress them. In my mind I was no longer Billy the Liquor Guy everyone on the unit idolized. I was an asshole who based my career around stupid mistakes. I didn't plan to be a bad guy during my role. I had turned into one.

I sealed myself in my room for two days before my wife and family members demanded I get help. They didn't like the guy that sat in front of them, avoiding the world. They wanted their husband, brother-in-law and father back. I'd like to say I wanted that guy back too, but I was so deep into my anxiety to know my own self. All I could think about was ending it. It was the only reasonable solution I could see that would make these horrible feelings and thoughts go away. "You're not well," my wife said, standing in our bedroom doorway. "You either get help or I'm going to do it for you."

And with that she dialed the number to a psychiatrist.

❦

"Billy, I want you to think of the mind like a rubber band," the psychiatrist said, looking up from behind his yellow pad. "It can pull in several different directions, but it can only go so far until it breaks. You've had more stress than most people experience in a lifetime. Your brain has only so many electrical impulses equipped to deal with day to day things."

For the first time I felt some sense of relief. I wasn't crazy, nor was I losing my mind. I'd just over-expanded it and it needed to be reset.

The doctor diagnosed me with PTSD.

"I thought PTSD was for people who'd been in war," I questioned.

"You've experienced just as much danger, Billy. You have to be kind to yourself and face the reality of everything you have done and been through these past years. Your brain has had trauma, just like those soldiers have."

Finally having a diagnosis provided me with something I felt I could hold on to. It was concrete and offered a light at the end of the tunnel. The doctor prescribed me some anti-depressants and anxiety medication, but they still didn't provide the cure I craved.

I continued to pace the hallway at home, feeling overstimulated at times and lethargic at others. The fact that the instant fix didn't occur like the pills had magically promised caused more worry and dread. My mind spun with what-if thoughts. What if I never got better? What if I always felt this way? What if people think I'm faking? Or, worse yet, what if people think I'm crazy?

I visited the psychiatrist twice a week for six weeks. Each time we played with my medication and worked on breathing and relaxation techniques.

"Give it time," he told me. "Practice your breathing. Go for walks outside. The medicine will work, but you have to try to calm your mind."

I did get there, slowly. I didn't feel 100 percent like myself, but I could feel things changing. I stayed outside of my room a little longer each time. I put the window down and enjoyed a car ride and I could take a walk by myself around my neighborhood. The walk would come with step counting or deep breathing, but it was a sign that I was headed in the right direction and that gave me hope.

I headed back to work. I took a few low-key smuggling cases so I could function, but it was clear that my love for my career was over. I went to work now only to go. I didn't enjoy being there and I couldn't help but wonder if the PTSD would dissolve if I didn't have to be.

For the next five months I made small steps. I still had to pump myself up to get in the car and drive to work every day, but I went. One morning I walked into work, counting the fourteen steps from the front door to my desk, to get called into the main office. I sat in my chair, closing my eyes and taking three deep breaths to calm my nerves from the surprise sequester, before I recounted the steps from my desk to the conference room.

My palms were clammy and the hair on the back of my neck was on end. Mentally, I was certain I was walking into an office filled with corporate suits about to fire me. Instead, they handed me an early retirement package.

"We wanted you to be the first to receive this, Billy," a representative from the Attorney General's office said, pushing a large manila envelope across the table. "Several law enforcement officials will be offered a package similar to this one by the end of the week, but we thought you deserved to be the first person to see it. You've done a great deal for the state, Billy. We'd like to think this is a great incentive to show our gratitude for you and your family."

"It's time," my wife said. "You've done a great job. Take your reward and close this chapter of your life. It's time to see what else awaits you."

I signed the papers that evening and returned with one condition. I didn't want a party. I didn't want a fuss or any attention. I wanted to close my desk and depart that afternoon. The higher ups agreed. I handed over my paperwork, badge and gun, and walked out of the building as if it were an average Tuesday. It felt wonderful. However, wonderful feelings only last so long.

The illusion that my PTSD would end as soon as I was off the field caused me to quit taking my medication. I began to feel invincible. I was overly excited, on a constant high and extremely energetic. I began walking around my neighborhood ten to twelve times before wanting to retreat to my porch. I began swimming again, taking twenty laps at a time. I joined the gym, went for long car rides and reconnected with friends and family members who I hadn't seen in years. It all seemed good. Until it wasn't.

The reality was my PTSD didn't care if I worked on the field or not. It was here to stay, no matter how soothing my surroundings. And within a month my symptoms returned. Fear kept me bound to the house, flashbacks haunted me at night and sleep again became hard to come by. My wife convinced me to go back to my psychiatrist, who I'd stopped seeing at the same time as I stopped taking my pills.

"That was not happiness, Billy," he stated when I told him how great I felt when I stopped taking my pills. "You were having a manic reaction. It's a beautiful high that your mind uses to mask how badly you are hurting."

Begrudgingly I began my medicine again that evening and decided to try a local support group that the psychiatrist recommended. It took everything I had to walk into that first meeting. My mind ran wild with embarrassing scenarios.

"You're here to get better," my wife said, squeezing my hand as I tried to work up the courage to go inside.

As I walked down the stairs into the beige-colored basement, I noticed that the majority of the people appeared to be Veterans. My sense of flight kicked in. I was ready to turn and bolt just as an older gentleman, sporting an old army jacket and long hair, walked up to me.

"The coffee ain't too bad, but the cookies are worth the meetings," he said, extending his hand. "My name is Mike."

I shook his hand, my guard slightly falling, and followed Mike to the round circle of chairs filled with gentlemen of different statures and origins.

I listened to everyone introduce themselves before they came to me.

"Name's Billy," I said, wiping my sweaty hands on the top of my pants. "I'm a former officer who spent over ten years working undercover to take down some hard criminals in and outside of New York State. I'm here to help cope with my recent diagnosis of PTSD."

My mouth flooded with the taste of bile as soon as I stopped speaking. I was waiting for the angry mob of veterans to yell at me, hit me or tell me to leave. Instead they began asking me questions. What had I done? Who did I work for? Would they know of any big arrests?

My body shook so badly that I couldn't speak. Mike came to my rescue, talking to the group about other things, while I sat trying to breathe and get myself together.

After that the group meetings became easier. And, after that, they became something I looked forward to. I awaited my weekly meetings with the guys and even purchased coffee so they could enjoy the soft butter cookies the nice church ladies donated with a "good" cup of coffee.

As my strength grew my psychiatrist recommended I keep a journal.

"Tell the truth, admit your mistakes and share your stories upon those blank pages. Let them become the canvas of your life," he told me. "You always showed up in your career, no matter how scared you were, and completed your job. You owe it to yourself to show up and complete this now, no matter how scary the words that come out."

Through the journal I learned that I'd transformed from a young man who spent his youth avoiding abuse, alcoholism and the chaos that came with family functions to a man who placed himself back in line with fearful situations, searching for a way out.

"Billy, you don't have a journal," my psychiatrist said after reading my notes. "You have a book."

It's taken a lot of time and strength to hand my words over to the public. To show what I've really done and to be honest about who I am. It's scary to consider what people may think of me after they read my words. But just as I couldn't pull myself out of the line of fire when it was too deep, I can't filter how people are going to feel about the work I have done. The only thing I can do is expose the truth. And that's exactly what I have done.

EPILOGUE

I'VE STILL GOT IT

Staton and I remained close after everything ended. His private security business thrived and took on large cases for business and law enforcement around the country. I took jobs with him from time to time. Ten years later, once we were officially cleared of taking any money and the findings showing the money was illegally displaced by a borrowing agency, which we were legally bound to remain quiet about, Staton placed a new offer on the table.

"I'd like you to go to Tunisia and hunt down Sayid," he said. "I need him to come back. The FBI no longer has him under watch."

Staton explained that Sayid was living with his family off the coast of Africa.

"You always said you dreamed of swimming in all parts of the world. Here's your chance," he added.

Intrigued, I ran the idea past my family.

"Why would you want to do this?" they questioned. "What's in it for you?"

Minus an all-expense paid trip to Africa, I saw this as a test. I wanted to prove that I still had it. That I'd worked my way through PTSD, conquered a fear of getting older, and could still handle the best of cases with ease.

Despite my family's misgivings, I boarded a plane to Tunisia with only a phone number. I had no return ticket, because I wasn't sure how long it would take before I could turn back.

The heat and humidity hit me as soon as I stepped out of the airport. My body was tired from the flight, and I could feel my nerves beginning to settle in. A gentleman speaking broken English approached me and asked me where I was going. My hotel was a five star, so his eyes automatically lit up as he grabbed my bags, called me sir, and welcomed me to ride in his cab.

As I slid onto the cloth seats I told him to put the meter on.

"No, meter broke," he replied.

I casually leaned forward, pulled out my badge and said, "No it isn't."

The driver laughed and flicked the switch on.

Tunisia reminded me of Haiti, except there were a lot less walls and a lot more guys with machine guns. When we pulled up to the hotel there was a large iron gate with two cone-shaped cement pillars that looked like missiles. Out of the security shed came two gentlemen with badass machine guns and mirrors, which they placed under the car to look for bombs. I questioned if ignoring my family and coming here was a smart move after all, but what was done was done.

As I exited the taxi the driver handed me his number, suggesting I contact him for any travel I needed to do while I was there. I took the number and checked into my room. The trip had been long, so before I started my pursuit of Sayid, I walked down the coast and went for my very first swim in the Mediterranean. It was cold. After a few laps I pulled myself from the icy water and walked to the pool, which was cold too. I swam a few laps to relax myself anyway before I headed back to room to watch a little Arabic TV that I couldn't understand. I called Sayid. He didn't answer.

The next morning I woke early, hoping to catch Sayid before he headed out for the day, and this time he answered.

It took me twenty minutes to convince Sayid that I was Billy.

"This doesn't sound like you," he said.

"It's been ten years! I swear it's me. I'm here to talk to you."

"You're here? In Tunisia? No, it can't be," he said.

"Tom sent me here to talk to you about coming back to the states," I said.

The line went silent.

"Sayid? Are you there?" I questioned, hoping the line hadn't broken.

"For what do you want?" he asked.

"What do you think for what?" I said in the normal Billy the Liquor Guy tone. "Parties are interested in you coming back to the United States to work."

Again, Sayid stayed silent.

"Remember how I always told you I'd be there for you? Well, here I am. Certain people would like you to come back to do things like you did before. If you're interested, I'd like to talk to you. I'd also like a tour of this place."

After a little more convincing, Sayid agreed to meet me. I called my famous taxi guy and handed him the directions to Sayid's house. We pulled up to an old faded white structure no more than 1000 square feet. Sayid came out to greet me with his wife and his three teenagers by his side. It was funny to see them grown, as they were little children when I last saw them. Sayid's wife had made a traditional lunch, which included rice, carrots and a type of meat that Sayid told me not to ask about.

After lunch Sayid and I piled into his little car, which was a touch bigger than an old Volkswagen, for a grand Tunisian adventure. Sayid showed me the ruins, the lost city that had been buried by a tsunami a thousand years ago, and the site of the Battle of El Guettar in World War II. It was one of the 10 greatest battles ever recorded, and one of the largest tank engagements fought by the U.S. Army at that point.

Sayid also remembered my love of swimming. So he brought me to another part of the African coast to add an additional swim to my list. For the record, it was cold too.

The rest of the day consisted of visits through Tunisian cities, such as Kairouan, Hammanei, and Matmainsfax. It was extensive, but it was something I would never experience again and Sayid knew that.

"You want me to get closer to Libya?" Sayid joked.

"Are you fucking crazy? Absolutely not!" I said.

"Good," he said. "Because I wasn't gonna take you closer anyway."

By the time we finally stopped for a bite to eat, Sayid had grown comfortable with me, so I knew it was the best time to land my pitch. I told Sayid the benefits he'd have if he came back to America. Staton only needed him for less than 90 days. He'd be well paid for his time, and he'd clear his name at U.S. Borders.

We spent the evening laughing about the past and joking about the crazy things we did during our previous operations before he brought me back to my hotel.

I spent a few more days with Sayid, which was a little longer than I'd planned. I didn't have access to a washing machine, and between the humidity and salty air, my clothes and body were beginning to stink. I found myself missing the states, longing to watch real TV with real sports, and using a shower that I could fit into. And ice! For some reason getting ice was very difficult there.

Luckily, after the third day, with a cheap $8 flight to Morocco to visit Casablanca, I convinced Sayid to return to the United States. I was psyched. I finished my paperwork, said goodbye and headed straight to the front desk to book a return flight to the U.S... all while dreaming about a regular sized toilet and a nice iced coffee from Dunkin Donuts.

Back at home, Staton was impressed with what I'd done.

"You've still got it!" he said. "I never doubted you for a minute. Billy the Liquor Guy will always be within you. It's a talent you were gifted, and you've transformed agencies because of it. But you don't need me to tell you that. You've known that all along."

Regardless of what I knew, one thing was for sure. My work here would finally be done—officially.

THE END

ACKNOWLEDGMENTS

During my career I was fortunate to work in the line of duty with excellent law enforcement members who rose to the occasion and performed extraordinary deeds. These men and women did tasks unseen by many and happily returned to their normal lives without anyone the wiser.

As for the task force I was assigned to, whether it was Operation Spirits in New York, Operation Keystone in Pennsylvania and Virginia or one of the many more operations that ran up and down the East Coast of the United States, the dedication and outstanding investigative skills of the people I worked with led to hundreds of arrests. They brought down drugs, firearms, trafficking, tax evasion and several money launderers who supported the terrorism organizations our country still fight to this day. Due to time and the length of this book, several operations, arrests and fellow individuals were omitted. To those that were there, we will always know the full story and the length it took to get here.

Lastly, I would like to make a final roll call:

Tom, John, Paul, Tony, Jeff, Brian, Randy, Bruce, Mike, Rob, Mary B, Bobbi, Joe, Chad, Ernie, Jo, Timmy, Russel, Gary, Michelle and the Deerslayer, who to this day I still don't know his real name, thank you for making me Billy the Liquor Guy.

ARTICLE REFERENCES

https://ag.ny.gov/press-release/cuomo-announces-multi-city-takedown-part-upstate-guns-gangs-and-drugs-initiative

http://www.westchesterda.net/pressreleases/90918tax.htm

http://nypost.com/2011/02/13/910-memento-a-botched-clue-in-911-puzzle/

http://thetimes-tribune.com/news/feds-bust-tax-evading-cigarette-ring-1.701190

http://www.pressreader.com/usa/new-york-post/20090919/282643208593560

http://www.nydailynews.com/news/crime/sting-cracks-cigarette-smuggling-ring-article-1.403868
http://www.richmond.com/news/yemeni-s-wtc-pass-mystifies/article235d12e3-9565-5820-a413-ef401439b711.html

http://dailygazette.com/article/2011/03/09/0309_bar

Made in the USA
Columbia, SC
09 February 2020

87709012R00170